JUDI
DENCH

with a crack in her voice

By the same author

An Actor and his Time
(with John Gielgud and John Powell)

Acting Shakespeare (with John Gielgud)

An Englishman's Home

Broadcasting: Getting In and Getting
On: A Careers Guide

Ralph Richardson. The Authorised Biography

JUDI DENCH

with a crack in her voice

The Biography

———

JOHN MILLER

Weidenfeld & Nicolson

LONDON

First published in Great Britain in 1998
by Weidenfeld & Nicolson

© 1997 John Miller

The moral right of John Miller to be identified as the author
of this work has been asserted in accordance with
the Copyright, Designs and Patents Act of 1988

A CIP catalogue record for this book
is available from the British Library.

ISBN 0 297 81963 1

Typeset by Selwood Systems, Midsomer Norton

Set in Monotype Bembo

Printed in Great Britain by
Butler & Tanner Ltd, Frome and London

Weidenfeld & Nicolson

The Orion Publishing Group Ltd
Orion House
5 Upper Saint Martin's Lane
London, WC2H 9EA

For John Gielgud
to whom I owe so much

Contents

Contents

Illustrations

Irina with James Cairncross as Solyony in *The Three Sisters*, Oxford Playhouse 1964.[1]

Frank Hauser, Artistic Director of the Oxford Playhouse Company, 1956–74.[1]

Silia in *The Rules of the Game*, Oxford Playhouse 1966.[1]

Lika with Ian McKellen as Leonidik and Ian McShane as Marat in *The Promise*, Oxford Playhouse 1966, Fortune Theatre 1967.[1]

Sally Bowles in *Cabaret*, Palace Theatre, 1968.[6]

Hermione in *The Winter's Tale*, RSC 1969.[7]

Viola in *Twelfth Night*, RSC 1969.[7]

Madame Ranevskaya in *The Cherry Orchard*, BBC TV 1980.[8]

Juno in *Juno and the Paycock*, RSC 1980.[9]

Grace Harkaway with Donald Sinden as Sir Harcourt Courtly in *London Assurance*, RSC 1970.[10]

Beatrice with Donald Sinden as Benedick in *Much Ado About Nothing*, RSC 1976.[7]

Madame Ranevskaya with Michael Gough as Firs in *The Cherry Orchard*, Aldwych 1989.[11]

Mr and Mrs Michael Williams – 5 February 1971.[1]

Between pages 242 and 243

With Finty as a child.[7]

With Finty.[1]

With Michael and Finty at Buckingham Palace in 1988 after becoming Dame Judi Dench.[12]

With Richard Warwick, Susan Penhaligon and Michael in *A Fine Romance*, LWT 1980.[1]

With Maurice Denham and Michael at the premiere of *84 Charing Cross Road*, 1986.[1]

With David Hare on location for *The Crew*.[13]

With Edward Jewesbury, Emma Thompson, Kenneth Branagh and Gerard Horan – the cast she directed in *Look Back in Anger*, 1989, at Birmingham Repertory Theatre, and on TV.[14]

The spy-chief 'M' in *Goldeneye*, her first James Bond movie.[1]

Christine Foskett with Corey Johnson as Butch in *Absolute Hell*, National Theatre 1995.[11]

Desirée Armfeldt with Laurence Guittard as her lover Frederik in *A Little Night Music*, National Theatre 1995.[15]
Esmé with Samantha Bond as Amy in *Amy's View*, National Theatre 1997.[11]
Queen Victoria with Billy Connolly as John Brown in *Mrs Brown*, 1997.[16]
Nominated for Best Actress at the Academy Awards ceremony in Hollywood, 23 March 1998.[17]

The author and the publishers offer their thanks to the following for loaning photographs:

[1] Judi Dench

[2] Tenniel Evans

[3] Wendy Toye

[4] Alec McCowen

[5] Jon Vickers/ Mander & Mitchenson

[6] Zoë Dominic

[7] Joe Cocks/ Shakespeare Centre, Stratford-upon-Avon

[8] Richard Eyre

[9] Catherine Ashmore

[10] Patrick Eagar

[11] John Haynes

[12] Press Association

[13] Martin Jarvis

[14] Moira Williams

[15] Mark Douet

[16] Mark Tillie/ Ecosse Films

[17] Camera Press

If any copyrights have been inadvertently infringed the publishers will make appropriate attribution in any future editions.

Introduction

When I approached Judi Dench in the summer of 1996 about writing her biography, she was initially very reluctant. She had previously refused two similar requests from distinguished theatre critics; one of her expressed reasons was that she had cooperated in an earlier biography published in 1985 and, ever since, she had dreaded any prospect 'of all that talking about myself again'.

I explained that I was planning to talk to as many of her friends and colleagues as possible and would come back to her only at well-spaced intervals for her side of the story. Fortunately, I had interviewed her husband, Michael Williams, for my previous book on Ralph Richardson and she said that that had made her laugh so much that she eventually allowed herself to be persuaded.

Our first meeting to discuss how best to proceed was held in the canteen at the National Theatre, before a performance of *A Little Night Music*. We made a preliminary list of her directors and fellow-actors and I asked to see her schedule for the next eighteen months. Without consulting any paper, she rattled off a list of her commitments to the National, the BBC and for two movies – one as Queen Victoria in *Mrs Brown* and the next as M in her second Bond film. I said I would like to come and watch her at work as often as possible, to which she raised no objection whatsoever and gave me the contact names for each project so that I could obtain all the other necessary permissions. Not all directors are happy to have their most intimate moments of the creative process in rehearsal exposed to outside eyes, as I was to discover.

When I had finished jotting down a list of her commitments right up to Christmas 1997, including a string of Sunday recitals, often for one of the 183 charities of which she is a patron★, it appeared to me that she was working a seven-day week for most of the time. When I gently suggested this, Judi said briskly, 'Oh no, we're having a couple of weeks in Barbados in March and I always take two weeks' holiday in August to recharge my batteries.' But my first impression was only reinforced over subsequent months, as I watched her in action.

We parted after an hour's discussion, saying that we hoped to meet next on location for the first film; meanwhile I would start to contact the first names on our list. As I left the building, neither the stage door keepers nor I realised just how often over the next few months I would be reappearing there to see an actor, director, writer or to attend a rehearsal. Judi told me often how much she loved working at the National Theatre, an affection which is clearly shared by virtually all our leading players.

The first time I ever saw Judi on stage was as Anya in *The Cherry Orchard*, with John Gielgud as Gaev, and he was one of the first people I went to talk to about working with her. With his customary forthrightness, he remarked, 'Isn't it a little early to be writing her biography. Shouldn't you wait until after she's dead?' I pointed out that we were much the same age and that it might therefore never get written if I waited that long. In any case, although I had loved writing the life of Ralph Richardson, and found his final days very moving, this time I really wanted to tell the story of a living figure at the very peak of her profession, when I could study her at work now, as well as trace the history of her rise through its ranks.

That dual objective has largely dictated the structure of this book, in which the story of her first six decades is interspersed with my diary observing her work-in-progress. The initially guarded response of her colleagues to this note-taking figure in the corner soon gave way to much good-natured ribbing; when Judi fluffed and corpsed during the final run of a scene in *As Time Goes By*, Geoffrey Palmer swung round and looked out past the camera, saying loudly, 'Make sure you put this in your book, John, she isn't always perfect!' Chatting to Billy Connolly on location for *Mrs Brown* as Queen Victoria swept up to us for the next scene, he hissed to me in a stage whisper that would have reached the back of the gods in the Glasgow Empire,

'Sssshh, she's coming, I'll finish telling you later', and then the two stars grinned knowingly at each other.

Laughter is the emotion that most of her admirers associate with Dame Judi Dench and that is even more so of many of those who know her well – family and friends as well as professional colleagues; but she has also shed many tears, off-stage as well as on, and I have endeavoured to capture those differing moods and passions, as well as the multi-faceted aspects of her genius. One of her most distinctive features is that unmistakable crack in the voice, which brings the hearer's heart into the mouth. Many of those to whom I talked spoke with awe of her innate instinct for acting, her speed of reaction, her gift for verse-speaking; and with enormous affection for those personal qualities that have made her, in the phrase used by so many, 'the best-loved actress' of our time.

Casting directors in the performing arts can call on an astonishing array of British talent, but the step up from being a very good actor to a great one is open to only a handful. That Judi Dench has made that leap, I am in no doubt – watching her develop a character in rehearsal is as spellbinding as seeing the finished role in performance – and I spent many fascinating months trying to establish the point at which her feet left the springboard.

She has been compared with Ellen Terry and Peggy Ashcroft and indeed they triumphed in many of the same parts, but a great actress is great in her own special way. I hope that the pages which follow help to show why Judi Dench is such a special actress, as well as a very special woman.

John Miller
1998

---

* Over a third are connected with the theatre in some way, ranging from the Actors' Centre and Shakespeare's Globe to Worthing Youth Theatre; many more are for medical charities, from the Arthritis and Rheumatism Council to York Against Cancer; some combine the two causes, such as the British Theatre for the Disabled and the Talking Books Service.

14 November 1996

Her Majesty Mrs Brown
(later retitled *Mrs Brown*)

Location – Wilton House

8.30 a.m. Arrived on location. Met Geoffrey Palmer striding across the car park to make-up, munching a bacon roll. He greeted yet another strange face with a cheery 'Good morning', but this didn't seem the moment to introduce myself. Followed his example and got myself a bacon roll and coffee from the location caterers and found Douglas Rae in the crew dining-bus. He and I had worked together in the early eighties at TVS; now he ran his own company, Ecosse Films, and this was its first drama for television. He told me about the storms they had endured on the shooting in Scotland and how he was lost in admiration of Judi's stamina and professionalism. She had never complained once about her 4 a.m. calls, or the lashing rain and gale-force winds.

8.50. We walked up to the House and went into the Double Cube Room, standing in for the Queen's sitting-room at Windsor Castle. There was the usual hive of crew activity, which looks so disorganised to outsiders, but everyone is concentrating on their own tasks. Judi was having a quiet discussion with the director, John Madden. When they had finished, she wandered around, deep in thought, until she was satisfied she had absorbed all his notes. Then she looked up and saw me, smiled and came over to give me a most unqueenly hug.

She said, 'We had such a good time filming in Scotland.'

'But I heard you had the most terrible weather and barely got any sleep!'

'Oh, but that's Scotland. I do so love it up there. We go every year to Eriska.'

Then she was called for opening positions for a rehearsal.

9.20. Rehearsal of Scene 86.

Windsor Castle, the Queen's sitting-room. Lady Ely enters.

VICTORIA.   Well?

LADY ELY.   Mr Brown is unable to attend today.

VICTORIA.   Why?

LADY ELY.   I believe he is unwell.

VICTORIA.   Unwell?

LADY ELY.   I understand he was in a fight.

VICTORIA.   Has he been hurt?

LADY ELY.   I believe not. (Pause). I understand he'd had rather too much to drink.

VICTORIA.   (Pause). You may go.

This scene was shot first with the camera facing the window and the two actresses in profile, long-shot. Take 3 was printed.

Brief break. Judi took me outside to the coffee urn and told me, with many giggles, how her pony, Bluey, farted right through her first tender scene with John Brown, which required endless takes before it was safely in the can.

9.50. Rehearsed reverses of Scene 86. Camera facing door.

During the long relight, Judi sat at the desk practising Victoria's left-handed signature, following a photocopy of the original, for a close-up of her hands needed later.

10.22. Shot 276. Take 4 OK.

The writer, Jeremy Brock, had now arrived and Judi greeted him with a kiss and asked if his wife's baby had arrived yet.

'Any moment', he said, with a rather worried look.

10.40. Shot 277. Other angle. Take 3 OK.

11.30. Shot 278.

The floor creaked on Take 1 and Judi corpsed. After Take 3, the director said, 'Judi, on the turn, it's more a denial of Brown's drunkenness than elegiac.'

Judi: 'Yes, I know, exactly.' On Take 4 she swept away with a much more emphatic walk.

Shot 279. Same angle, different lens. Take 2 OK.

Shot 280. Ditto, wide angle for the last line and Judi's move.

Relight for the next scene. Judi was whisked off to make-up, and I was introduced to the three co-producers from WGBH in Boston.

12.45 p.m. Scene 88. With Geoffrey Palmer as Sir Henry Ponsonby.
Geoffrey arrived on the set, now wearing a magnificent full set of whiskers. Judi introduced us and we had a long talk about *As Time Goes By*, in which he co-stars with Judi. We agreed to talk further during the rehearsals for that show next month.

Shot 281.

After Take 1 the director gave a note to Judi: 'The line "My family is quite capable of communicating with the Queen in person" should be said as a dismissal.' On the next take Judi introduced a new piece of business, picking up a glass of water to take a sip. Then she paused, as she realised Ponsonby was still standing there, finally saying irritably, 'What is it?'

Ponsonby said diffidently, 'They are demanding the dismissal of Mr Brown on grounds of drunkenness.'

After the take Judi was immediately concerned about the need for continuity over the position of the glass on the retakes from other angles. Take 3 OK.

1.20. Break for lunch. Judi queued for her food with the rest of the crew and took it off to her caravan. I decided not to bother her during this break, knowing that she was concentrating on her lines for the next scene. Bumped into Richard Pasco, an old friend from other shows, who is playing Dr Jenner. Just as I finished my lunch, Judi appeared at the window of the bus and beckoned me to join her. 'I missed you at the lunch break. You should have come to my caravan.' It was so hot inside that she left the top half of the door open. After about ten minutes we were interrupted by a Scottish voice saying, 'I was watching you doing the *Acting* this morning.'

'Billy Connolly, don't you dare say *Acting* like that with a capital A! We've got your implacable scene this evening.'

'Shall I show you my implacable look? And my placable look? Did you notice the difference?'

Then she introduced me to him and a wicked gleam came into his eye. Shortly afterwards, she was called for make-up and, as she disappeared into the trailer, Billy stood on the top step, holding the door open, and bellowed after me, as Richard Pasco and I went off for a coffee, 'That's John Miller,

7

the *biographer*. Tell him I'll see him later, when Judi's not about.'

A regal voice from inside rang out, 'Now Billy, just you behave yourself!'

3.15. Rehearsal of Scene 91. Confrontation with the family.

Brief discussion between the director, Judi and Geoffrey about which angle for the Queen to dismiss the family, to get the best cutting-point. The actors thought it unnecessary for her to add, 'Do I make myself clear?' The director said the line was to enable her to be more emphatic. On Take 2 Judi was much fiercer; Take 3 fiercer still.

Long relight for reverse angle shot.

Judi sat on the long sofa under the seventeen-foot Van Dyck of the Pembroke family and commanded her two ladies-in-waiting to get paper and pencil. She then taught them one of her many word games with which she whiles away those long waits that are so often the lot of actors on set or on tour. This one had a grid of twenty-five boxes, and they each called out a letter in turn and put it into a box of their choice to make up a word – a kind of combination of Scrabble and noughts and crosses. They got so engrossed in this that they seemed almost sorry when they were called for positions in the next shot.

Shot 287. Tracking shot of Queen's entrance, ending on the family. Judi preserved the intensity of her performance, even though out of shot, to help the family reactions. Her own daughter, Finty, had been cast as the Queen's youngest child and in the break Judi said to me, 'I told Finty this was her one chance to play the rebellious daughter, so she'd better make the most of it!'

When this scene was finally in the can, the Double Cube Room was finished with. There was a long break to reset and light the corridor and a costume change for Judi. Billy Connolly was already made up and in costume, so I took advantage of the opportunity to ask him about the filming with Judi and his reactions to his co-star.

'She's wonderful. She gives you so much power that she forces you to act, and react, naturally. And she's always so quick that, when you have a line she interrupts, she never leaves you hanging. You can confidently launch yourself on the speech, knowing she'll come in, wham! She's such fun to work with. We travelled to the locations together quite often and we had a lot of laughs. She has a marvellous, full-throated belly-laugh; none of this swallowing it back down her throat, like some people do.'

It was now getting late and the final scene was tricky, with the camera mounted on rails, tracking back with Victoria and Ponsonby, as John Brown is rebuked.

6.15. Shot 290.
On Take 3 the cameraman said, 'Cut. We'll have to go again, I lost focus on Geoffrey at the beginning.'

Geoffrey made a mock-bow of apology, saying, 'Sorry everybody, my fault!' and Judi giggled. It had been a long day's filming, towards the end of the third week of shooting with many early calls and late finishes, but there was no discernible sign of irritability from anyone in the large crew or cast. This happy working atmosphere under pressure was one I was to observe as so much the norm wherever Judi was involved, and to hear about again and again from her colleagues from the earliest days, that the odd exception occasioned surprise.

one

1934–54

York – an actress is born

It was medicine that brought the Dench family to York, but it was the city's strong associations with drama, amateur and professional, that kept them there. Reginald Dench was born in Weymouth, but his parents moved to Ireland when he was still a little boy. He met Olave Jones at Sunday school when they were both fourteen, and they were married after he graduated in medicine from Trinity College, Dublin.

Reginald was a keen amateur actor and distinguished himself in that field at Trinity. There was a university tradition on Founder's Day that the Master of Trinity would come out onto the steps on one side of the quadrangle and read a long pronouncement, while a student would perform a take-off on the opposite steps at the same time. The rag audience was always larger than the official one and Jeffery Dench remembers seeing photographs of his father, dressed as Shakespeare, writing sonnets on rolls of lavatory paper and tearing them off.

After qualifying as a doctor, he and his wife moved to Tyldesley, near Manchester, and it was there that the two boys were born, first Peter and then, four years later, Jeffery. But Olave was unhappy with the quality of life in that area. Their move to York in 1934 was to bring happiness and fulfilment to the entire family, which shortly increased to five when, after a six-year gap, Olave gave birth to a daughter on 9 December of that year.

She was christened Judith Olivia and she was known from the beginning as Judy; she always knew she was in trouble whenever she was addressed as Judith. The change of spelling came much later when she arrived at the Central School of Drama to find another girl called Judy in her year, so she changed to the more distinctive Judi, by which she has been known ever since. (In the interests of clarity, that is how it is spelt throughout the rest of this book.)

Her arrival had been a little unexpected; her mother was then thirty-seven, coincidentally almost exactly the same age as Judi when she gave birth to her daughter Finty. Judi's father might have spoilt her if her mother had not been so firm with her, and the age gap with her brothers meant that they did not become really close until Judi was in her teens. Peter says, 'I didn't realise I had a sister until she was fifteen or sixteen, and I was in practice. She was eight when I went to Cambridge.'

Peter took up his father's profession and, after his National Service, returned to York to join his practice where, as he puts it, 'A chair was kept warm for me.' He and his wife Daphne both then became very close to Judi; they have followed her career with keen interest from the beginning. Being on-call as a GP restricted Peter's chances of seeing her earliest performances, but he managed to catch most of the later ones. He and his wife now regularly house-sit when Judi and her family are away on holiday; tall, like all the Dench men, he frequently bangs his head on the low beams in his sister's house.

The activity that united the whole family derived from their love of the theatre. The Settlement Players was a very good amateur dramatic group in York and Reg was soon playing leading parts, while Olave became a highly skilled wardrobe mistress. At a pre-war Stuart masque and fair all the amateurs dressed up as Caroline characters; Olave was an imposing Lady Castlemaine, Charles II's mistress, and Jeffery remembers her surprise 'when she discovered what a naughty lady she was'.

All this industry seemed the most natural thing in the world to the youngest member of the family. 'I thought all families were dressed up; we had the most wonderful dressing-up box. I remember them going to a great party. Daddy went as Shakespeare and Mummy went as Elizabeth I; she made the most incredible dress and they both looked marvellous.'

Dr Dench was the official GP for the Theatre Royal in York and frequently invited visiting actors home to their house in Heworth Green. Phyllis Calvert remembers Judi as an enchanting little girl there, but had no premonition that she would grow up to join her profession. Nor did the young Peter Woodthorpe, who was a patient of Dr Dench's. He says now, 'I can't forget her voice – I never thought she'd succeed as an actress because of her voice; she always sounded as if she had laryngitis. But she trained it.'

That distinctive feature is something derived from both parents. Her father had a very deep bass voice and her mother possessed a striking Irish brogue. But Judi's affinity with the Celts is not limited to the land nor the time of her parents' youth. 'The first recorded Dench in Scotland was in 1580 in Gairloch. I suppose that is also one of the reasons I love Scotland so; it is a question of finding one's roots.'

She regrets that she only ever knew one of her grandparents, Reg's father. 'Gampy was just adorable. He remarried and had a son when he was in his seventies, and my uncle is much younger than me. I realise that Daddy was very like him; he was a wonderful swimmer, very ebullient and enthusiastic. I went to Castle Howard once when I was very little. I had water-wings and he said, "Now come along, get the wings off, get in there and take the wings off." I was quite frightened, but I did, and I swam about three strokes for him.'

Her father was captain of water polo at Trinity. For Judi, too, swimming soon became a favourite activity and remains so. One of the reasons for buying her present home in the country was the presence of the pool in the garden. The long, low proportions of the Tudor cottage are a great contrast to the narrow and tall Victorian terrace house in which she grew up. Her bedroom was right up in the attic, where she could draw on the walls with impunity. The doctor's surgery and waiting-room were on the ground floor.

Cycling was another joint family activity and on Reg's Thursday afternoon off they would often all mount and ride the fifteen miles to Castle Howard for a swim. For longer trips to Scarborough, they all piled into the family car and, after a swim, would attend productions in the open air of *Faust* and *Hiawatha*.

The first professional play Judi saw was lighter fare – Ben Travers' farce *Cuckoo in the Nest* at the York Theatre Royal. 'I can never forget that when a man appeared in long johns from a basket at the bottom of a bed I screamed with laughter so much that my parents took me home because they thought I'd make myself ill. But Ma did take me

again the next night to see the rest of the play, which was very tolerant
of her. I can still clearly remember that place. It was cleaned with
something like Jeyes Fluid, and a string trio played from the pit. Even
now I can evoke that particular smell, and hear that unique sound of
the trio.'

The parental enthusiasm for things theatrical naturally fanned an
interest in all three of the children. Peter and Jeffery went to St Peter's,
in York, the oldest school in the country, and took part in the annual
school play, produced by the classics master, Leslie Burgess. He was
also a playwright, married to an actress, and a very skilled director.
Jeffery says, 'He taught me more stagecraft than I ever learnt at
Central.' Before his voice broke, Jeffery played Cleopatra to his
brother's Caesar in the Shaw play, a rare change from the school's
usual Shakespeare. It was noteworthy enough to be reviewed by the
Yorkshire Post under the headline treasured by Peter, 'Surprise, surprise,
Cleopatra was Caesar's brother!'

Jeffery went on to play Kate in *The Taming of the Shrew*, Cassius and
Macbeth. After Judi saw the last, 'I thought it was very, very racy to
bring out the piano stool at home and say, "What bloody man is
that?" That's all I knew of the play, but I did say it a lot.' Judi was
thrilled to see her brothers on-stage, and they supported her, too.
Jeffery remembers seeing her at Clifton Preparatory School, known
to everyone as Miss Meaby's, 'playing a snail, and rehearsing at home,
so she started very early, about three and a half or four'.

Miss Meaby encouraged all the children to take part in readings
and performances. Sometimes this meant inventing extra parts to
include everyone, which peeved the budding young actress. 'They
said, "Now Judi, you're going to play a fairy." I can remember
thinking then that there's not a fairy in the Nativity Play; I knew it
was a cobbled-up part. I was quite cross and you can see I'm cross in
the picture. Angela Bedford played Mary, with my doll, and in the
picture my friend David Rymer has put the gift right on top of the
doll's head, for *spite*!'

She might have been less cross if she had known that she would
get her chance to play Mary on a much bigger stage at the outset of
her professional career. But even at Miss Meaby's, she got to play the
title role in *Alice in Wonderland*.

Her boundless energy was much in evidence from the beginning, though not everyone was appreciative of her high spirits. The young Peter Woodthorpe *was*: 'Hers was the best party I ever went to, with a very funny treasure hunt; there was a sense of fun in the house, and a sense of fun all the time.' But the local magician, Mr Bull, who used to entertain at all the York children's parties, was less entranced by Judi. 'I used to know his act, so I used to say, "Watch, *watch*, here comes the rabbit." So he said to the hostess, "I'm absolutely not doing my act if she's there, because she ruins it." Poor man, can you imagine? I can't imagine anything worse.'

Her reputation for jokes, now usually indulged by her famous colleagues, was less fondly regarded by the young men of York. One little boy named James Conyers would not even stay for one party, saying loudly for all to hear, 'If Judi Dench is here, I'm going, and taking my brother with me.'

But more often, Judi made friends easily and there was a constant flow of children through the house and garden. When war broke out holiday trips became more difficult, though even then in most summers the family took the train to Cornwall, where Judi first developed her addiction to lobster. A French friend, Daphne, whose family had fled to England in 1940, came to Cornwall with them one year and collected snails for the pot, but they all escaped. Nine years older than Judi, she soon became closer to Peter and eventually became his wife. She remembers Judi at this time as a cute little girl with two plaits, who loved cats and used to take them for a walk, dressed up in doll's clothes. She still loves cats and has five of them at home, but now lets them take their own exercise.

The first really formative decision in her life was her expressed wish to go to The Mount school. It was a good school, which fostered her natural talents; it was also a Quaker school, whose faith has become one of the sheet-anchors of her life. But, when pressed, she admits that neither of those qualities was the one that attracted her. 'It was the uniform. I rather fancied that bright blue shirt and huge white collar.'

All the girls had to board, even if they lived locally, and they were not supposed to slip home, though Judi soon found a way of circumventing that rule. 'When it was wet and we couldn't play games, they used to send us on the brown wet walk, or the blue wet walk, or the red wet walk. I used to go with my friend Susie Marshall, and we'd go round the corner and telephone, and Daddy would say, "Hang on, I'm seeing a patient. After this patient I'll come and pick you up." So we'd hang around in a doorway and he'd come round and pick us up, take us back and give us tea, then water us with the garden hose, drop us somewhere near school, and we'd rush back. We did that a lot. Of course, it was absolutely illegal.'

Her eldest brother softens his faint disapproval of all this with the full-hearted Dench laugh. 'She was always getting into mischief. It was said The Mount was never the same after she'd been there. She was always getting into scrapes.'

Margaret Drabble was a pupil at the same school, three years younger than Judi, 'so she was somebody I looked up to very much. Her light-heartedness was not something that was readily encouraged by our school. All of us were always being ticked off. We had a headmistress, Kathleen Carrick-Smith, who was extremely nervous and repressive; she was afraid anything we did would go wrong. The irrationality of some of the taboos was just ludicrous. There was a lot of emphasis on silence at school, not making a lot of noise, and not running, and I wonder if that's good for growing girls. There was an attempt to make it unnaturally subdued and I'm sure a lot of us wanted to break out of it. We were positively discouraged from selling ourselves. We were not supposed to advertise; we were supposed to let virtue shine forth without doing anything about it ourselves.'

Subdued is hardly the description one would apply to Judi, then or now, but she certainly still finds arguments about the size and placing of credits distasteful and positively hates having to give promotional interviews of any kind. Many of the other school rules that at the time she jibbed at, she now believes were character-forming. 'At The Mount you weren't even allowed to ask for the salt. You couldn't ask for anything; you had to be invited to have it, and it's good, it teaches you a lot of good manners later. You used to get to the stage where you'd say, "I bet you're enjoying that salt on your table", because you'd get desperate. You had to sit there waiting until someone would say, "Is there something you'd like?" "Yes, I'd like some salt, and about time too!"'

The Mount had a strong academic tradition and was keen for all its girls to go on to university, but one of its special qualities in Judi's eyes was that it catered entirely for the individual and encouraged her in all the things she liked best. 'Molly Humphries taught maths and I said to her about algebra, "I just have to know why I need to know that $2x + 2y$ = something?" She just looked at me and said, "I don't expect you will ever have to know that." It was such an adult thing to say. Then I coped with it – not very well, I was better at geometry, because I understood geometry.'

She was much keener on art, which was taught by Phoebe Brook. She encouraged them all to do well in whatever they did, but not to compete. That school philosophy was also carried over to sports matches against other schools; even there, winning was not the important thing.

But the activity for which Judi was best remembered at The Mount is acting. As so often in a school with a reputation for its theatre productions, there was one key figure, in this case a former professional actress, Joy Harvey, who taught drama there under her married name of Mrs McDonald, usually abbreviated to Mrs Mac. She had a profound influence on Judi. 'She was quite dissipated, and she used to drink, and she smoked like a chimney, but she'd suddenly talk about the theatre, as someone who'd acted in it. She was a good laugher, but she took it seriously, and she was a terrific teacher. That's why I'm now so against getting people in to talk to students who don't actually work in the theatre. It's fine academically, but you need somebody to tell you actually what it's like to be in a company, how you should behave, and the homework that you do, so you don't take up a lot of people's time. She was very like that; she was amazing.'

Judi played Titania in *A Midsummer Night's Dream* and Margaret Drabble played one of the fairies, roles which they were both to repeat at Stratford in 1962. Margaret also remembers her vividly in *The Tempest* as Ariel: 'She had a gift for verse-speaking already at school; she had a natural ear. When she came on–stage she just lit up for the audience.'

Julius Caesar was the first play Judi saw at The Mount. 'With all these big girls in bigger togas, that's not at all a good play to do. That so put me off the play that I've hardly ever been to see it since.' But later in her time there, joint productions were put on by The Mount and Bootham, the twinned boys' school, where John Kay possessed a similar skill to Leslie Burgess at directing and enthusing young players. He cast Judi as the Queen in *Richard II* but, true to the Quaker precepts, The Mount insisted that she share the part with another girl, Rachel Hartley, so they took it in turns on alternate nights to play the Queen and her lady-in-waiting.

Her acting as a girl was not confined to school productions. When the Settlement Players did Christopher Fry's *The Firstborn*, she played Pharaoh's daughter, Tuesret. But much the biggest theatrical event was the York cycle of Mystery Plays. These were revived in 1951 in an adaptation by Canon J. S. Purvis and produced by E. Martin Browne, who specialised in religious dramas with huge casts combining amateurs and professionals. This series of medieval plays, based on scenes from the Bible, was played in the open air in the grounds of St Mary's Abbey.

All the young professionals in the cast, and some of the even younger amateurs, went on to distinguish themselves in the theatre. Joseph O'Conor played Christ, John van Eyssen was Mephistopheles, David Giles (who later became a successful TV drama director) played the Archangel Gabriel, and Tenniel Evans was the Archangel Michael, in his first professional engagement. Other leading parts were taken by the best local amateurs – Reginald Dench as Annas the High Priest, John Kay from Bootham School as Caiaphas, and Mary Ure from the sixth form at The Mount as the Virgin Mary. The younger girls, like Judi, were cast as angels. 'There were about eight of us and I got a part as a very, very forgetful angel. We had white robes with a gold collar, and gold wigs. Mummy had made the costumes and the wigs came from Bert, the famous wig-maker. It was so exciting. Martin Browne was an adorable man, like a kind of crane, with huge hands, a very storky kind of person. His wife Henzie Raeburn played Mary Magdalene.'

Judi was not the only one entranced with the way she looked in this production; Tenniel Evans' eyes still sparkled forty-six years later: 'I just fell madly in love with her, but I thought, "Be careful. Baby-snatching!" She was nearly eighteen, but I thought she was about fourteen. We became great friends then, and we've been friends ever since. She always sends me a rose on my birthday.' He may have been the first, but he was far from the last of her fellow-players to fall for her.

Joseph O'Conor's initial acquaintance was less close. 'I got to know her a bit; she used to listen earnestly to my guitar-playing in the garden. But three years later I came up to do it again. I came into this huge hall with 150 people there, and my eyes went like a compass needle to Judi. There was something magnetic about her even at that time, when the eye took in not 149 other people, but Judi. She played the Angel at the Tomb, which was one speech. I wasn't surprised when, at the next Festival, she played Mary; I think that moment of magnetism is significant.'

Judi's own memory of that second production is a little more mixed. 'I played the young man guarding the door of the tomb, in white clothing, and I wasn't allowed a chair. Henzie said not, so I had to sit there with bent knees, while the three Marys came on and said, "Oh look at that, there's no stone in front of the tomb", or words to that effect. It was most uncomfortable.'

Three years later, she followed in Mary Ure's footsteps to play the Virgin Mary, though she had actually auditioned for the part of Eve. But in this part, too, she had to endure some discomfort. 'I was always rained on. I used to bend over for the birth of Christ and then just part the straw and the baby was there; I used to look up and everyone was putting their macs on. There was a sea of plastic macs.' Since the production was four hours long, she did not blame the audience for coming prepared for all the rigours of the English summer.

Given all this growing success on-stage in and out of school, it is surprising that acting was not her first choice of career, particularly as by now her brother Jeffery had been through his training as an actor at the Central School and joined the repertory company in York. That year, 1953, Judi enrolled at the School of Art in her home town, thinking that she might become a painter or a stage designer. (Interestingly, two great actors of an earlier generation, John Gielgud and Ralph Richardson, had both made exactly the same false start before realising that their major talent was for the performing rather than the visual arts.)

She had always enjoyed art classes at school and it was one of the subjects she passed at A Level. English was another, so line and language were of equal importance to her then. But she might have guessed that designing was a second-best choice, since her very first ambition was to be a ballet dancer. Her father always encouraged all his children to follow their ambitions, but he knew exactly how to dissuade his daughter from an unsuitable decision for her. 'I can remember Daddy talking to me and saying, "Well if you do take up dancing, by forty you'll have to teach or something, because you just can't go on, it is quite short." I remember that as if he said it to me yesterday. I wouldn't have liked that; I don't like the thought of anything packing up.'

The only residue of those youthful leanings is her habit, when first rehearsing her curtain call, of running straight off into the wings as if she were wearing a tutu, with her arms held out before and behind.

Her six months at the art college were unhappy and frustrating. Her decision to abandon the course was again influenced by her family, in both positive and negative ways. The first was through her brother Jeffery, whose stories about his three years at Central had enthralled them all at Heworth Green, but none more so than his little sister, especially his tales about the fights he had to learn. When he moved back to York to join the repertory company, she was exposed even more regularly to his tales and evident excitement in his chosen career.

But the die was cast when her parents took her to see Michael Redgrave's *Lear* at Stratford-upon-Avon in 1953, directed by George Devine, with costumes and sets by Robert Colquhoun. It was the last that were the real revelation to the putative young designer from York. The stage was dominated by a huge saucer and a rock, which became in turn the throne, the cave and everything else required. 'I'd never seen a set like that, where you didn't need to bring the lights down to change the scenery. So I thought, "Gosh, I'm very old-fashioned about how I think." I saw this great saucer with this revolving thing in the middle and the lights never went down, they only ever changed; it was just incredible.'

In the same season, Judi also saw Redgrave play Antony to Peggy Ashcroft's Cleopatra, little knowing that one day she would not only become a close friend of Dame Peggy, but recreate many of her great classical roles. It is indicative of the power and charisma of the actress who became her mentor and model that all Judi can remember today of that production is the Cleopatra.

When Jeffery told his parents he thought Judi should be the second member of the family to go to Central, it fell on receptive ears. They knew that they would have to pay for her three years there, as they had for his, but they were confident that she had the talent to succeed, having watched it blossom as she grew up. The prospective student herself had much less confidence, which was not helped by going down with tonsillitis during the application period. The written part of the examination was sent to her at home. 'They asked a lot about Greek theatre, which fortunately I knew a lot about.'

Thus far, that is the full extent of her brush with the Greeks. It is the one branch of theatrical tradition that she has shunned, with an especial fervour if a production is to hide the actors' faces behind masks, in the classical Greek style.

Any trepidation about the challenges she would face at Central was proved groundless in her first term there, but that nervous anticipation before a new experience is one that has recurred before every fresh departure in her career. Fortunately, she has always been able to conceal her nerves at the time and channel them into the required adrenalin. She had made one false start in her career, but any fears that she might have made another were soon dispelled.

two

1954–57

Learning her craft – from Central School
to the Old Vic

The three years that Judi spent at the Central School of Speech and Drama coincided with the end of its tenure of rooms at the Royal Albert Hall; the year she left, it moved up to the Embassy Theatre in Swiss Cottage. Unfortunately the student records so carefully packed up and delivered there by one of Judi's teachers, Vera Sargent, seem to have been lost or mislaid since, but the bare list of her achievements at Central speaks volumes – a First Class Diploma, the Spotlight Prize, the William Poel Prize, the Gold Medal and the Elsie Fogerty Prize.

The last of these is awarded to the outstanding student of the year and is named after the actress who founded the school in 1906. It is no accident that Speech precedes Drama in its title, for that was Miss Fogerty's speciality; many famous players went to her for voice-coaching, including John Gielgud, Laurence Olivier and Peggy Ashcroft.

The Principal when Judi enrolled in September 1954 was Gwynneth Thurburn, who succeeded Elsie Fogerty and maintained that concentration on speech and diction. Cicely Berry was one of the teachers and Judi has continued to work with her throughout her career, especially when they were both on the strength of the Royal Shakespeare Company.

Cicely remembers that 'she was a very bright student, very alert and receptive. She always wanted to work, and I do remember that we had a lot of fun in class. The voice is not fully developed when the student arrives at her age, so it was just a matter of developing it, getting the breathing working, so that it increased the capacity of breath, and opening out the resonators in the chest and the throat.' They did a lot of work on the speaking of poetry, to open the ears of students to different rhythms, from the Elizabethan and the Meta-physical Poets right up to the modern writers.

Judi has fond memories of several other members of staff. 'Clifford Turner couldn't do an accent, and he used to teach us dialect; but he was a brilliant voice teacher. He looked a bit like George Sanders. I used to adore movement classes with Maggie Rubell – leaping about everywhere, relaxation, and coordination of your body. Nobody ever cured me of falling over, though', (a tendency particularly on first nights, which disconcerted more than one of her leading men later).

Oliver Reynolds took classes in mime, not of the white-faced Marcel Marceau variety, but a basic acting exercise performed without dialogue or props. He remembers Judi being good at this and very attentive in class, although at the time he had some reservations: 'She had a nice sense of comedy, but in much of what she did I could hear the background noise of hockey sticks bullying off. There was the touch of the tomboy about her, but she was very popular with the men at the school; she went about in a rather grubby raincoat, but that didn't put any of the men off.'

On one occasion Judi had forgotten to prepare a mime exercise and, on the spur of the moment, decided on 'Walking in a familiar garden'. One fellow-student, Charles Lewsen, recalls 'the image of a girl wandering in a garden, sitting for a moment on a swing, and then departing – simple, unemphatic: the work of someone who could already achieve repose in the presence of an audience, and who probably had the capacity to live fully in the present. After forty-three years, I have the strong sense of the imagined garden being stocked with tall flowers, and that they are visited by butterflies. I think it is that scene that has made me feel that Judi came to Central fully formed as an actress – by which I mean not that she had nothing to learn, but that in some vital way she knew her artistic self.'

However, if she did arrive fully formed, it was buried quite deeply in Judi's subconscious, because she felt uncertain in her first term. She cites this exercise as the moment she felt she had it in her to be an actress.

The school believed in bringing in established actors to act as adjudicators on the students' work and in Judi's time the best-known of these was Walter Hudd, known more familiarly as Dicky. 'He told me off terribly for laughing because the ceiling fell down on me. In *Time and the Conways* Richard Page-Jackson had to pull the curtain aside and catch me. He pulled it aside so hard that it came off the rail and the whole thing came down on my head. My next line was, "I suppose you do this to all your girlfriends." Well, the audience howled and I howled. Dicky Hudd said, "This is a very naughty thing to do. You mustn't ever do that, Judi." Then, when we were doing *Henry V* at the Old Vic, he played the King of France when I was Princess Katharine. In one of the scenes I saw him corpse really badly on stage and I thought, "Oh my cup is full, it's gone full circle." '

She loved it at Central and made the most of its base at the Albert Hall, sometimes cutting lectures to watch rehearsals in that huge arena, including one for Gigli's last concert, and on one occasion James Stewart filming *The Man Who Knew Too Much* with Alfred Hitchcock. Despite her limited allowance from her parents, she managed to see virtually every play at the Old Vic and in the West End, everything from the classics to new plays, farces and musicals. 'Barbara Jefford and Dorothy Tutin both had a big effect on me; I saw Dottie in *I am a Camera* so many times; so did Peggy Ashcroft of course, but she was a kind of icon to me.' Judi's interest in the whole gamut of theatrical forms has, if anything, grown in intensity and although the choice of her next role has frequently astonished audiences, it has been perfectly consistent with her never-ceasing wish to try something new.

For the whole of her time at Central she lived next door at Queen Alexandra's House, a hostel run by Charis Fry, daughter of the Test cricketer C. B. Fry. It also took students from the Royal College of Music and Judi made friends with both groups; she shared a room with Jennifer Daniel for all three years. The only real restriction was that the front door was locked at 11 p.m. Old family friends from York, the Moffats, now lived in Maida Vale and Judi often visited them with one of her first regular boyfriends, another student at Central called Jeremy Kemp. 'Oh my God, the times Jeremy and I went to Auntie Jean and Uncle John's. He was always saying, "There's a tube", and we'd leave and of course there wasn't, so we'd be walking back and we'd be locked out.'

Other contemporaries at Central included, in the year above her, Ian Hendry, Rowena Cooper and Philip Bond (whose daughter Samantha would much later play opposite Judi), and Stephen Moore two years below; the other leading light in her own year was Vanessa Redgrave. 'Vanessa was very good and very serious. She was the only person in our year who could do Restoration comedy. She just got up and did it; we were all open-mouthed.'

In her autobiography published in 1991, the subject of Judi's admiration reveals that, as far as she was concerned, the boot was on the other foot. 'I was nervous, self-conscious and my throat tightened hard when I came to speak on stage, far worse than any other students. I looked at Judi and was both admiring and jealous. She was confident enough to speak in her own voice; she skipped and hopped with pleasure and excitement up the stairs, down the corridors and onto the stage.'

Another of Judi's contemporaries, and the one who would come to have the most important influence on her future career, was Julian Belfrage. 'Julian had just come out of the Navy, and never used to wear a jockstrap. He used to wear the most terrible black tights with the crutch just below his knees, and a green sweatshirt. Jules used to send everything up. He wasn't really a good actor; he was too aware of the absurdity of acting.' He worked only briefly as an actor before abandoning the boards to represent others. He offered to become Judi's agent and she became his very first client, a professional relation-ship that built on their friendship and proved of great benefit to them both.

Julian was one of the very few students at Central who possessed a car and whenever he drove Judi from the Albert Hall to the outside lectures at 52 Hyde Park Gate, he used to charge her tuppence per lift; so he was clearly a born agent. Judi often taxed him with this later, threatening to deduct it from his ten per cent.

In the summer term of the final year, the school examinations and adjudications paled in importance beside the audition speeches for invited theatre representatives and agents talent-spotting. Judi chose two Shakespearean passages – Miranda's second scene with Ferdinand in *The Tempest*, which begins 'Alas now! pray you, work not so hard', and a speech of Julia's from *The Two Gentlemen of Verona*. She was able to study Barbara Jefford playing the latter part at the Old Vic and she was coached in both pieces by Beatrix Lehmann, who was then on the staff at Central.

Julia Wootton had been sent by the Old Vic, which decided to act quickly on her report and called Judi for an audition at Waterloo Road a couple of days later. Tennent Productions was also interested in her, but they were slower off the mark.

Frank Hauser from the Oxford Playhouse was very keen to engage her, too. 'I saw her public show from the Central School at Her Majesty's Theatre in 1957, and I put in a bid for her straight away, she was obviously very talented; but no, she was going to the Old Vic, and she did.' He had to wait nearly ten years before he at last succeeded in luring her to Oxford, when she totally vindicated his faith in her.

When Judi arrived at the Old Vic Theatre she was more than nervous. 'I was terrified. There were so many people, masses and masses of them queuing. John Dexter (then an ASM) was organising it all, and he said, "Oh Judi, would you come forward please?" At the time my hair was all pulled back and I had an artificial plait round it. Michael Benthall asked me to let it down, so I took off the plait (which got carried on to the stage that night, as one of the props!). I did Miranda's speech again and then Michael said, "Will you go away and learn, 'O, what a noble mind is here o'erthrown?'" I said, "Of course I will", so I went away and learnt it.'

There was a Saturday matinée the next day, so she reported back the following morning, wearing a yellow linen dress (which she kept and her daughter now wears). An old Central friend, Bill Johnson, who had already joined the Old Vic, waited for her outside. After she had performed Ophelia's speech, she was asked to go up to the Artistic Director's office. Michael Benthall's questions puzzled her. 'I thought it was to walk on at the Vic, but he kept asking me my height. Then he paused and said, "I'm going to take an enormous risk; I'm going to cast you as Ophelia. If it doesn't work, I'll ask you to step down and you can understudy. I don't want you to tell anyone, OK? Not even your friend Bill Johnson." Bill was waiting for me down the road, sitting on the wall of that church by Waterloo Station, and I had to tell him I thought I'd got a part walking on.'

She couldn't resist telling her parents, but had to swear them to secrecy for the time being. In the interval between the audition and joining the Old Vic Company, she returned to York to play the Virgin Mary in the Mystery Plays. When she told people which theatre she was going to join, the response was innocently enthusiastic: 'Oh wonderful, maybe one day you'll be playing parts there.' But still she managed to keep her secret.

When the news broke in the press, the least astonished were the staff who had observed her so closely for the previous three years. Just after she left Central, Stephen Moore was surprised to see a notice go up on the board announcing that Judi Dench was the student most likely to become a star, which so far as he knows has never happened again since. But that prediction was more firmly based and longer term than the premature headlines prior to the opening: 'ENTER JUDI – LONDON'S NEW OPHELIA – Old Vic make her first-role star', in the London *Evening News*, and 'The girl with the week's biggest break', in the *Daily Express*.

The competition for the part of Ophelia had been fierce, with about forty other actresses desperately keen to play opposite John Neville's Hamlet. If Judi had let this go to her head she might have had a sticky time with the existing company, many of whom had just returned from an American tour – and were wearing 'I love Elvis' badges. The first people she met were Barbara Leigh-Hunt, Adrienne Hill and Juliet Cooke, who were sharing a flat together. 'I said, "How do you do." Everybody called each other Mr and Miss; it was what you did then. Bill Johnson had gone off somewhere, so I'd got his flat in Queen's Gate, which supplied sheets and laundry, and I got this awful allergy. The day I arrived to do the nunnery scene, my left eye was completely closed up and I was covered in spots.'

On her way home that night, she went into St George's Hospital in Knightsbridge and sat down with others who were waiting. After she had been there about an hour and a half, someone asked her what she wanted and when she said she was waiting to see the doctor, they said she didn't have a number and sent her away. 'I vowed I'd never go into that place again, ever, and I never have, even though it's now that posh hotel, the Lanesborough.'

It transpired that Judi was allergic to the soap powder used to wash her bed linen. Coral Browne, who was playing Gertrude, took pity on her and suggested she move into the top-floor flat of her house in Chester Terrace. Coral had a famous acerbic wit, but her bark was much worse than her bite and she mothered several of the young girls in the company; it was Coral who first coined the affectionate monosyllabic abbreviation to 'Jude'. She and her husband, Philip Pearman, were well-off and glamorous and she would often quietly pass on her elegant clothes to the struggling young actresses. Judi's salary in her first year was £7.10s, which rose to £9 in her second year – the Old Vic ever since Lilian Baylis's day had always offered the best parts in the best plays for the least pay in London.

So when Barbara Leigh-Hunt asked Judi if she would like to share their flat for £3 a week, as Adrienne Hill was leaving, she jumped at it. It was at the top of a tall house in Eaton Terrace; Barbara recalls that often the attractions of this smart central address were outweighed by the location of the actual flat. 'The hours were very long. We were on our feet rehearsing from ten o'clock until one, and from two till five, and then quarter past seven till eleven for the evening per-formance. We were busy changing, running around, understudying, and all the things that young actors do, so we were weary. We'd go home and start to drag ourselves up these interminable flights of stairs. The question always was, when we'd got halfway up, one of us would turn and say, "I wonder if anyone has sent us a hamper from Fortnum and Mason?" When we got to the top, whoever pulled our flat door open would turn and say, "No hamper." A couple of Christmases ago a carrier arrived with a large parcel containing a miniature Fortnum and Mason hamper with two huge cups and saucers decorated with cats, and two large tins of Charbonnel and Walker drinking chocolate. Judi said she'd found it in an antique shop and said, "Oh I know who that's for, it's got Bar's name all over it." She couldn't wait to send it off to me.'

Michael Benthall shared a flat opposite with Robert Helpmann and he would often give them a lift in his car to the theatre, which saved them having to catch an earlier bus. The girls discovered to their mischievous delight that, if they pulled the tall Victorian pine chest of drawers up to their window, put a chair on top and stood on it tiptoe, they could just see into their Director's rooms. Barbara confesses a little shamefacedly, 'We did give Michael a very nasty fright. He nearly crashed the car when we told him we could see into his flat; he was horrified until we let on the truth about it.'

Michael Benthall ran a happy and mostly very successful company at the Old Vic and confounded the doom-sayers who rubbished his Five-Year-Plan to present all the Shakespeare plays over that period, including *Hamlet* twice, a feat never repeated since then. He had a gift for spotting potential talent and then casting them to their strengths, in often unexpected roles. Many of the actors who appear in these pages expressed the same view – that his achievements at the Old Vic were never given their proper recognition – and they were angered that he was allowed to leave at the end almost under a cloud.

Paul Rogers says, 'Most of us canonised Michael Benthall. He was a marvellously sweet, no-nonsense person, wonderfully steadying to an actor on a first night because, with a great twinkle in his eye, he would come round and say, "It's only a play you know." That's been a talisman for all of us.' It certainly was for Judi, who has been heard to echo that advice on many occasions.

Benthall had a gift for handling crowd scenes, honed from working with Tyrone Guthrie. Joss Ackland was very impressed by him: 'He would say to people in the crowd, "You say – 'What light from yonder window breaks?' You say, 'To be or not to be'; you say . . ." What he meant was, "Say something, live", and if they followed his directions literally, of course, it would have been disastrous, but he meant "Be alive." He was very astute.'

He was quietly spoken and blinked a lot; he was known, not unkindly, as 'Mick-the-Blink' behind his back, though it was always 'Mr Benthall' to his face. He had long experience of Shakespeare; he had directed the famous Paul Scofield 'Victorian' *Hamlet* at Stratford in 1948, and in 1957 he was tackling the play for the fourth time. He used the First Quarto text of 1603, rather than the Folio, which transposed the 'To be or not to be' soliloquy from the third act into the second, making much more plausible Hamlet's progressions in mood and improving the placing of the nunnery scene with Ophelia which follows that soliloquy.

In those days there were no such things as previews before the press night, so it was decided to open it out of London, at the Royal Court Theatre in Liverpool. Whatever help this was to the actors, it failed to gain them a favourable verdict from the daily newspaper critics when it opened the Old Vic season on 18 September.

The Times thought it was 'organised extremely well and spoken extremely ill', dismissed John Neville as 'this clockwork Hamlet', and failed to mention Ophelia at all. Thomas Wiseman did in the *Evening Standard*, but only damned her with the faintest of praise: 'Ophelia is played by a girl called Judi Dench, whose first professional performance this only too obviously is. But she goes mad quite nicely and has talent which will be shown to better advantage when she acquires some technique to go with it.'

W. A. Darlington in the *Daily Telegraph* began by saying, 'Last night's *Hamlet* at the Old Vic gave me a deeper and more continuous pleasure than I have had in the theatre for a long time past', and particularly praised John Neville, Jack Gwillim's Claudius, Derek Francis's Polonius, and 'Coral Browne's Gertrude was one of the best things I have seen her do', though even for Darlington, 'Judi Dench made a nice little Ophelia, if not much more.'

There was even less comfort in the normally more measured judgements of the Sunday newspaper critics. Kenneth Tynan praised Michael Benthall's production in the *Observer*: 'Textually and conceptually it is as near to a definitive *Hamlet* as anything I have ever seen ... The production has the clean, physical dexterity I associate with Mr Benthall at his best.' However, the only performances which gained his approval were those of Claudius and Gertrude: 'The Ophelia, Judi Dench, is a pleasing but terribly sane little thing, and there is little in the way of a Hamlet.'

But the real hammer-blow fell in a diatribe from Richard Findlater in the *Sunday Dispatch*, under the headline 'Miss Dench was built up too soon'. He began as he meant to go on: 'Heralded by some windy homage, the latest victim of our theatrical girl-fever stepped out into the Old Vic limelight last week, tripped over her advance publicity, and fell flat on her pretty face ... Hamlet's sweetheart is required to be something more than a piece of Danish patisserie. Is it surprising that Miss Dench did not succeed where other actresses, less blankly inexperienced, have failed? The debut was, in my view, a débâcle.' Having hailed the other leading players and the production, his parting shot at the main target of his ire was loftily dismissive: 'Judi Dench, in time, may well be a prime asset of our theatre. A few years' hard labour, in proper obscurity, will do wonders.'

This lack of percipience in the critic, who was usually one of the best and most evocative judges of great acting, would come back to haunt him years later; when it did he had the grace to apologise handsomely and publicly for what he came to recognise as an intemperate and over-personal attack.

John Neville blames the Old Vic's PR department for Judi's bad press. 'I begged them not to emphasise the great discovery of Judi prior to the opening. I thought, and still think, that it would have been best just to let the media discover her for themselves. I'm convinced she would then have received the great reviews she deserved, had they taken my advice. Judi was a very fine Ophelia. She had exactly the right quality – vulnerability. My Hamlet interpretation was based on the disillusionment of youth (the worst kind of disillusion in my view); Judi's Ophelia matched this in vulnerability.'

He denies the critics' charge that she was given the part long before she was ready for it. 'She was *very ready* for it. I must admit that when Michael Benthall told me he was casting Ophelia with a young actress straight out of drama school I was horrified and told him so! But I was wrong. Michael, whom I adored, was a great and under-rated director and, above all, he was the *greatest* discoverer of talent.' A glance at the cast lists of the Benthall years at the Old Vic proves that claim up to the hilt – the vast majority of those names are now top-line stars with long and distinguished credits behind them and it was Michael Benthall who discovered them. But it was difficult even for him to resist an overwhelming critical tide.

The critical drubbing was not the end of the afflictions Judi had to endure over her first professional part. At the end of the season, the company was scheduled for a six months' foreign tour and she was summoned to a meeting in the Director's office, where he told her that in the United States Ophelia would be played by Barbara Jefford. 'He said, "You didn't get very good notices as this, Judi." I think he found it quite difficult to say to me, because when I went in he was standing looking out of the window; and every night when I come home from the National I look up at those little windows at the top of the Old Vic, and I know that that was where he standing, on the right-hand side. He said, "Do you still want to go?" I said, "I do, I do still want to go", and he said, "Well, you'll be out of *Hamlet* altogether. I wouldn't ask you to go to be in it. I want you to play the Princess of France, and Maria." Both of those were very good parts. So I had a very, very good cry afterwards. I remember John was waiting for me, because he knew what was coming, and I cried a great deal. Then I went and had all my hair cut off.'

Michael Benthall's reluctant decision put John Neville and the rest of the company in an awkward position too, because by now Judi had a firm hold on their affections. Barbara Leigh-Hunt was placed in a particular dilemma. 'It was very difficult for everybody really, because we had to make it possible for Barbara Jefford to play it, and yet we all felt a loyalty to Jude. She was devastated, naturally; any young actress would be in those circumstances, particularly as she was going to America with the company in another play, so that was doubly difficult for her. It was very unfortunate, but you have to learn these things very early on; you have to take the blows.'

This whole unhappy sequence of events might have been enough to destroy totally the self-confidence of a young actress with less steel and determination to succeed. It was a tribute to Judi's resilience that for the rest of her formative years at the Old Vic, she happily played smaller parts for a year or two until her success and growing experience led to the first great smash hit of her career.

three

1957–60

The Old Vic – from Juliet to Juliet

Hamlet was an unhappy experience for Judi, but the next production at the Old Vic, *Measure for Measure*, was unhappy for the entire company, the blame for which can be laid squarely at the door of the guest director from America, Margaret Webster. She was known to her friends as Peggy, but she never succeeded in getting on those terms with her cast. She arrived on crutches, with a broken leg in plaster, then got off on completely the wrong foot with John Neville, who was playing Angelo, when she turned to Barbara Jefford and said, 'I wonder what it was that made Sir John so wonderful in this part?' Barbara had played Isabella before in the 1950 Stratford production with Gielgud but, if the director was tactless enough to ask such a question in front of her own Angelo, the actress had far too much sense to attempt to answer it.

Things went from bad to worse. The director was rude to every-body; she never learnt their names, and would call the boys walking-on Soldier 3 and Soldier 4. Barbara Leigh-Hunt laughs ruefully at the memory of her giving notes on-stage: 'She'd swing her crutch in a great circle above her head to get it in a position to move, and John always used to overact terribly behind her back; he would shy and cower. He swore she'd leave on crutches with both legs in plaster, "because I'll break the other fucking leg", he said.'

Judi came in for her share of abuse, too. Her costume as Juliet was stiff and flared, falling from her shoulders to the floor, so it looked a bit like a playing card. She wore a board over the front, hanging down to her waist, with 'Adulteress' written on it, and a wig of long straight hair. When she walked on at the dress parade, Margaret Webster shouted, 'Oh my God, why do all ingénues look like parcels?'

It was the explosion over the designs that was the last straw for the company. She insisted that Barry Kay design the costumes and passed all his sketches without query. The cast hated them, but when they put them on, Margaret Webster screamed abuse at the designer in front of everyone and the actors immediately took his side. Whenever they were off, they escaped to the pub next door – John Neville used to lean against the door at half past five and when it was opened, he would fall in and say, 'Sorry I'm late.' At the technical run, which overran with endless stopping and staring, he was a little the worse for wear and past caring whom he upset. On one entrance he struck a match on the vast timber set and announced, 'I name this ship *Disaster*.'

It nearly was, too, but at least Judi was spared being picked out by the press, which barely mentioned her at all, though W. A. Darlington provoked some ribaldry backstage with his reference to 'Margaret Webster, who obviously is one of those creative directors by whom actors are inspired to do their best.' This experience failed to put her off the play, to which she would return to play Isabella twice, in productions which were both happier and much more successful.

Michael Benthall took over the reins of the next production, *A Midsummer Night's Dream*, where the import from outside produced laughter instead of tears – Frankie Howerd as Bottom. Judi has fond memories of him, with only slight reservations: 'He was lovely, except he couldn't learn the lines, and he was also very, very mean. At lunchtime we used to go to the pub and he'd always manage to be the last in. So they all got wise to this and one day Dan Thorndike, Ronnie Fraser, Jimmy Culliford and some of the others waited for him to come out of his dressing-room, and they all hung back and followed him. When he saw them he stopped to do his shoe up and said, "'Ere, what are you lot doin'?" They said, "We're waiting for you to buy us a drink." He was nice, though.'

After an uncertain start, as he grew more familiar with the Shakespearean text he remarked at one rehearsal, 'What a scriptwriter!' He never quite got over his awe of his classical colleagues and twenty-five years later, when Judi and Barbara Leigh-Hunt were both playing in *Pack of Lies*, he went round to see them and said diffidently, 'Do you remember me, my name's Frankie Howerd?' They laughed and said, 'Don't be silly, of course we do.'

The costumes and make-up were strikingly designed by James Bailey with a greeney-bluey tinge to everything. Judi was the First Fairy; the other fairies came from the Royal Ballet School. They had gauze costumes with gauze wings and tight-fitting little headdresses; they were choreographed to come down a ramp with their heads down and their arms out behind them, quivering with the gauze of their skirts blown behind them by fans to accentuate the swooping movement. When they knelt down too quickly, the fans lifted their skirts in the air and slowly deposited them right over their faces. This was too much, especially for the First Fairy, and they all collapsed in a heap on the floor. As they struggled to get their move right, Michael Benthall delivered a rebuke she still quotes: 'Miss Dench, will you try not to knock the other fairies over. You're coming in with your hands like a pair of finnan-haddies.'

John Neville was not in this play, as he was due to go into hospital for a tonsillectomy, so he told Judi he was going to send up the designer at the costume parade. She still giggles at the memory. 'James Bailey was very small and rather effete, and he wanted very ethereal-looking fairies. At 11.20 they said, "OK, the fairies please", and John went on in a figleaf he had had made out of green lurex, a pair of long green socks and nothing else except a huge pink hat with buttons all round it that had been made for David Dodimead in *Measure for Measure* and thrown out by Margaret Webster. James Bailey had to be carried to a room at the side of the Old Vic. He had the vapours, he absolutely had the vapours, I'll never forget it. He laughed so much he was completely overcome. When James asked why he wasn't in his production, John said, "I can never, ever be in any of your productions James, because I am so very, very common, and you are such a lady".'

The fun the cast had communicated itself to the audience, but the critics only gave it a qualified welcome, most of the qualifications being expressed about appearance rather than performance. Tynan called it 'one of Michael Benthall's chillier productions . . . it was hard to tell whether the fairies were blue from cold or make-up, even their smiles looked frozen'; and in the *Daily Telegraph* Kenneth Young thought that Titania's 'attendant fairies had been too close to the flour bag. But it was a brilliant, shining evening, as lively as vaudeville, and more magical than Maskelyne ever was.'

One non-critic was even more taken aback by the special Max Factor 'ghostly make-up' used by the immortals. When the Queen and the Duke of Edinburgh met the cast after a performance, the fairies were all lined up at the end of one row and Prince Philip looked up and said, 'Good heavens, they look like a very nasty car accident', because they all looked like ghosts.

The performances most singled out for praise were Coral Browne's Helena, Derek Godfrey's Oberon and Frankie Howerd's Bottom; Judi was not mentioned by name. However, when Joyce Redman's husband came to see her as Titania, he told his wife afterwards, 'That young girl playing the First Fairy is going to be a big star.'

Titania was one of the parts in which Judi would vindicate his prediction before long, and the next play in the repertoire – *Twelfth Night* – was another that she would revisit to acclaim, in a bigger part. Michael Benthall cast her as Maria. 'I played it straight and then one day Michael said to me, "Could you play it in anything else?" I said, "Yes, I'll play it Yorkshire", and it fitted actually very well. We had a lovely time doing that.' For her brother Peter, this was his favourite performance: 'I thought, "Gosh, that's my little sister", though she's moved me in so many things.'

John Neville received most of the critical plaudits for his foppish and very funny Sir Andrew Aguecheek and his by now large fan club laughed almost before he said the lines, but he is quick to share the credit. 'Her Maria was perfect. She is a wonderful comedienne, as well as a great classical actress. She showed an aptitude for Shakespeare from the very beginning.'

Not all the critics shared his admiration. *The Times* disapproved of 'a Maria played as a soubrette with a northern accent instead of as a lady-in-waiting', but W. A. Darlington eulogised the whole production, calling it 'an evening of enchantment . . . in which the May-morning gaiety and laughter is tempered with a tinge of melancholy'. He enjoyed Barbara Jefford's Viola, Richard Wordsworth's Malvolio, John Neville's Aguecheek, and Derek Godfrey's Feste, and only muffed his praise for the Maria by misspelling her first name: 'In the frankly comic scenes the spirit of laughter irradiates everything. Judy Dench is light and quick and happy as Maria, flitting about the stage in an orange frock, making no secret of her adoration of Sir Toby, who is played by Paul Daneman as an elderly mischievous schoolboy.'

Her flitting about was less carefree in the three parts of *Henry VI*, in which she had several walk-on, or rather rush-on, appearances, playing various citizens or Cade rebels. The set had a curved forestage, with steps leading down into the orchestra pit to what were called assembly entrances. The rebels were given pikes, pitchforks and staves, which were real instead of the usual lightweight stage props, and therefore quite dangerous. As the angry mob rushed off into the dark assembly entrances one night, Judi was knocked out by one of these too, too solid poles. *Henry VI* was dogged by accidents. Derek Francis was playing Jack Cade and at the second performance, a matinée, he leapt from a cart onto the steeply raked stage and injured his leg. He was carried off and taken to hospital and the rest of the Cade rebel scenes were cut, which made the plot quite hard to follow. He had not returned by the evening as he had, in fact, broken his leg. In that performance, all the Cade rebel scenes were cut, which made a total nonsense of the plot, though the cast had the consolation that for once during that play they made the pub before closing time.

Other misfortunes reduced the ranks in that difficult trilogy. A virulent strain of Asian flu in 1958 laid low many of the company, for some reason hitting the men first, so at one performance the assembled rebels consisted only of the three occupants of the Eaton Terrace flat, which somewhat undermined the dramatic tension of Jack Cade's command: 'Now go some and pull down the Savoy; others to th'Inns of Court; down with them all.' The giggles on-stage were drowned by the involuntary laughter of the audience.

The requirement to play every night, in either a speaking or non-speaking capacity, meant that it was impossible for Judi to get home to York at weekends, though her parents faithfully came down to see her in every production. Barbara Leigh-Hunt was just able to catch the last train to her home in Bath on a Saturday night and the early one back on Monday mornings in time for rehearsal, so she invited Judi to go home with her on many weekends, and also one Christmas when they had only a short break between performances. Judi got on so well with Barbara's mother that she christened her the O.M. – the Other Mother.

In the late summer of 1958, the Old Vic Company set off on their long American tour with *Hamlet, Twelfth Night* and a new production of *Henry V*, which opened first at the Edinburgh Festival. This long absence meant that the girls had to give up the flat in Eaton Terrace. After the last night of the season in *Hamlet*, the three of them piled into a cab at the stage door and, as soon as they had packed ready for their early-morning departure, they were on their knees washing the floors of the flat for the last time – from stardust to dust within a short cab ride.

The tour opened in Paris, Brussels and Antwerp just with *Hamlet* and *Henry VIII*, which starred Harry Andrews as the King, John Gielgud as Wolsey, and Edith Evans as Queen Katharine. This was Judi's first contact with Sir John, whom she had admired only from afar until now. The second play was not accompanying them to America, but Gielgud was to give his one-man Shakespearean recital, *Ages of Man*, in New York at the same time. Judi went round shyly after one performance and joined a queue of visitors backstage. Sir John came out of his dressing-room, spotted her and said, 'Oh, Judi, how nice to see you', turned to the others and explained, 'We were at the Old Vic together, you know', as if she had co-starred with him instead of just playing one of the Queen's ladies-in-waiting.

Her actual co-star in *Henry V* was Laurence Harvey and she found that that was a stickier relationship. 'He never, ever looked into my face, he just looked above my head – you couldn't be that tall! He was perfectly polite to me, but there was a suspicion that he was only there to promote his film, *Room at the Top*. I don't think he was very good as Henry V. I always think Henry's a soldier-king and one of the boys, and Larry was very much more of an aristocratic king, not one of the boys.'

Joss Ackland joined the company for the tour and goes further than Judi in his criticism: 'I was very fond of Larry Harvey, but he was lousy as Henry V, although he got rave reviews. He was a lousy stage actor; he could only ever manage the first performance in anything. And he'd leave great pauses, which impressed the Americans a lot, and he got away with it.'

Joss introduced Judi to jazz and took her and several others to hear Kid Ory, Earl Hines, Louis Armstrong and Billie Holliday. They all seized the chance to let their hair down after a performance. In Boston, Joss and Judi were leaving a restaurant in the very early hours with John Neville, Laurence Harvey and Richard Wordsworth, when they came across a lavatory bowl with a chain attached, left unattended in the middle of the pavement on a street corner. In their convivial condition they thought it might come in useful, so the men picked it up and carried it. As a police car approached and slowed down, Judi yelled out in her broadest Yorkshire accent, 'Officers, stop those men, they've stolen that lavatory.' After a brief conversation, the bemused police just grinned at them and told them to carry on – if they wanted it, they could keep it. When Douglas Morris, the company manager, awoke the next morning he found an extra loo in the middle of his room, wrapped in pink tissue paper.

The company played from coast to coast, travelling across the States by train to San Francisco, a journey which took three days, while they all goggled at the spectacular scenery. Harold Innocent got very excited when he claimed he had seen a bear, which none of the others was able to see. Joss Ackland snorted, 'He was probably pissed!' They progressed from San Francisco to Los Angeles and Dallas. Judi's main memory of Texas is of the man from the Nieman-Marcus store coming to say goodbye to her on the train and getting caught on it as it departed. They had to stop it quickly so he could get off, as it was a long-distance express, but that memory is an early indication of Judi's huge enthusiasm for shopping.

The only real on-stage hiccups happened in Philadelphia, where the cast kept getting lost between the dressing-rooms and the stage during *Twelfth Night*. Judi and Jane Downs as Olivia had to improvise for a while, waiting for Viola to enter, until Barbara Jefford at last found her way. Judi had the same trouble not once, but twice. On the second occasion her line was, 'Get ye all three into the box-tree. Malvolio's coming down this walk', and John Neville hissed, 'Wanna bet?' which convulsed them all. Not that it seemed to throw the audience, which gave them, as everywhere else in America, an ecstatic reception, if occasionally a confused one. One American woman looked at Judi's short cropped hair and, despite the fact that she was wearing a grey skirt with her navy-blue blazer, asked John Neville, 'Does your son come with you everywhere you go?'

As promised, Judi was not required to walk on in *Hamlet*, so she used some of her nights off to see other shows, particularly on Broadway, which was where she saw Gielgud's *Ages of Man*. But she was not too proud to watch Barbara Jefford as Ophelia, an experience she profited by when the company returned. They were invited to go to Yugoslavia, but Barbara was already committed to do *The Cenci* with Hugh Griffith, so once again Judi was summoned to that top-floor office. 'Michael said, "Now Miss Dench, I think you've learnt a lot in six months." I said, "Well I hope so." He said, "Well, I think you ought to play Ophelia in Yugoslavia." We played Belgrade, Zagreb and Ljublana; it was so exciting. I felt I played it better. I'd watched Barbara play it; I couldn't copy her performance because I'm not like her, but I felt I understood it better.'

They played to packed houses, but the students could not afford to come so a small group, including Judi, went to the universities instead and did scenes from the play, for free.

Between New York and Yugoslavia, Judi and Barbara Leigh-Hunt briefly shared a tiny flat in Notting Hill, then Judi moved for the duration of her second Old Vic season to lodgings in Elm Park Gardens in Chelsea. She bought her first car at this time, a second-hand MG which she used to get to and from the theatre. She learnt to drive at sixteen, but only got round to taking her driving test when she was fifty.

The MG broke down one night when she was driving John Neville, at about one o'clock in the morning, and a policeman stopped. 'Do you know you've only got one light?'

Judi said hastily, 'I do, I'm on my way to get it replaced.'

'Are you a learner driver?'

'I am, yes.'

'Where are your plates?'

When Judi hummed and hawed, he said, 'You're going to be reported.'

She was summoned to go to Bow Street. 'I didn't go. I wrote the judge a letter and said, "I did have adhesive L-plates, but you know what the weather's been like, my lord." I was fined £1. I was very, very lucky indeed, because I was a criminal.'

Even then, she could not be bothered to take her test and she might have gone beyond her fiftieth birthday without doing so, had not Barbara Leigh-Hunt passed her test just before it, which galvanised Judi at last into doing the same.

Michael Benthall's new recruits to the company included Donald

Houston, John Woodvine, Maggie Smith, John Moffatt and Alec McCowen. The last arrived feeling very conscious of being the new boy in the company: 'At the end of the first day's rehearsal of *The Double Dealer*, people were getting their coats and hats and preparing to go home; Judi was with a big group of actors near the stage door and she just called to me, "Come on Al, we're going to tea." Nobody else has ever called me Al, before or since, but I was suddenly a member of that company, which she just did by that one little act. She spent Christmas at this time with me and my family in Tunbridge Wells and my father fell madly in love with her; he always used to call her "The Mighty Atom", which is in fact a very good description of her.'

The Double Dealer played for a week at the Edinburgh Festival, before the opening of the Old Vic season, and was much acclaimed in both cities. It had not been seen in the West End since 1916 and even then only in a club production, but Michael Benthall's production disproved the conventional view that it was only minor Congreve. None of the reviewers even attempted to summarise the complicated plot, although Elizabeth Frank in the *News Chronicle* gave a snapshot of the players: 'Miles Malleson is a joy as a much betrayed and gullible husband; Alec McCowen sets off a shower of sparks as the pert coxcomb Brisk; and the ladies dispense venom, blandishment, coyness and sweet innocence in that order, in the persons of Ursula Jeans, Maggie Smith, Moyra Fraser and Judi Dench'; and Alan Pryce-Jones in the *Observer* thought that 'the Cynthia of Judi Dench is charmingly crystalline'.

Miles Malleson specialised in playing comic old men. As Sir Paul Plyant, he wore a full-bottomed wig over a bald pate and underneath was his own toupée, but his off-stage behaviour belied his years, which is Judi's abiding memory of that play: 'It was so extraordinary that, when we were in Edinburgh, Maggie and I had to spend the whole of the time between the matinée and the evening performance locked in a loo, because he was always after us.'

It was preceded onto the stage of the Old Vic by Wendy Toye's production of *As You Like It*, which she set in the Regency period. Highly experienced as a director of ballet, opera and films, this was her debut in Shakespeare, but she showed a sure touch, much admired by Judi. 'The designs were so clever. Rosalind left to go into the forest in a lovely dress and gradually you saw the dress being made into trousers; it got whittled down to all sorts of things, until it was just a scarf over the head. That's good designing, very clever; it told a proper story.'

The real star of this production was Alec McCowen. 'He was so funny as Touchstone; when he said with disgust, "So *this* is the Forest of Arden", it brought the house down.' But Judi was less happy than the critics with her own performance. 'I had a blonde ponytail as Phebe – what an arse-paralysing part! When everyone's shifting about and finding their handbags, and ready to go home, suddenly she comes on again, having a row with Silvius. "Oh good grief", they all think.'

Wendy Toye thinks she is too hard on herself, 'because she just made it mean something, she made it real, she made it truthful; maybe there are people who say she's not the greatest verse-speaker,' (said very disbelievingly) 'but to me she is.'

To her regret she has never had the opportunity to direct Judi since 1959, but if they have not worked together again they have frequently played together. They discovered a mutual passion for games of all kinds, especially elaborate and difficult word games, and a small group of friends, several from that early Old Vic company, still meet regularly for games sessions. These are taken very seriously, which can startle newcomers. Ian McKellen arrived twenty minutes late the first time and was severely ticked off by Judi: 'Where have you been? We're all waiting to start!'

After his triumph as Touchstone, Alec McCowen was cast opposite Judi, as the young lovers Algernon and Cecily in *The Importance of Being Earnest*. They enjoyed their scenes together despite their mutual propensity for giggling. Fay Compton was playing the formidable Lady Bracknell, but her command of Wilde's dialogue was less than precise, which only too quickly set Alec off. 'She was getting on in years and she did make a few mistakes, one of which was on the line, "Thirty-five is a very attractive age." On the first night she said, "Thirty-five is a very attractive name", which started us off. It also threw John Justin playing John Worthing, who then announced that he was "Miss Gardew's cardigan", and it steadily went to pieces. Judi and I were hauled into the leading lady's dressing-room and given a really sound telling-off – threatened with fire and damnation. We were very chastened and we tried desperately not to giggle again. Whether we succeeded, I doubt, but it was quite testing.'

Philip Hope-Wallace echoed Miss Compton in his Manchester *Guardian* review, where he observed at that first performance how they both 'occasionally obscure a brilliant line in a shame-faced mutter'. Judi has never conquered her weakness for corpsing, as we shall see, but she has learnt since then how to conceal it from the audience.

The play had not been done at the Old Vic for a quarter of a century, but it was the memory of the glittering Gielgud wartime production that cast the longest shadow, especially of Edith Evans as Lady Bracknell, against whom all later assumptions have been judged, and still are. This meant that even the favourable notices had a grudging tone, epitomised by Philip Hope-Wallace: 'The performance is, in sum, enjoyable, decent "People's Classical Theatre". The little extra polish may presently be added, though it seems unlikely.'

Anthony Cookman was more encouraging in the *Tatler*, giving the edge to the women for stylishness: 'Miss Barbara Jefford is deliciously remote in her avowal of the curious vibrations set up in her by the name of Ernest, and she and Miss Judi Dench make their scene of rivalry the comic highlight of the evening.'

Wilde was followed by Shakespeare, with *The Merry Wives of Windsor*, and the audiences seemed to enjoy John Hale's romping production, though looking back on it Joss Ackland thinks it was pretty dreadful, especially his own Falstaff. 'There was a knock on my dressing-room door at the end of the show, and Michael Benthall put his head inside and went, "Bub, bub, bub, bub . . ." and walked out. I wanted to jump off Waterloo Bridge that night, but he was absolutely right.' As Anne Page, Judi was again described as 'charming'.

Her first two and a half years at the Old Vic had had their ups and downs, but Judi had survived the critical savaging of her Ophelia and the devastation of losing the part, and learnt how to cope with unsympathetic directors like Margaret Webster. Michael Benthall had taught her a lot, but she had also gained much from her fellow-actors – and not just by playing with them. 'I used to watch all the time. I don't think actors do that any more. I don't think there's any standing in the wings watching people now, but we used to do that at the Old Vic all the time. I don't remember being in the dressing-room except to change.'

All this study now began to pay off. 1960 was the year when she was promoted to a series of leading parts and fully justified Benthall's faith in her. She began with an interesting and challenging double, the same role almost simultaneously in two different media – the Princess of France on stage and on television. Donald Houston wooed her as Henry V at the Old Vic, and then Peter Dews cast her in the same part in his 'Age of Kings' series of all Shakespeare's History plays for the BBC, where Judi played it 'with different cuts, different costumes, different moves, and a different Henry, Robert Hardy. He was absolutely wonderful – well, he thinks he's the incarnation of him.'

Peter Dews recruited a young company of actors, most of whom played in the cycle right through from *Richard II* to *Richard III*, playing everything from leading parts to rebels and spear-carriers, with the occasional guest performer just in one role, like Judi, though even she doubled as a young soldier in the background the night before Agincourt. A young member of the ensemble was Patrick Garland. 'Peter Dews brought her to the TV studios to watch *Richard II*, that was the first time I saw her and she made a great impression. She was exquisitely pretty, diminutive and bright, and I remember the merriment and intelligence in her eyes, and thinking what a heavenly girl.'

That merriment bubbles right through her TV performance, as she claps her hands to her mouth in a vain attempt to hide her giggles at Henry's awkward courtship; it shines through even in the murky old monochrome telerecording and is considerably enhanced by her impeccable accent, in both the French and the English dialogue.

Her last small part at the Old Vic was the Queen in *Richard II*, which she took over from Maggie Smith when Alec McCowen replaced John Justin as the King. Neither of the new pair appeared to satisfy the critics, but it was the next production, which opened the new season in October 1960, which caused the greatest sparks to fly, with reactions polarising into passions that echoed those on-stage.

This was over the famous *Romeo and Juliet* directed by Franco Zeffirelli, whose previous experience was in directing opera. Michael Benthall had been impressed by his productions at Covent Garden, particularly *Cavalleria Rusticana*, and told Zeffirelli he wanted him to bring to the production a feeling of Italy – 'something truly Mediterranean; not heavily carved furniture and velvet drapes, but sunlight on a fountain, wine and olives and garlic. New, different, real, young. Put like that it made some sense for me to do it and I agreed.'

Zeffirelli thought the original invitation was a hoax, as he had never directed any Shakespeare; indeed, he had only ever previously directed one play, in Italian, and that was not a success. His apprehensions were initially shared by his prospective cast before they met him, especially Alec McCowen, who was to play Mercutio. 'All we knew was that an Italian director was coming over, who had never directed Shakespeare before, so we thought Michael Benthall had gone mad and our feelings were very against Zeffirelli to begin with, because of what we saw as his lack of experience. But then he was so charming; he was more a seducer than a producer. We all fell in love with him and finally would do anything for him.'

Benthall suggested John Stride and Judi for the title roles, which was agreed on the spot. Zeffirelli told the cast he wanted it to be a real story in a plausible medieval city at the opening of the Renaissance, so he wanted no wigs; everyone had to grow their hair long – the girls and the boys. The embarrassment the latter felt at first soon evaporated when they realised how much easier it was to move, and to fight. The convincing sword fights became one of the high spots of the production and had audiences on the edge of their seats with excitement. Alec McCowen resisted this new approach at first, 'because in my death scene as Mercutio he said they should go on laughing at me and thinking I was playing the fool, much longer than was usually done. I foolishly protested, "But Franco, I'm dying, it's my great death scene." He said, "Yes, the more they laugh the more heightened the event will be", and of course he was quite right.'

The young lovers were similarly shocked out of their Englishness. The first time they played their initial meeting, the director cried out: 'No, no, what is it, the end of the world? You are at a party, you see a pretty girl, you want to meet her, to kiss her, to ... well, do it!' John Stride was instructed to play the balcony scene like a dog seeing a young bitch for the first time, which was not quite the way it had ever been played on the Old Vic stage before.

Zeffirelli would stand beside the actors, miming doing it with them, which was often an eye-opener, though Alec McCowen found it daunting in the Queen Mab speech when he watched him dancing round pinching people's bottoms, kissing them, and generally playing the fool. 'Then he said, "You do it." I said, "But Franco, I'm from Tunbridge Wells." He said, "Do it your way", and I managed it. It was a very happy production, and Judi and John were adorable.'

The lovers were adored by the audiences and so was the whole atmosphere of the production; the first night went well, even though the second half had never yet been done in costume on the complete set until that opening night. But if the audience loved it, the notices the next morning generally tore it apart, complaining that it lacked poetry, dignity and, curiously, speed and pace. In the *Daily Telegraph*, W. A. Darlington lamented that 'the tragedy had been swallowed up in a welter of over-production. Franco Zeffirelli, the Italian director responsible for this, has not avoided the pitfall into which nearly all foreign directors of Shakespeare fall – he has not realised how much the poetry matters to an English audience.' *The Times* was dismissive: 'Miss Judi Dench and Mr John Stride are young players who act their parts competently but cannot yet make anything like constant touch with the poetry within them.' The *Sunday Times* so failed to grasp the director's intention that it heaped abuse on the principals: 'There can never have been a Mercutio of less gaiety than Alec McCowen ... John Stride's Romeo, though well-spoken, is pasty-faced and sulky; and in the balcony scene Judi Dench flaps her arms about like a demented marionette. What has happened to youth? Where is its spring, its elan?'

Clive Barnes in the *Daily Express* was one of the few critics to get the point, praising Zeffirelli for giving the play 'a new, almost strange, vitality', and infusing it into his cast. 'Beautiful Judi Dench made a wayward, spirited Juliet, and in John Stride she found a boyish, ardent Romeo plunging to his destruction like an eager puppy-dog with a death-wish. Alec McCowen's sardonic Mercutio, spitting out his hate with bitter wit had, like the two lovers, the quality of timeless, misunderstood youth.' He even perceived how this new interpretation would divide opinion: 'Many will hate this beatnik *Romeo*. Many more will be stirred by it.'

But his lone voice was not enough to prevent the whole company being stirred to despair on the day after the opening. The cast were practically in tears and the director was convinced he had failed abysmally. Only Michael Benthall stood like a rock against the critical onslaught. When Zeffirelli rang him and told him he was leaving, 'he barked at me not to be so stupid and to be at the theatre before that night's performance. When I got there everyone was nervous – some were reading the afternoon reviews, which were just as ugly. Suddenly Michael called us on-stage and proceeded to give us a full-scale dressing-down and pep talk. We were fools to take note of critics with no vision, and fools not to realise that we had the most wonderful production, the most original vision of Shakespeare since Tyrone Guthrie's *Hamlet*. "Go on," he told them, "and listen to your hearts." And they did. That second night was fantastic and we all felt better.'

They all felt even better on the Sunday, when Kenneth Tynan pulled out all the stops in a long rave review in the *Observer*, under a succinct quote from Act IV of the play – 'This is as't should be.' He claimed that Zeffirelli had worked 'a miracle ... a revelation, even perhaps a revolution ... so abundant and compelling was the life on stage that I could not wait to find out what happened next. The Vic has done nothing better for a decade.' He was excited by the youthful vitality of the playing and touched by both the lovers' first meeting and the balcony scene which had been so criticised by his colleagues: 'Judi Dench, a calm, wise little Juliet, waits him aloft; their encounter is grave, awkward and extremely beautiful.'

This turned the tide and word of mouth did the rest. The box office was besieged and the run had to be extended to an unprecedented 122 performances.

The intensity of love and anguish that Judi poured into Juliet led to one extraordinary reaction from the audience, surprising because it came from a particularly regular and sophisticated theatre-goer – Reginald Dench. When he and his wife came to see it, he was so moved by Juliet's cry of, 'Where are my father and my mother, Nurse?' that an involuntary cry rang back from his seat in the stalls, 'Here we are darling, in row H.' Parental identification with a performance can rarely have been so publicly expressed. Fortunately, it caused the barest flicker of surprise on the stage and did not seem to break the spell on the audience.

As a young student at RADA, John Hurt went to see it four times.

'She was an absolutely stunning Juliet – the way she was just turning and yearning on that balcony, it was so sexy, and she did seem as if she was fourteen. Fantastic I thought, and so did the rest of the audience, so I don't know where the critics got it wrong; and also she speaks verse immaculately.'

It was the criticisms of the verse-speaking that cut deepest and to this day, when the subject of *Romeo and Juliet* comes up, Judi's immediate response is, 'Ah yes, the one without any poetry!' with an edge in her voice that reveals just how deeply they cut.

After its success in the Waterloo Road, the production was invited to the Venice Festival, where it was played in the exquisite Fenice Theatre, and the company watched the audience arrive in such numbers that there was a gondola traffic jam. Half the crowned heads of Europe seemed to be there, as well as the Lee Strasberg family from America, but Zeffirelli was much more nervous of the reception by his family and the rest of his compatriots. His fears were groundless, and the reception was even more tumultuous than in London. Judi was awarded the Paladino D'Argentino by the Palermo International Prize Committee for Best Actress of the Year, the precursor of many awards to come, and one she particularly prized after their baptism of critical fire.

The production went on to a tour of packed houses at home, and then on to Broadway, but Judi refused to go with it, much to Zeffirelli's displeasure. 'I thought he'd never forgive me for not going to America with it. He was very, very angry indeed; he wouldn't speak to me.'

The reason for her refusal was positive, not negative. The Stratford-upon-Avon Memorial Theatre was being transformed by Peter Hall into the Royal Shakespeare Company, and one of its associate directors, Michel St-Denis, was so taken with her Juliet that she was asked to join the new company, an offer which she eagerly accepted. Her four years at the Old Vic had seen her blossom into one of the brightest new hopes of her generation. Now she had the chance to spread her wings on new stages with a new company.

four

1960–62

From the Old Vic to Stratford-upon-Avon

Romeo and Juliet opened and closed the 1960–61 Old Vic season and its popular success tended to eclipse the two other productions which opened after it, and which also featured Judi as a young girl in love. Each of these characters had a happier fate in store than Juliet.

The first was Kate Hardcastle in *She Stoops to Conquer*, produced by Douglas Seale and starring the new young pop music star, Tommy Steele, as Tony Lumpkin. Judi thought that, like Frankie Howerd, when he arrived he was a bit scared of what he saw as grand classical actors, but he struck up a friendship on the first day with old Etonian Nicholas Meredith and the two of them used to go down together to the Eel and Pie Shop.

A lot of teenage fans came to see their idol and were not at all sure what they expected to see, which Judi found a bit disconcerting. 'I enjoyed that enormously, except that a lot of the audience were just restless until Tommy came on. It was like being bottom of the bill at the Palladium. One letter came to the stage door that said, "Dear Tommy, me and my friends are going to come and see *She Stoops to Conquer* on Friday night. Please could you put in 'Little White Bull', as it is our Maudie's birthday?"

The critics gave him only mixed reviews, but did acknowledge his popularity with the audience, and for Philip Hope-Wallace in the *Guardian*, 'the heart of the play, Kate's conquest by stooping, came off delightfully. Judi Dench plays it with such high spirit and delicacy of merriment that she scored the triumph of the evening and indeed made the play a success.' W. A. Darlington, in the *Daily Telegraph*, registered the ovation she received on her exit, after the scene with young Marlow when she masqueraded as a barmaid, and welcomed the chance she was given 'to show how sure her comic touch is now, and to flicker about the stage like a gay little female will-o'-the-wisp'. This was echoed by Kenneth Tynan in the *Observer*: 'Judi Dench, who improves with each new costume she dons, makes Kate an irresistible imp.'

A Midsummer Night's Dream was frequently in the Old Vic repertoire, as it was always popular with audiences, and it was revived in a new production by Michael Langham three years after Judi had played the First Fairy. Now she was promoted to Hermia, with Barbara Leigh-Hunt as her rival in love, Helena. It was perfect casting in terms of the text and their talents, but this only became apparent to them after it opened. Barbara still cannot contain her anger when she thinks about it. 'I thought Michael Langham was an absolute pig. He would reduce Judi and me to tears in front of the company practically at every rehearsal – if not one then the other, or both of us. I completely forgot we were doing a comedy; I hated every minute of it. He was very unkind to everybody and most of the company hated him.'

Judi is less harsh about him in retrospect. 'He was a disciplinarian, and I could put up with his saying, "Are you going to come in like that? You convey about as much as a bouncing ball!" because I believed he thought I could do the part.'

If he had a curious way of showing it, his belief in all of them was vindicated in front of an audience. For Barbara, 'it was a source of astonishment that he got amazing performances out of both of us. When the laughs started to come I was almost shocked, because I'd forgotten it was a comedy and that people were supposed to enjoy it, because the whole thing was such torture. But once we began to play it we enjoyed it enormously. My mother was sitting in front of Paul Rogers and his wife on the first night and Paul said, "Oh my two favourite girls in *The Dream*." So she had a good night.'

The girls' costumes had the lowest cleavage in London, reminiscent of Peter Lely's picture of Nell Gwyn, and in the fight between the two of them Hermia was supposed to pull off a piece of Helena's dress. 'But on the first night I pulled too much of it, and exposed poor Bar's bum to the audience for the rest of the evening.'

If any of them noticed, they hardly cared. *The Times* recorded that

The first picture of the young Judi centre-stage.

On holiday in Cornwall with sister-in-law Daphne, brother Jeffery and her father Reginald.

A rehearsal-break in the *York Mystery Plays*, 1951, directed by E. Martin Browne. The angels (Judi, third from right) listen to Tenniel Evans, the Archangel Michael, reading to them, with David Giles, the Archangel Gabriel standing behind.

The Virgin Mary in the *York Mystery Plays*, 1957, directed by E. Martin Browne.

'I was always rained on.'

Ophelia with John Neville as Hamlet, directed by Michael Benthall, Old Vic 1957.

'When Michael told me he was casting Ophelia with a young actress straight out of drama school I was horrified and told him so! But I was wrong; she had exactly the right quality – vulnerability.'

Phebe in *As You Like It*, directed by Wendy Toye, Old Vic 1959. John Justin and Barbara Jefford as Orlando and Rosalind centre left, John Stride as Silvius downstage left with Phebe.

'I had a blonde pony-tail as Phebe, what an arse-paralysing part.'

Cecily with Alec McCowen as Algernon in *The Importance of Being Earnest*, directed by Michael Benthall, Old Vic 1959. 'Judi and I were hauled into the leading lady's dressing room and given a really sound telling-off – threatened with fire and damnation.'

above left Juliet with John Stride as Romeo, directed by Franco Zeffirelli, Old Vic 1960. 'This is as't should be. The Vic has done nothing better for a decade.'

above right Michael Benthall, Director of the Old Vic 1953–61. 'Most of us canonised Michael Benthall; he was wonderfully steadying to an actor on a First Night.'

below Franco Zeffirelli adjusts Juliet's costume. 'I thought he'd never forgive me for not going to America with the production.'

Titania with Ian Richardson as Oberon in *A Midsummer Night's Dream*, directed by Peter Hall, RSC 1962. 'It is years since Oberon and Titania have been presented at Stratford more fittingly and mellifluously.'

The same scene in Peter Hall's 1965 film.

'Practically all that survived of Judi's costume were the pointed rubber ears.'

Isabella with Ian Holm as Claudio and Tom Fleming as the Duke, in *Measure for Measure*, directed by John Blatchley, RSC 1962.

'When she said, "Tis best thou diest quickly", there was no question but that Claudio was going to have to make the supreme sacrifice.'

Lady Macbeth with John Neville as Macbeth, directed by Frank Dunlop, in the Nottingham Playhouse/British Council tour of West Africa, 1964.

'When you're manifestin' yourself on de stage, what you thinkin' to stop yourself laughin'?'

on the opening night the play was received 'with vociferous applause', and in the *Guardian* 'the audience was in no two minds about Michael Langham's inventive, speedy and well-thought-out production'. In the rest of his review, Philip Hope-Wallace awarded the honours for the night to the quartet of young lovers. 'In these pride of place goes to Barbara Leigh-Hunt whose Helena is authentic and yet original, fetching and delightfully droll. Judi Dench again shows a fine little comedienne as Hermia, and the rivals Demetrius and Lysander are amusingly filled in by Michael Meacham and John Stride. It seems a long time since we saw the foursome so well taken.'

When W. A. Darlington commented in the *Daily Telegraph* that 'I can't remember that any director has ever driven his lovers so hard at it as Michael Langham', it was almost as if he had been privy to his cracking of the whip at rehearsals. 'When Judi Dench, as Hermia, dashed across the stage to try to get at Helena and scratch her eyes out she had the look of a nippy little fly-half making for the line, and but for that sure (though rather high) tackling of Lysander and Demetrius she would have scored several times. As for Barbara Leigh-Hunt as Helena, she was travelling so fast when she said the line "My legs are longer, though, to run away" that she had barely time to get the words out between mid-stage and the wings.'

For Kenneth Tynan in the *Observer*, too, there was no doubt which pair stole the evening: 'Barbara Leigh-Hunt makes Helena a large, clinging creature, sweeter than she is silly; and Judi Dench's Hermia, a baby spitfire, is a portrait which, when set beside her Juliet and Kate Hardcastle, completes a dazzling triptych of flirtation.'

It is hardly surprising that Judi was now casting as powerful spells off-stage as she was on. Patrick Garland, who had fallen for her during the televising of *Henry V* and became even more enamoured by her Juliet, began taking her out and then home to his parents, who very much hoped they would marry. Marriage was not in the minds of either of them, though Patrick has fond memories of that summer romance. Being of Judi, some of them have a comic tinge. 'We went to a French restaurant together, and she didn't like meat rare. The waiter said, "'Ow do you want your steak?" She said, "Very, very well-done, extremely well-done, charred, quite honestly burnt." I ordered a medium-done steak and mine was brought first, so Judi said, "Well, where's my steak?" And he said, "Still burning, mad-emoiselle." '

Another conquest was David Jones, who filmed some scenes of *Romeo and Juliet* for the BBC arts programme *Monitor*, and sub-sequently took her out a few times. Like Patrick Garland, he came back into her professional life again much later on.

By the time Judi left the Old Vic in 1961, she recognised that the two greatest influences on her time there had been Michael Benthall and John Neville. The latter she was to work with again, though to her sadness she never did with the former. But she never forgot what she owed him and when he died in 1974 she spoke at his memorial service, together with Barbara Jefford, Paul Scofield and Paul Rogers.

It was perhaps as well that her last director at the Old Vic gave her such a hard time *en route* to her triumph in *A Midsummer Night's Dream*, or she might not have survived a much greater ordeal at the hands of her first director with the Royal Shakespeare Company – Michel St-Denis. He had had a long and distinguished record of producing the classics, especially Chekhov. In 1938 he had directed *The Three Sisters* in the famous Gielgud season at the Queen's Theatre but, more fatefully, as Judi was about to discover, he had seen *The Cherry Orchard* in the first performance by the Moscow Art Theatre in Paris after the First World War.

The Russian actress playing Anya had left an indelible impression on him even forty years later, as Ian Holm recalls. 'Apparently she had this wonderful tinkling, bell-like laugh, which rang round the theatre before she appeared at her first entrance. For the first two weeks Judi never got on-stage, because Michel would stop her: "No, no, no, no, you have to laugh, we have to hear this laugh." Poor Judi got so fed up with this.'

The company had eight weeks' rehearsal, twice the usual length, which stretched out Judi's misery. The other members of the cast reached out to help her. Dorothy Tutin was playing Varya. 'After a week of rehearsal at Stratford I said to Judi, "Why don't we go to the Duck?"' (The Dirty Duck is the actors' pub opposite the theatre.) 'We had some Guinness and I said, "Let's go back to the rehearsal room", and we rehearsed our scene together, a little bit drunk. The next time we did that scene we remembered the emotion of our private late-night rehearsal, and we both cried.'

Peggy Ashcroft was Ranevskaya, and she had worked with St-Denis before. She told Judi that he always had a whipping-boy and unfortunately this time it was her, but she was not to let him see her cry. Gaev was played by John Gielgud, who offered his support at exactly the right moment for Judi. 'It was a run-through in the rehearsal room which is now the Swan Theatre. At the end of Act I, which was the scene Michel gave me such hell over, John said to me, "If you'd done that for me in one of my productions, I would have been very proud." I thought, "Well he's won my heart, and he's got it now forever; whatever he does with it, he's got it." '

Dorothy Tutin echoes that affection. 'We both adored acting with John as Gaev and he treated us as if we were both his daughters. He was like a child as Gaev and we were all children together.'

John Gielgud was not over-happy with St-Denis' production: 'He was a bit too set for me, somehow, but I always remember the scenes with the two girls were very enjoyable indeed; they were charming to work with.'

Kenneth Tynan bracketed the three of them together, in his *Observer* review, as the best performances of the night. 'Gaev was exactly right – elegant and gravely foolish, in John Gielgud's sympathetic reading. Judi Dench, probably our best classical ingénue, was all softness and volatility as Anya, perfectly setting off the sadder, sterner merits of Dorothy Tutin's Varya.' Tynan delivered an unwitting rebuke to the director's attempt to force Judi into creating a carbon copy of an earlier Anya, when he praised this production, 'in which, for long periods in the first and last acts, one ceased to reflect how much better these things were done by the Moscow Art Theatre'.

In the *Illustrated London News*, J. C. Trewin praised 'an ensemble that is unmatched', and in his evocation of the individual qualities of each player he found that Judi was 'an Anya freshly true'.

That freshness and truth won her the Clarence Derwent Award for Best Supporting Actress in 1962, which was presented by British Actors' Equity. The prize was a cheque for £50 but, more importantly, the award was made by a formidable and expert quartet of judges – the producers Sir Bronson Albery and Gilbert Miller, the director Sir Tyrone Guthrie and the critic W. A. Darlington. This made up for the hard times in rehearsals, but she had forgotten all about that when it came to accepting the award itself at the Equity meeting. Nothing makes her so nervous as when she has to appear just as herself, which was clearly apparent to the recipient of the Best Supporting Actor for his performance in *Luther*, John Moffatt. 'We stood in the wings and she was reciting to herself, "Shake hands first, and take the money afterwards, shake hands first and take the money afterwards, shake hands . . .", and then went straight on and took the money first.'

The Cherry Orchard was the first time I ever saw Judi on-stage, and I can still see those moving performances in Abd'Elkader Farrah's elegant settings; I remember how naturally she laughed and skipped about the stage and how touching she was in her scenes with her mother and uncle. Above all, it is that characteristic gurgling laugh that I associate with her Anya and I was astonished to discover long afterwards that such an experienced director could have been so wrong-headed and insensitive to her innate qualities as an actress.

That she survived his treatment of her, and succeeded with her own interpretation, is evidence of that inner steeliness and determination which has carried her to success in several parts mistakenly thought beyond her. Not that that was the case with her next three parts during this first stint with the RSC.

In *Measure for Measure* she was cast as Isabella, with Ian Holm as her brother Claudio. They had first met in *The Cherry Orchard* and his initial reaction was, 'I just fell in love with her, which was fine because we were playing Anya and Trofimov. Her Isabella was cer-tainly the best I've seen, a radiant performance.'

Ian Richardson was playing Lucio and, at their first meeting, 'I discovered to my astonishment, when I complimented her after the read-through of the play, that she herself does not necessarily read the whole work. She told me that the read-through was terribly valuable to her because she now understood what it was all about. What is difficult about the role of Isabella is how she always hangs onto her virginity and says to her brother, "Well, you're just going to have to die." I've never seen it really brought off as cleverly as Judi did. When she said, "'Tis best that thou diest quickly", there was no question but that Ian Holm as Claudio was going to have to make the supreme sacrifice. She was not going to submit to Angelo. You believed it and applauded it, which is an enormous accomplishment on its own.'

He observed how her presence in the company made Isabella even more of a focal point than usual in this complex play. 'What was so marvellous about *Measure for Measure* was she's so divine that we chaps couldn't help falling in love with her a bit. Tom Fleming, that confirmed Scottish Presbyterian bachelor, was crazy about her, it was quite obvious, and the fact that he was playing the Duke meant that it added a certain *je ne sais quoi* to the production.'

Judi and Tom Fleming became very close; when they were rehearsing at Stratford she used to cycle out to his cottage at Hampton Lucy for breakfast. 'I used to collect the cream, and Tom would have the porridge on, then we'd put the bike in the car and come in to rehearsal. We had lots of picnics – one where I brought a chocolate cake and Tom stepped on it – oh, we had such good times there.' There was talk of marriage, but Judi was not ready to make any such lifelong commitment yet.

Life at Stratford seemed to be full of surprises for both of them. 'On Shakespeare's birthday we were invited to that big civic lunch, so we got ourselves all dressed up. I had a new black dress and Tom came in full Highland dress – I felt like a peahen. The beadle said, "Name?" and Tom said, "Tom Fleming." This man announced "Mr Albert Finney", and then he said to Tom, "A horse, a horse, my kingdom for a horse." We never did piece that bit together.'

Ian Richardson quickly realised how Judi is always very close to laughter and how the slightest thing can set her off on-stage. Lucio had a line to Isabella: 'Your brother and his lover have embraced', meaning that the girl had been made pregnant. 'I came on this night; Judi was right downstage, facing out front, and I said, "Your lover and his brother have embraced." She spun round and went, "Oh!" and darted away upstage and shook for a bit in the corner, and then came back and carried on.'

The critics seemed a bit nonplussed by John Blatchley's production, querying the very low-cut gown designed by Alex Stone, instead of the usual nun's habit, and fearing that Tom Fleming's towering performance as the Duke disturbed the balance of the play. Harold Hobson in the *Sunday Times* found 'the glowingly robust Isabella of Judi Dench more fitted to the breezy pastures of East Anglia than to the cold seclusion of a convent'. In the *Guardian* Philip Hope-Wallace, too, had his reservations, though crediting her with 'a most intelligent shot at a part which is full of pitfalls. She very cleverly plays down the prig; but she doesn't for me suggest either the sense of vocation or the temptingly innocent child of nature.' In describing the great confrontation scene with her brother, he referred to her in a way that always made her hackles rise: 'little Miss Dench was content with sincerity and an orderly, if not very affecting, use of language.' Her height of five feet one and a half inches has not stood in the way of her playing any of Shakespeare's great heroines, with the possible exception of Rosalind, but 'little Miss Dench' was too often used by one or two critics in the early years to diminish her powers as an actress. Caryl Brahms became a particular *bête noire* for this, compounded by her other regular habit of citing her as 'Dench J.', as if she were in a school production.

Her height was never a casting consideration for Peter Hall, who was only interested in the depth of her talent, and directed her now for the first time in *A Midsummer Night's Dream*. 'People become actors because they think they're too tall and want to be short, or too short and want to be tall, and so on. That's not very surprising. By the time she did *The Dream* Judi had a colossal, reckless freedom about her acting, and she just dared to plunge in. I remember it being a peculiarly happy rehearsal period, because if you've got Judi in the company it's very rarely an unhappy company.'

The intriguing thing about the production was that although it was a revival of the one first seen three years earlier at Stratford, unusually in the theatre the revival was generally acknowledged as a great improvement on the original. Peter Hall is in no doubt about why that was. 'We just did it better. Although on paper we had the most glittering cast in 1959 – Albert Finney and Vanessa Redgrave, Robert Hardy and Charles Laughton – it was a very disparate group. By the time we did it again it was a company; I think that was the real reason.'

The only actor who appeared in both productions was Ian Holm. 'For me it was the happiest experience ever playing Puck, the most wonderful sense of power one had on the stage, with the audience in the palm of your hand. I thought Judi was a devastating Titania; she doesn't just come onto a stage, she flies onto a stage.'

The illusion of flight was perfect for the Queen of the Fairies, but it presented an initial challenge to her Oberon. Early in rehearsals Peter Hall took Ian Richardson quietly on one side and confided, 'You know, I'm worried, Ian, because you're very solidly on the ground, whereas look at Judi, she's actually some feet up in the air.' He puzzled for a while about what he was failing to do. 'I remember sitting and watching Judi, and Ian Holm too, thinking, "How is it that they are giving this impression of being in the air?" Then I realised that they were barefoot and I was wearing shoes, so I took off my shoes and that helped a bit.'

Alec McCowen thinks that the thing that distinguishes Judi, quite apart from her truthfulness and wit, is her speed. 'She was the fastest Titania I've ever seen, rushing around the set stamping on fairies. It was an extraordinary performance, and yet so feminine. Her speed is phenomenal and she can make you gasp at the quickness of her speech, which is always crystal clear. She doesn't hang about.'

But her speed and lightness about the stage creates its own pitfalls for her. Ian Holm says, 'I've seen Judi trip and fall probably more than most actresses.' On the opening night, Judi told Ian Richardson, 'Ian, I want to warn you, sometimes, on a first night in particular, with nerves and everything, especially if I have to run about a bit, I have a tendency to fall down.' He said, 'Oh I'm glad you told me. I'll try to be on hand to pick you up.'

Everything went without a hitch up to their very last entrance, when they came into the hall to bless the house where the marriages were going to take place, swooping right from the back of the stage via conveniently placed chairs up onto the great refectory table, and thence down to the ground. 'We came on, we got up onto the table, went down and Crash! Titania was flat on her face on the floor and, as I picked her up, she said, "I told you so!"'

Margaret Drabble was now in the company, playing a fairy again to Judi's Titania, just as they had done a few years previously at The Mount school, but this time of course there were many more performances, which only added to her admiration. 'I can still hear her intonations even now. I particularly remember Judi's long speech, "The seasons alter", as I was on-stage throughout it, and she orches-trated that speech superbly well.' During that season Margaret was completing her second novel, *The Garrick Year*, and the other actors could hear her typewriter clacking away from her dressing-room whenever she was off. Her husband, Clive Swift, was also in the company and they had a year-old baby boy, Mark, of whom Judi made a great fuss.

Peter Hall was a great believer in encouraging the family life of the company, so on a Friday, which was pay day, all the wives and children used to arrive in the Green Room. Ian Richardson noticed that Judi always made a point of being there too. 'She was just wonderful with all these children and I remember thinking, "Judi, you're a born mother. Isn't it time you married and had one of your own?"' But he refrained from saying so.

Peter Hall's well-known affection for small children must have helped him create the childlike atmosphere of the production, which lifted it out of the usual perception of the different worlds of the play. Tynan both perceived and rhapsodised about this approach. 'The Fairies are children pretending to be grown-ups, as you may guess from the fact that they wear outsize grey wigs; the latter sprouting from their scalps like thickets of steel wool, are weirdly, impressively sinister ... Ian Richardson and Judi Dench play the royal elves superbly, and when Miss Dench delivers the "wonted liveries" speech, the ailing cause of Shakespeare-designed-to-be-read-as-word-music receives its most powerful shot in the arm for a very long time.'

J. C. Trewin picked up on this theme in the *Birmingham Post*: 'It is sound, the shining of moonlight sound, a silver glory, that we always seek first in *A Midsummer Night's Dream*. We had it in the speaking of Ian Richardson, not a syllable misplaced, and in Judi Dench, who looked like spun crystal. It is years since Oberon and Titania have been presented at Stratford more fittingly and mellifluously.'

Gareth Lloyd-Evans enthused in the *Guardian* about the mechanicals, led by Paul Hardwick as Bottom, 'the best one has seen ... The fairy world is equally successful. Ian Richardson's Oberon has a mellifluous authority and Judi Dench, as Titania, has a crispness of movement and speech which avoids the usual parade of mincing nasality in this part.' Since no one commented on her fall on the opening night, she must have leapt up as crisply as she fell and convinced everyone watching that it was intentional.

What cheered Judi as much as the notices was a letter from Zeffirelli, apologising for writing afterwards instead of sending her a good luck cable beforehand, but he had muddled up the date:

Accept my love just the same, for what it's worth to you, you unfaithful heart!

Incidentally, seeing how clever you've been in Stratford I have completely forgiven you for having abandoned Juliet.

You known I've missed you deeply, I've hated you immensely – Now I see that altogether you were right.

One must never get too sentimental in work. It can be a disaster. One day I shall perhaps learn this tiny, little truth.

I am tempted to come to Stratford for Easter, hoping to see the Dream, I wonder if there would be any chance for tickets.

I would like to see the Dream.

I would like to see you in it.

I would like to see you – Period.

Love, more than ever –

Franco.

It had taken two years, but Judi was much relieved that he had at last forgiven her for refusing to play Juliet on Broadway.

A Midsummer Night's Dream was one of the first great successes for the RSC 'ensemble' that Peter Hall was so keen to achieve, where the stars would be created from within the company, rather than being brought in from outside for just one or two plays, so it was only natural that he should want to capture this production on film.

However, he realised that the gorgeous artificiality of Lila de Nobili's costumes, which would have perfectly dressed any of those Elizabethan figures in Nicholas Hilliard's miniatures, would also have looked quite out of place in the back-to-nature woodland where he wanted to set the film. So practically all that survived of Judi's costume were the pointed rubber ears that had been her idea. The only other covering she wore was a minimal chamois leather G-string, two tiny chamois patches strategically placed and a strand of ivy. Oberon was similarly practically naked, until the designer decided at the last minute to pluck a lump of moss from the ground and slap it onto his shoulders. The cameras rolled, but Judi was now rooted to the spot. 'It's a w, it's a w!' she blurted out. She has a phobia about worms and, encouraged by the heat of the lights, a little worm was crawling out of the moss, stopping the action for some while until Judi had recovered her composure and a new patch of moss had been carefully screened as worm-free.

The location was by the lake in the grounds of Compton Verney and, far from being midsummer, it was now late autumn. It rained all too frequently, but perversely not on the day Peter Hall wanted the effect of rain falling on the surface of the lake in the background. So the Warwickshire Fire Brigade was brought in to provide the rain. To stop their teeth from chattering during the take, Oberon and Titania were allowed to keep their blankets on until the very last minute. A young fireman was dutifully hosing the lake. When he heard the clapper board go he looked round and did the most enormous double-take, but as he did so he brought the hose round with him and hosed the two actors straight into the lake. Ian pulled Judi out in hysterics and she promptly fell flat on her face in the mud, which retained the top half of her costume, not to mention ruining all her green body-paint. Filming had to be abandoned for the day.

Subsequently Ian Richardson was surprised by her control in another difficult situation, when she had to run through the woods, followed by all the children playing the fairies. 'Peter stopped the camera and said, "Judi dear, is it possible for you to run without your breasts bobbing up and down?" Judi looked at him and said, "You've got to be joking. You're asking me to keep my boobs in order, and I've got nothing on except two little bits of chamois leather?" He said, "Well, could you try?" She went back and, do you know, she came down through the glade and I swear to God her bosom didn't move at all. I don't know how she did it, but she controlled it!'

It was impossible to record a clean soundtrack in that open-air setting, so all the dialogue was added to the pictures in a post-synching studio later, permitting a control over the verse-speaking that made it, in the opinion of many, including its director, the best-spoken *Dream* ever. 'I saw the film again quite recently, and it stands up quite well; it looks very sixties now, the young people look terribly flower-power, but I was really quite pleased with it.'

It was made for CBS Television in America, where it drew a Sunday night audience of millions, but it only had a brief life in British cinemas.

Judi was already fairly well-stretched at Stratford in 1962 when she was offered the title role in Shaw's *Major Barbara* on BBC Television, with Edward Woodward as Adolphus Cusins. This was still in the time of live drama on television, when Sunday transmission was followed by another live performance for the Thursday repeat. This held no terrors for Judi, who had already played a handful of live TV performances and accepted it as the normal practice. The televised *Major Barbara* caused few ripples of interest, but the experience was doubly valuable to Judi – for her stage assumption of the role for the RSC in 1970 and for the huge TV role she undertook in 1966 in *Talking to a Stranger*.

For the moment, however, she had reached a crossroads in her career and, in a hasty decision she came to regret, she missed a major opportunity. It occurred towards the end of her season with the RSC, during her last play with them, *A Penny for a Song*, directed by Colin Graham.

John Whiting's play is set in Dorset in 1804 and concerns the differing responses of a small community to the threat of a Napoleonic invasion. The cast included Marius Goring, Michael Gwynn, Newton Blick and Gwen Ffrangçon-Davies. Judi only had the small part of Dorcas Bellboys, but it remains one of her favourite memories. 'It's such a brilliant play and the critics didn't like it at all. We actually worked with John Whiting on it and we had such a nice time.'

As the end of the run approached, Judi began to worry about where to go next as her contract with the RSC was due to end. When she was offered a part in a crime thriller, *A Shot in the Dark*, due to open in the West End in the early summer of 1963, she reluctantly decided to accept it as the only offer she had. No sooner had she signed and despatched the contract than a telegram arrived at the stage door of the Aldwych which said, 'Dear Judi Dench. Will you come to my first season at Minneapolis to play Ophelia, Marianne in *The Miser* and Irina in *The Three Sisters*. Tyrone Guthrie.'

Judi knew of Guthrie's famous work as a director at the Old Vic and Stratford-upon-Avon before and after the war. Now he was designing and operating new theatres to stage the classics in Stratford Ontario, and this newest one in Minneapolis, which was named after him. Desperately keen to work with him, she wrote to explain her dilemma, but very properly he would not countenance her breaking her contract and said that there would be other opportunities to work together later. This proved a vain hope and the occasion never arose again before his death. Judi has worked with most of the great stage directors, but deeply regrets that she has never numbered Guthrie among them.

However, as one door closes in Judi's career another always seems miraculously to open for her. To fill the gap between the end of *A Penny for a Song* and the opening of *A Shot in the Dark*, she suddenly received a call from her first leading man at the Old Vic and now very close friend, John Neville.

He had gone to lead the company at the old Nottingham Playhouse in 1961, where in my last year at university I saw him play a memorable Thomas More in *A Man for all Seasons*. Two years later he was invited to become the Artistic Director of the handsome new Playhouse in that city, with two associate directors – Peter Ustinov and Frank Dunlop. Now the company was to embark on a pioneering tour of West Africa and John Neville asked her to play Lady Macbeth, and Viola in *Twelfth Night*.

She leapt at the chance, with very little idea of what it would mean, or how the experience would enrich her as an actress in the most surprising ways.

five
_____

1963–65

Lady Macbeth goes to Africa, and the
Russians and French come to Oxford

The Nottingham Playhouse company took three plays to West Africa - *Macbeth*, *Twelfth Night* and *Arms and the Man* – but Judi was only in the two Shakespeares. The cast John Neville assembled for the tour included, as well as Judi, Paul Daneman, James Cairncross, Peter Blythe, Polly Adams and Jill Gascoine, and they played mostly in the open air because of the heat. It was the first professional British company ever to perform in Nigeria, Ghana and Sierra Leone and not everyone was convinced it would be a success. When the British High Commissioner in Lagos, Lord Head, heard of the visit, he exclaimed, 'Oh God, no, no, they're not ready for that. Bring a circus!'

It was true that the audience was markedly different from that which the actors were used to at home. The African audiences who flocked to all the performances became very audibly involved in the action on stage. When Judi played Lady Macbeth's sleepwalking scene, she heard someone in the audience call out, 'Oh my God, she's washin' her hands in no basin.' They howled with laughter whenever the actors touched each other, and particularly at the rhyming verse. Judi soon learnt to expect a gale of laughter on 'The Thane of Fife had a wife', and there were frequent calls of, 'Please say that line again.' After one performance, she was asked with real concern, 'When you're manifestin' yourself on de stage, what you thinkin' to stop yourself laughin'?' It is a definition she delights in: 'manifesting yourself on the stage – that's acting in West Africa! I went down with malaria in Accra, in the middle of *Twelfth Night*. I passed out and Peter Blythe had to carry me off, and there was thunderous applause – they thought it was all part of the play.'

The doctors told her she was not well enough to travel, but she could not face the prospect of being left behind, 'so I went with them and James and John carried me. I don't remember much about it, to tell the truth, because I was really ill. But I didn't miss any performances, because we had a four-day rest period and in those four days I recovered.'

When Polly Adams could not play because of an impacted wisdom tooth, Judi stepped in and played a Witch as well as Lady Macbeth at a moment's notice, emulating a double Sybil Thorndike used to perform regularly on her wartime tours.

On another occasion, one of the British Council staff stepped in to play the Third Witch without time for rehearsal, but her memory failed her at the spell over the cauldron. After 'Double, double, toil and trouble' she went blank on her second line and gamely improvised: 'Scale of dragon, tooth of wolf,/Witches' mummy, two pork chops.'

This provoked some extra capering by the other two witches before they could carry on.

In normal circumstances, *Macbeth* is considered a dangerous play for actors, but Judi observed a new hazard one night when she spotted several vultures perched above them, watching the action. 'I said, "For God's sake twitch when you're killed", because they were all sitting there waiting to pick our bones.'

James Cairncross was thrilled by the audience responses: 'A great highlight was a performance of *Twelfth Night* at the University of Accra in the open air, when I don't think the audience were ever less than about two inches above their seats. Playing Shakespeare to people who don't know the story is simply wonderful; at the end when the twins met at last, they threw their programmes in the air and cheered. I think I can also claim that we were the only company to play *Macbeth* where a lady in front gave her child the breast without removing her eyes from the stage; she just hoicked it open and plugged it in. That kind of attention was extremely rewarding.'

The impact of the tour was endorsed in the slightly more formal wording of the British Council Representative in Nigeria, who reported that it was 'a revelation to the great majority of Nigerian audiences and an inspiration to the development of the theatre and arts generally in Nigeria'. (Judi's pride in their achievement was still strong enough three decades later to contradict Peter Brook in public. When he claimed at the National Theatre that his company was the first ever to take Shakespeare to Africa, she was quick to put the record straight.)

It was an eventful tour for the actors as well as the audiences; during it, Judi was suddenly overwhelmed by an impulse that one would hesitate to write into a work of fiction. 'We went out to lunch with a man from the British Council called George Baker and I had a funny premonition at his house, strong enough for me to ask if I could phone home to England, in a total stranger's house. I rang home and Daddy had just had his second heart attack.'

Reginald Dench had made a good recovery from an earlier attack in 1954, but this one was much more serious. Somehow that fact had communicated itself to his daughter thousands of miles away. It was not to be the last time she would display such sensitivity where her family were concerned.

After three gruelling months and seventy performances in thirteen far-flung locations, the tour came to an end with a final performance of *Macbeth*; John Neville was so glad to tear off his hot breast-plate for the last time that he threw it on the ground and, in a suitably symbolic gesture, urinated over it and abandoned it. Unfortunately for him, he had not reckoned with the faithful loyalty of their new fans. A little boy retrieved it, and delivered it proudly back to its owner at the hotel.

Judi would not have missed the whole experience of that tour for worlds. 'When you've played those West African audiences, nothing can ever, ever throw you on-stage again.' It is perhaps no coincidence that the two parts she played for the first time in Africa, Viola and Lady Macbeth, would become two of her most brilliant successes when she tackled them again with the RSC. She was also so taken with that part of the world that she returned in 1969 for a two-handed Shakespearean recital tour with James Cairncross.

But for now she was committed to the much less attractive prospect of *A Shot in the Dark*, scheduled to open at the Lyric Theatre in May 1963. The danger signals were there from the beginning. Marcel Achard's *L'Idiote* had been translated into the American idiom by Harry Kurnitz and it had succeeded both in Paris and on Broadway, but nobody bothered to adapt this Franco-American hybrid for English ears.

To compound the problem, the director of the American production, Harold Clurman, was brought over to direct the English cast, and he seemed unable to erase the memory of what Julie Harris had done in the part now taken by Judi. Peter Sallis played the judge's clerk and recalls the cast's dismay: 'Harold had a high reputation and we were all thrilled to hear he was going to direct it, but he was not very helpful to any of us, to say the least, because he tried to reproduce on the British stage what he'd done on the New York stage. Poor Judi got a very raw deal; he'd say, "Miss Harris would sit down on that line, walk across the stage on that line." The nadir was when he wanted her to wear identical clothes to Miss Harris.'

It is difficult to credit that two such experienced directors as Harold Clurman and Michel St-Denis could both make the same disastrous misjudgement of Judi's own imaginative powers and attempt to shackle her into a mere reproduction of a predecessor's performance.

In this uneasy combination of whodunit and comedy, Judi played a parlour maid accused of murdering her lover, a Spanish chauffeur, and much of the play consisted of cross-examination of her and her millionaire employer.

Milton Shulman, in the *Evening Standard*, thought it 'hardly worth all that has been lavished upon it'; Philip Hope-Wallace growled in the *Guardian* that 'one would surely have had to be very hard up for entertainment to leave home for this kind of rubbish'; and the anonymous reviewer for *The Times* laid the blame at the door of 'Harry Kurnitz's script, which represents Broadway at its sniggering, priggish, blunt-witted worst ... The cast, in whom one detected symptoms of embarrassment, brazen it out as best they may.'

They did not have to brazen it out for long. It closed after only a few weeks, which increased Judi's chagrin that the offer had just preceded Tyrone Guthrie's invitation to join his new company in Minneapolis.

Her first foray into the cinema at this time was even less encouraging. *The Third Secret* starred Stephèn Boyd as an American reporter in London who gets sucked into investigating the murder of his analyst. A galaxy of British talent played the other patients and suspects – Jack Hawkins, Paul Rogers, Alan Webb, Diane Cilento,

Patience Collier, Peter Sallis and Rachel Kempson; Richard Attenborough played the owner of an art gallery and Judi's boss. She only had half a dozen lines and all she now remembers of the experience was that the director, Charles Crichton, 'was adorable'. He was a gifted director of comedy (originally for Ealing Films), but this mystery never caught fire.

Then, after a period of not so much marking time as moving backwards, things shifted smartly into forward gear with an invitation from Frank Hauser to join the Meadow Players at the Oxford Playhouse to play Irina in *The Three Sisters*. After being unable to play that part for Tyrone Guthrie, she was reluctant to risk losing it a second time, but was convinced there must be some mistake. She rang her agent and said, 'You've got completely the wrong person. He loathes my guts. Who's he asked first?' Julian Belfrage replied calmly, 'Well, why don't you go to lunch and find out?'

When the two of them had met in a pub on an earlier occasion, each had thought the other had snubbed them and Judi had also been told, wrongly, that he had walked out of the Zeffirelli *Romeo and Juliet* at the Old Vic. Happily these misunderstandings were cleared up at their second meeting because, according to Frank Hauser, 'the moment you start to talk to her it's love at first sight, or love at first giggle. We got on very well indeed, and I became devoted to her.'

He had assembled a very strong cast that included Joseph O'Conor, Roger Livesey, Elizabeth Sellars, James Cairncross, John Moffatt, John Standing and John Turner. It was Frank Hauser's first Chekhov, which he regards as one of the best productions he ever did. He particularly recalls one conversation with his Vershinin. 'I'd known Jo O'Conor for a very long time, and we were having a drink after a rehearsal. I said, "Wonderful company feeling about this", and he said, "Yes, that's of course because the company is being properly led." I said, "By you?" And he said, "No, no, not by me, by Judi." Now Jo is an authoritative man, and it was perfectly true; if anyone was unhappy, or couldn't confess to unhappiness, she would look after them. But if people misbehaved, or were late, or hadn't learnt their lines when they were obviously required to, then she was not pleased at all and would weigh in, and be quite strong.' (Judi says, 'that can't be true, I don't remember that'.)

Judi had come quite a long way since she had stood out in a large crowd at York and caught Joseph O'Conor's attention, and he thinks she was the best Irina he has seen. 'I remember vividly a very sudden passing thing during *Three Sisters*, how wonderfully her face changed from happiness to sudden melancholy. I'd never seen those lines of Keats: "But when the melancholy fit shall fall/Sudden from heaven like a leaping cloud" illustrated so perfectly. I've never seen in any other face that suddenness and absolute reality achieved.'

In his review for the *Financial Times*, John Higgins spoke of the production in the same breath as two other Chekhov productions in London – Olivier and Redgrave in *Uncle Vanya* at the National Theatre and the Moscow Art Theatre's production of *The Cherry Orchard* in the International Theatre season at the Aldwych. Higgins' sharp eye and ear also caught that moment which so impressed O'Conor. 'Judi Dench has the radiance for Irina. Her sense of excitement for three acts that she alone might get away from this awful town makes the final realisation that she too is trapped all the more poignant.'

All the reviews were generally enthusiastic. Mervyn Jones wrote in *Tribune* that 'in an excellent cast, I shall especially remember Judi Dench's brightly flickering Irina, Roger Livesey's fruity old doctor, and the remarkable success of James Cairncross in explaining how that strange character Solyony ticks'.

It is more remarkable that the Chekhovian mood was not broken for the audience by the antics of several members of the company, like John Standing. 'As Tuzenbach I went off to get shot by Solyony, and I was lying in the wings demonstrating positions in the *Kama Sutra* to John Moffatt, when Judi looked off and absolutely creased with laughter.' Judi tried in vain to stop herself looking out into the wings at this point, as John Standing would hold up his fingers to signal that this was position 43 or whatever other number took his fancy.

John Moffatt had an even trickier situation to cope with on-stage. Kulyigin had to shave off his moustache between Act III and Act IV. 'It's very unnatural to take off a moustache in the middle of a performance, and one night playing at Southampton I forgot to. I came on and sitting underneath this tree were Roger Livesey, John Standing and Judi Dench. That blush came over Judi, a tremendous smile that's just under the surface of the skin, and when I saw this

look on her face I knew the moustache was still on. Aaaahh!! So I
did a little twirl round, looking at the trees, and whipped it off just
in time for her to say, "You've shaved off your moustache." I questioned people afterwards who had seen it that night and of course no
one had noticed.'

But two of his colleagues dispute his version of the dénouement.
Judi insists that after saying Chekhov's line, 'You've shaved off your
moustache', she added hastily, 'and grown it again,' and, as he turned,
'and shaved it off again.'

John Standing claims that it happened more than once. 'He kept
forgetting to remove it at the end and one night he turned upstage
to try to rip it off quickly. All he succeeded in doing was to rip off
both the ends, leaving him looking exactly like Adolf Hitler.'

The end of the first act offered further opportunities for larking
about, as the lunch party was going on upstage while Natasha and
Andrei were playing their love scene downstage. The *sotto voce* conversations round the lunch table reached ever dizzier heights, which
fortunately never reached the ears of either producer or audience.

Russian plays have offered rich opportunities for Judi, which she
has seized with both hands. Frank Hauser's policy during his long
tenure of the Oxford Playhouse was to offer the best of European
drama, much of which had never before been seen on the British
stage, like his next play – *The Twelfth Hour* by the contemporary
Russian dramatist Aleksei Arbuzov.

It was set in Russia in 1929, in the shadow of the beginning of the
first Five-Year Plan, as the Soviet Government considered the takeover
of the remaining capitalist concerns. Joseph O'Conor played Dor,
'the most famous confectioner in Leningrad', who waits anxiously
for news of his fate; Judi was his daughter Anna, bored with her
husband, John Hurt, and having an affair with her father's manager,
played by John Turner. This pairing presented a bit of a staging
problem that the director had to solve for Judi. 'I had to kiss John
Turner passionately, but he's so incredibly tall that Frank had to devise
a kind of tree stump, that John fell over when we were doing a dance,
because there was no other way I could kiss him passionately.'

Fortunately by then she had overcome her initial fear of him, which
was based more on his dietary habits than his size. 'During the
rehearsals for *The Three Sisters* he used to send out for a quarter of a

pound of completely raw steak and then he used to mix an egg in with it and eat it. I was very, very frightened of him.' For someone who likes all her meat practically charred, steak tartare seemed a most uncivilised dish.

Frank Hauser was skilled at bringing out the best in Judi. She hates to feel she is just going through the motions. One day, when James Cairncross was watching her rehearse, she sighed, 'Frank, I'm simply sitting here saying lines. What's the matter?' He just said, 'All right, darling', and James says that 'within ten minutes they'd got it all sorted out, and she was away.'

Arbuzov came over to see the production in rehearsal, during the tour of *Three Sisters* to Southampton. He arrived on a hot summer's day, two hours earlier than expected, when the company were all having a lunch break, so they quickly pretended they were rehearsing. Frank Hauser noticed with some surprise that Judi was initially intimidated by the presence of the author. 'She was so frightened at one point when we were doing a run for him, she was standing on the side of the stage waiting to come on and suddenly there was this terrible pause. Everyone looked at her and she screamed, "Oh my God, I'm off", and took two steps and was on. Everyone was frightfully nervous, but he was deeply impressed with Judi. I'm fairly sure he wrote *The Promise* [his 1966 play] for her after seeing her in *The Twelfth Hour*. He also wanted to bring the *Three Sisters* production to Moscow, and he flatly refused to believe it had been done in four weeks. "We take two years to do a play like this", he said.'

John Hurt was thrilled to be playing opposite the Juliet he had watched so often. 'It's marvellous to be on-stage with her, because she serves her character, she's not serving herself, so you're playing with the character, which is precisely what one wants, and oddly enough it's a rarity to that degree.'

The character she was serving was a deeply unpleasant one, but it had considerable impact. *The Times'* reviewer praised the production, singling out the performances of John Moffatt, John Hurt and Ursula Jeans, and 'Judi Dench's Anna is a voluptuous destroyer whose whip-lash arrogance conveys all her underlying self-hatred.'

Ursula Jeans' success came as a bit of a relief to the company. Judi giggles as she pictures her rehearsing with the script in her hand right up until almost the opening and remarking unworriedly to the director, who was showing definite signs of concern. 'It's all right, Frank, I know it will only take me an evening to learn this part, it's just that I haven't chosen the evening yet.'

The consecutive triumphs of the Chekhov and the Arbuzov prompted talk of bringing both the Russian plays to London, which disappointingly came to nothing this time.

In the summer of 1964 Judi made her first great mark in the medium of film. *Four in the Morning* interwove two separate storylines of unhappy young women. It began with river police finding a body in the Thames; the tension came from trying to guess which one of the two had drowned herself. Judi played a young mother stuck at home with a crying baby, while her husband was out drinking with an old friend, who were played by Norman Rodway and Joe Melia. Judi was now living in a flat in Regent's Park, which was used for rehearsals. The director was Anthony Simmons and he asked them to improvise situations around the basic idea, from which he wrote the script. One result of the improvisations was that all three characters ended up with the actors' own names – Jude, Norm and Joe.

Norman Rodway was a bit sceptical when he was first approached, 'until Tony said, "I've got Judi Dench", when I said, "*Yes, yes, yes,* certainly." Then we shot it in this crummy little house in Putney, overlooking the river, and the three of us had a wonderful time – she's got a great knack of turning a serious or tragic situation on its head and finding an ironic joke in it.' He adds regretfully, 'I got a little smitten, but nothing came of it.'

For Judi it was a tough initiation into the problems of location filming on a shoestring. 'That must be the noisiest location in the whole of London – on the flight path to Heathrow, by a railway bridge, by a road bridge, and opposite where all the river tankers come up and dump their rubbish. So we never got any kind of a run on anything without being interrupted.'

However, despite all these trials, the film is so convincingly naturalistic that it feels more like a documentary than a drama, and it won Judi the Most Promising Newcomer Award from BAFTA. John Hurt thought she was more than promising: 'She was absolutely brilliant, our answer to Simone Signoret; she has that same quality – deeply sexual and at the same time tremendously vulnerable and moving.'

After the filming, she rejoined the Oxford Playhouse Company for rehearsals of *The Alchemist*. Barbara Leigh-Hunt had a standing invitation to stay with Judi at her flat in Regent's Park Terrace whenever she was in London and she happened to be there at the end of November 1965. The front door had a mortice lock, which had to be locked with a key from the outside or inside. Judi was going off to rehearsal and asked Barbara to lock her out and keep the key. No sooner had Barbara got into her bath than she heard Judi's footsteps on the steps outside and her calling, 'Bar, Bar, will you let me in again? I'm awfully sorry darling.'

She got out of the bath and let her in, saying, 'You're going to be so late, Jude.'

'Yes I know I am, but I just had to come back.'

'What is it? What have you forgotten?'

'I haven't forgotten anything, I've got to ring home. Go and have your bath. I'm going to ring home.' Judi was on the phone to her mother and father for about twenty minutes and Barbara said, 'Well you've really torn it now, you'll be so late. What was the matter?'

'Oh nothing was the matter. I just knew I wanted to speak to Daddy'.

Judi went off to rehearsal, now very late, which was totally out of character – normally she is so early she is the first to arrive. Her father died that day, just after noon. He came back from shopping with his wife, said he felt a bit tired and, when Olave took him a cup of tea, he had gone. Judi said, 'I didn't know he was going to die, but I just knew I had to talk to him.'

When her brother Peter rang to tell her the news she was devastated. She called Frank Hauser and he did not need her to tell him why she had telephoned; he said he would come straight over. He sat quietly with her while she packed and then said simply, 'I presume it's one of the family.'

After the funeral he rang Judi in York and invited her to bring Olave back to Oxford with her, saying he would find her some work to do. He had met Olave before and knew of her wardrobe skills; his thoughtfulness did much to help both Judi and her mother over their immediate grief.

Fortunately Judi was plunged into a very busy schedule of work, with three new productions in as many months, beginning with *The Alchemist*, which opened in January 1965. At Frank's suggestion Judi cropped her hair for the part of Dol Common and wore a very long wig when she masqueraded as the Queen of Faery. She had huge fun playing with John Turner and Alan MacNaughtan as the two confidence tricksters, Face and Subtle – a partnership much admired by *Theatre World*: 'Alan MacNaughtan in a magician's robe, John Turner in a military tunic and Judi Dench in a golden wig made a lively coney-catching trio. A most dramatic moment came in the first scene when Miss Dench, enraged, snatched off her wig and stamped on it. Since Jonson provided little or no build-up in his plot, little incidents like this are important.'

In *Plays and Players*, Derick Grigs also enjoyed the performances of the two con-men and their accomplice: 'An actress of astonishing range who was the gentle, dreamy Irina of the recent *Three Sisters*, Judi Dench was as firmly inside the grubby skin of Dol, her hard sensuality offsetting the coy eccentricity she assumed for the benefit of Sir Epicure Mammon ... effectively underplayed by David Swift.'

John Higgins in the *Financial Times* thought that 'Judi Dench makes a good Dol Common, brazen, bawdy and busty, an admirable trollop'.

During the run, Edith Evans invited her to play Juliet to her Nurse in the TV celebration of the living theatre, *The Golden Hour*, on Sunday, 31 January. Dame Edith had not much enjoyed Zeffirelli's production at the Old Vic, telling her, 'Oh you all looked so dirty', but she was a good judge of fine acting and Judi felt suitably flattered by the invitation.

Her next play at Oxford coincidentally had Romeo in its title, but this was *Romeo and Jeannette* by Jean Anouilh and the only real parallel with Shakespeare was that the young lovers both committed suicide. Nicholas Pennell played Frederic, torn between his love for Julia (June Murphy) and her sister Jeannette. As the latter, Judi made her, for Alan Brien in the *Sunday Telegraph*, 'as much Cressida as Juliet, gamey as well as tender, dangerous as well as defenceless. The conventional boor of a brother (played with lip-smacking, self-hating relish by John Turner) turns into a modern Thersites.'

It was a play of difficult moods, skilfully directed by Tony Tanner. In one scene, Frederic takes his respectable parents to visit Jeannette's wild and volatile family and his mother tries to smooth over the awkward meeting by offering to cook something for lunch. Frank Hauser was deeply impressed by how the acting conquered a situation fraught with perils. 'She goes into the kitchen and comes back and says, "I've only managed to find a dead chicken." This terrible family say, "Oh my God, just wait until Jeannette sees it, that's her favourite chicken." After a bit more dialogue Judi comes in, carrying the dead chicken in her arms, saying, "Who did this?", guaranteed I would have thought to bring the house down. It's a very funny idea – you know perfectly well it's not a dead chicken – and nobody laughed. She came on in a blazing entrance; if she'd come on carrying a golliwog it would have made no difference at all, she just dominated the audience, and she did it again and again.' His admiration of the power of her blazing entrance did not inhibit him from gently admonishing Judi. 'I got a note from Frank saying, "When you come in will you refrain from lifting the entire back set off the floor." '

One of the perennial complaints of the Oxford Playhouse was that the university showed little interest in its productions, but this one certainly caught the imagination of a keen undergraduate critic in *Isis*, Andrew Snell, who was carried away by it and especially Judi's Jeannette. 'It is a gem of creation that goes far beyond the merits of this play. Always changing, at one moment brash and rude, at the next she shows great tenderness: sometimes she flashes around the stage with the instinct and irrationality and sensuousness of a young faun, and then suddenly you will have a mature woman with a strange foreboding feminine intelligence. Perhaps Miss Dench's greatest achievement is to have given us a slut with more purity in her than all of the other characters put together ... It is a pity that not enough people in Oxford realise their fortune in living in a town which has a repertory company of the standard of the Meadow Players.'

That last sentiment was repeated almost word for word at the end of Alan Brien's review in the *Sunday Telegraph*, but it fell on deaf ears. Frank Hauser shrugs resignedly and says that throughout his long tenure at the helm, the university, both the staff and the students, usually waited to hear if a production was any good, left it until the last week to book and then complained that they could not now get tickets. A sell-out in the last week could never make up the losses on half-empty houses in the first two or three weeks, and if it had not been for the returns from the London transfers of a number of the more outstanding productions, the Meadow Players would have foundered much earlier than they finally did.

After opening the season with two Russian plays, Frank Hauser closed it with a French pair. The Anouilh was followed by Alfred de Musset's *Le Chandelier* under the English title of *The Firescreen*, not seen on this side of the Channel since an adaptation by Alfred Sutro in 1910. The wife of a doddering lawyer is having an affair with a dashing captain of dragoons, who suggests that to distract suspicions from themselves she should encourage a young clerk in her husband's office, who naturally falls so passionately in love with her that she reciprocates his feelings and rejects her former lover. The French ambience and comic spirit were convincingly created by the Greek director, Minos Volanakis, though Judi was not so keen on all his bright ideas. 'Minos said, "What they are getting for the food is very dull – you have to get something that is not so dull-looking." So the stage manager went out and bought a huge bottle of maraschino cherries and emptied them into a tin of Irish stew and on the first night that's all we were given. Simon Ward was laughing so much that he blew it into his glass and it went everywhere. Red wine dripped all over him, and we had to play a love scene.'

Her lover's discomfiture was equalled by her husband's at another performance. Frank Shelley as André opened the play by finding his wife in bed, supposedly asleep. On this occasion Judi had been out to lunch, put on her make-up and costume, got into bed and really fell asleep. The unsuspecting stage manager took the curtain up. 'Frank came on and said my name, "Jacqueline", and I woke up and said "Frank!" in great surprise.'

The Times thought her performance 'a near-revelation', and the *Stage* also paid handsome tribute: 'Jacqueline … wilful, amorous, coquettish, as hard as nails but almost softened into real affection, is a gift to any actress as accomplished as Judi Dench, who plays her with her brilliantly-calculated verve in a considerable comic tour-de-force.'

Judi spent a large part of the sixties shuttling between Oxford and Nottingham, chalking up successes in both and helping to establish their reputations as major centres of theatrical excitement, whose work could not be ignored by the London-based critics of the national press. When John Neville sent out his second call for her, she bade au revoir to Frank Hauser and set off for Nottingham again for another rich quintet of parts.

six

1965–66

Having fun with the classics in Nottingham, and tearing the emotions on Television

The Nottingham company that John Neville invited Judi to join for the 1965/6 season included Alan Howard, Edward Woodward, Harold Innocent, Michael Craig, John Shrapnel, Job Stewart and James Villiers – a cast list that in itself does much to justify his ambition of the time: 'I wanted the Nottingham Company to be the best in the UK. That was the aim quite simply. It was often referred to as "the signpost for the future" *vis-à-vis* regional theatre. I believe we, in many ways, were worthy of that reference; Judi was an obvious choice to be part of that.'

Worthy should not, however, be interpreted as dull – not in a company of mutual jokers of whom one of the biggest was the director himself. His opening production was a modern-dress interpretation of *Measure for Measure*. As Isabella, for the second time, Judi's costume did now resemble a nun's, a white shift, but Edward Woodward wore a white raincoat and dark glasses as Lucio. The moated grange was transformed into a nightclub, which momentarily flummoxed Judi. 'I said, "How do I come into this nightclub?" and John yelled at me, "The way any fucking nun comes into a nightclub after hours!"'

John Neville remains 'immensely proud of that production; Judi was a very fine Isabella, she seemed very at ease'; but there was the occasional hiatus during the run.

Edward Woodward confesses that he has a great facility for making up his words very often – the only way to survive the treadmill of learning lines for weekly repertory in which he had begun. He says that actors who had come up by that route 'can never learn DLP [dead letter perfect] and of course you have to be pretty dead letter perfect for Shakespeare. As Lucio I had to say to the assembled company in *Measure for Measure*, "Did not I pluck thee by the nose for thy speeches?" For some strange reason I couldn't think of the word "nose" but I didn't want to stop, so I said, "Pluck him about the speeches", and Judi said, "Pluck him about the speeches!!??", giggle, giggle, giggle, turned her back and went on with that husky quality in her voice, which gets even huskier when she is laughing.'

The modern setting, with cocktail parties and jazz singing, and the bowler-hatted Duke departing with his airline luggage, met with a mixed reception but played to near-capacity audiences. The Special Correspondent of *The Times* was distinctly uneasy: 'Here is a robust, entertaining and utterly misguided production of a great, uneven play ... That the play holds together is largely the merit of Miss Judi Dench. Her Isabella, though lacking in some initial coldness, is a triumphant portrayal of righteous zeal and fierce humanity, intelligently controlled and at times immensely moving ... Mr Edward Woodward's Lucio was a perfect gem of comic characterisation but, like all the good things in the production, his talent would have shone through Elizabethan garments. The best of Shakespeare cannot be improved and, though it is a very pretty production, Mr Neville, you must not call it altogether Shakespeare.'

A month later these two actors opened in a production of *Private Lives* that was altogether Coward. Ronald Magill set it firmly in its inter-war period and at the dress rehearsal, when Judi donned her dark red, marcelled wig, her co-star totally failed to recognise her. 'Teddy passed me on the stairs and walked straight past me. He had no idea who I was.'

If they had fun in the Shakespeare, the Coward was a near-riot. The author warned the leading man, 'I do hope the girl's going to give you everything. I played it once with the most ghastly actress, and it turned out to be turgid beyond imagination, no laughs at all.' Noël Coward acknowledged much later that his fears had been groundless, though it was perhaps as well that when he went to see it the actors had no idea that he was in the audience. It was certainly fortunate for everyone that he was not present at the opening, when the cast needed all their aplomb. 'My bracelet flew off into the audience, the lid came off the coffee-pot and Teddy put it in his top pocket; he pushed me into the top of the trolley, I couldn't get out and he wouldn't help me. It was the most riotous first night; the audience just couldn't let it go.'

More than most plays, *Private Lives* only succeeds when the players feel it is just like going to a wonderful party every night, and Edward Woodward says it was exactly like that opposite Judi. 'We had to be very careful, because it was so fast and furious. The fight scene is very tricky to do, because the one thing Elyot must not do is to rip Amanda's clothes, and the one thing she must not do when she hits him over the head with the record is to use the side of the record; one night she did, which caused no end of amusement, from the audience and from Judi.'

Sometimes the two of them corpsed each other so much that one of them would actually have to walk off the stage to recover, while the other improvised a bit of business to fill the gap. John Neville disapproved of all this fooling about, but admired both their performances.

But audiences and critics were carried along on the bow-wave of their delight in the play, which Benedict Nightingale told his *Guardian* readers was perfectly judged. 'Edward Woodward is remarkably assured as Elyot and injects humour into such simple lines as "Like your mother? I can't bear her," by producing the intonation that is natural and right, but never the least obvious. Judi Dench, an Amanda that smoulders with the constant heat of egoism, has timing as splendid. Together they successfully suggest that any honest love necessarily involves anger, frustration, jealousy, and even violence. Women, as Coward puts it, have to be struck regularly, like gongs.'

Judi, Edward and Alan Howard soon formed an inseparable trio in their off-stage relaxations, going ice-skating and riding, and Judi took them both to the local Quaker meeting, though Alan refused to go again after his first visit, when the woman next to him spoilt his concentration by noisily opening a packet of biscuits. Edward had a few qualms at the Nottingham ice rink. 'I remember thinking, "My God, this is so dangerous. If John Neville knew we were doing this he'd say, 'Why did you let her go and break a leg?' " '

His fears for her safety on the ice were overshadowed by his own in the saddle. The riding stable was known as Bunny's. When they returned one afternoon for the evening performance of *Measure for Measure* Edward sank exhausted into a chair in the Green Room.

Harold Innocent was a little upset at not being included in their jaunt and asked with a slight edge to his voice, 'Oh, so you've been out have you?' 'Yes', said Judi. 'Bunny's I suppose?' asked Harold. Edward snapped back, 'No, I wish to Christ they were!' He still hates having to play a part on horseback and only Judi could have persuaded him to mount one when he was not paid to do so. 'Most of my good times as a youthful actor were with and around Judi, and I suppose that is the experience of a great number of us.'

Judi was not in the next play, *Richard II*, but at the dress rehearsal the cast were mystified when John Neville as the King was followed onto the stage by a curious figure bundled up in a cloak and boots and so unrecognisable behind a wig and beard that he thought at first it must be a protest by someone he had rejected at an audition. He refused to continue and was amazed when Judi removed her beard to a huge roar of laughter from the company. Her unscheduled walk-ons in costume have shaken other actors during performances since then, though she seems to have escaped reprimand by transfixed directors watching from the front.

Judi has done surprisingly few of the great Restoration comedies, but she showed her talent for them as *The Country Wife* by Wycherley, again directed by Ronald Magill, in which Harold Innocent as her jealous and puritanical husband tried to protect his new bride from the lecherous attentions of the rake Horner, played by Michael Craig. Benedict Nightingale zeroed in on her performance, 'a husky-voiced upper-crust milkmaid with a lively eye for a fellow, a natural coquette under the awkward knees and elbows. Miss Dench can present a very matter-of-fact veneer . . . and evoke a marvellous sense of life through it.'

She enjoyed it much more than *The Astrakhan Coat*, a new play by Pauline Macaulay, a thriller in which she was part of a gang with Job Stewart and James Villiers who plot a murder. Under Donald McWhinnie's direction they did what they could with it, but Judi thought it was 'a dreadful play'. She had one exit when she opened a door to reveal a figure of a blackamoor holding a tray, and her performance was not helped 'when Michael Craig got rather merry, and when I opened the door instead of the blackamoor there was Michael Craig blacked up with a towel round him. I don't know that anybody else saw, but I saw!'

The best known practical joke, involving not just Judi but the entire cast, was in the final play of that season, when she played St Joan. Harold Innocent was playing the Inquisitor and the cast began to feel that he was making rather too much of his great fourteen-minute speech in the trial scene, so they asked John Neville, who was directing, if they could have a complete run-through of that scene at the warm-up on the day of the opening. Job Stewart was playing Stogumber, and he and Judi laid an elaborate plot.

As Harold launched into his marathon speech, Job produced a flask and poured cups of tea for all the monks; Ronald Magill as Cauchon sitting beside the Inquisitor took out a great length of knitting, the colour of his purple cassock, and everyone else was doing a crossword, playing chess or cards. Judi says, 'Oh God, it was wonderful. Harold was so mad with us all. He said, "Do you want me to go on with this, John?" Johnny had to lie down between two rows of seats, he laughed so much. I wish Harold was alive to tell you himself, and Job.'

John Neville says it could only have happened because 'the company was a great one, solid, unified, accomplished, and confident in themselves and each other; it was a typical incident among colleagues who loved and respected each other.'

Gareth Lloyd-Evans acknowledged in the *Guardian* the power of this team, though his review had a sting in the tail. 'The production ... has every kind of acting. The formal dignity of Harold Innocent's Inquisitor, the driving passion of John Shrapnel's superb Dunois, the bland cruelty of Job Stewart's well-timed English Chaplain, the perky petulance of Jimmy Thompson's Dame-Dauphin. In the midst is Judi Dench's St Joan, appealingly courageous in its moments of elation, winsome in its fear, almost cockily compact in its times of certainty. Her strength is in her constant radiation of strangeness, her weakness is the necessity she seems to feel occasionally to respond to every acting style that lies about her ... Its parts – the scene before Orléans, the inquisition – are stronger than the whole. Perhaps time and Miss Dench's own power will eventually bring about cohesion and consistency.'

The Times was more struck by the youthfulness of Judi's portrayal: 'She gives to Shaw's relentless but superbly innocent saint a touching and unusual quality of a daring child.'

Looking back on it now, Judi feels that her playing of the part was not earthy enough, a view refuted by her director: 'Judi was a superb St Joan. I felt she *was* earthy enough.'

Judi has always worn period costume as if it were her everyday dress, but her highly developed sense of the ridiculous on occasion got the better of her in this play. 'When we were delayed in Act II, I was standing in the Green Room and I looked out of the window and saw a woman with two children and a whole lot of bags pushing a pram. I turned and looked at all this knitted chain mail on everyone, and I thought, "Oh God, what are we doing?" '

What they were doing was drawing packed houses to the new Playhouse; Judi cannot remember ever seeing an empty seat there. It was in Nottingham, too, that Judi first tried her hand at recitals late at night or on a Sunday. 'John came to me and said, "We do poetry and jazz evenings with Johnny Southgate, and you ought to have a go at them." I was frightened about it, but I'm very glad I did it.'

She so enjoyed doing these two-handers with John Neville that she has honed her technique in this performing art-form in the succeeding years to a high level, and frequently gives recitals for one of her many charities.

John Neville pioneered the use of the theatre building all the time, not just for the regular performances; people flocked to these other attractions and to see the exhibitions and use the restaurant. Not many theatres buzzed like this in the sixties. Sadly his efforts did not always please the city fathers and, after a spectacular public falling-out, the first director of the new Playhouse, a man who had attracted huge new audiences into the theatre, shook the dust of Nottingham from his feet in 1968. Even more sadly for British audiences, he took his talents off to Canada, where he has founded and run a succession of new theatres. As Judi says, 'It's our loss and Canada's gain that they've got him, but my goodness it is a loss.'

Their partnership had grown especially close during this, their last, season together and she is unstinting in her acknowledgement of what he taught her. 'There's nobody holds a candle to John for leading a company, nobody I've ever met. He was brilliant at teaching you basic things that I don't think young actors are taught any more – the whole business of getting in on time, being prepared, and not taking up the director's time while you sort out the problem of what is actually your homework. He had a great sense of fun, which is terribly important, and there's no doubt that if a company is led like that it comes over to an audience that it is a unit which works together, and it's something you can't manufacture. He used to *hate* it if anyone said they were tired and he's quite right, acting requires discipline, and if they're too tired well, frankly, I feel they should let someone else do it then. When I caught Asian flu during *Hamlet* at the Old Vic, one night I cried *during* the scene and went to pieces and John came off and said, "If you can't do it, let your understudy do it. Don't go on and show something that's nothing to do with Ophelia." I thought that's a very good lesson to learn.'

No one who has seen any of her performances since would doubt that she had learnt it. Some actors may have off-nights, when it is clear they are just walking through it, but no one has ever accused Judi of merely going through the motions. It has to be something really paralysing, like a snapped Achilles tendon, to prevent her going on.

1966 was a richly varied year for her. After shedding St Joan's chain mail in Nottingham, and before returning to her Oxford stamping ground, Judi embarked on a quartet of television plays which for many people, particularly in that industry, is the first thing that springs to mind when asked about her. This was *Talking to a Stranger*, written by John Hopkins, the creative force behind *Z-Cars*; Judi had played the character of Terry in embryo in an early episode he had written for that police drama. The BBC's acquisition of its second TV channel in 1964 opened up the possibilities of longer and more challenging plays; as the director Christopher Morahan says, 'It was a time when the BBC was very audacious, BBC 2 hadn't been going very long, and it was quite an extraordinary patron of new writing.'

He had seen her Juliet at the Old Vic and went up to Nottingham to see her St Joan, when he gave her the Hopkins script. Judi believed she was really second choice for the part, though Christopher denies this: 'I'd talked to Eileen Atkins, but I hadn't offered her the part. It took some time to get the balance of casting right. I was very keen to create a family.'

When she read the script Judi was on the brink of turning it down. 'I thought, "I can't do this, I really can't. The girl was such a complex character." I said to John Hopkins, "There are so many things I wouldn't understand. How would I manage?" John said, "I will sit outside in the car, so that you can come and ask me." '

In fact, he attended rehearsals every day and it was not only Judi who depended on him. Maurice Denham was playing her father and he was equally nervous. 'It's a very sparse script and consists of a lot of "Yes" and "No" and "Why?" and so on. He'd say, "When you say Yes there, you don't mean Yes, you mean no." So that what you saw on the page bore no relation, unless it was pointed out by John, to what was really happening.'

Michael Bryant played her brother and Margery Mason their mother. Judi's character was brittle and volatile; her sharp-edged humour conceals her panic at her pregnancy and her inability to tell her family. The tensions between the women erupt over the teacups on a Sunday afternoon when Terry makes a sarcastic crack about presenting 'the Jesus of Nazareth Award for suffering humanity' to her mother, who immediately slaps her face. When Alan says he has been offered a job in Australia, his mother's despair leads her to break all her precious china, and commit suicide by slashing her wrists. During the police questioning the following day, Alan exposes the rawness of the family's emotions when he says bleakly, 'As a family we don't exist.'

Each of the four ninety-minute episodes looks at their relationship from the perspective of a different member of the family, beginning with the daughter's. But they recorded the second episode first, the father's view, so that Judi did not have to begin with what was in effect a huge, twenty-minute monologue to her flatmate Jess, played by Judi's real-life friend Pinkie Johnstone, who remembers them both being reduced to tears during rehearsals.

It was only a couple of years since the death of Judi's own father and Maurice Denham looked not unlike him. 'Judi and I became really like father and daughter. There were days when we really got involved as a family, when she came in and said, "I can't do those scenes today, I can't say those things to my father." It was as intense as that; I've never known it before or since. Each of us, at one time or another, blew up.'

Judi's explosion happened during a lunch break in the pub in Hammersmith opposite the rehearsal room. 'Michael Bryant said he was feeling a bit down and I said, "If I was the director I'd give you the afternoon off." Well, Christopher hit the ceiling. Nobody spoke, so Maurice put his hand on my knee under the table. That made it worse of course. So I got my money and just put it down for my lunch, and got up and rushed out of the pub. There was the most unbelievable screech of brakes and they came racing out after me. A car had run into the back of a jeep. John Hopkins and I walked around until the end of lunch, then we went back for notes and I smoked a packet of fags, and I don't smoke. But it was an incredible feat of direction by Christopher.'

Michael Bryant says they were all a bit emotional during the three months they worked on the series and they had to break the tension by some larking about and giggling, 'otherwise you'd have gone potty. Judi was a great example to us all, the way she put it on like a skin, and could come out of it just like that.'

Christopher Morahan admired the way she relied on her instincts, 'and the most amazing vigorous gift of being able to realise it. She embarks on dangerous solutions, dangerous in that they're not necessarily conventional. Her Terry was recognised as being quite, quite vivid. She had to show herself subjectively in the first episode, and objectively in the others as she was seen by the three members of the family, which is fascinating because you get a many-faceted portrait.'

The camera crew who worked on the studio recordings of the first three episodes were supposed to be on holiday during episode four, but they too became so fascinated and involved in the developing story that they all gave up their holiday to come in and record the last episode, which, as Maurice Denham observed, 'makes a huge difference on the set if you know everyone already'. It is rare for television crews to get that involved in a production, though Judi has exerted her magnetism to that effect on other occasions since.

The audience response was similar – the cast received an avalanche of mail, much of it identifying with the characters and the situations rather than commenting on the performances. The press was generally admiring, if a bit equivocal. Both J. C. Trewin in the *Listener* and T. C. Worsley in the *Financial Times* would have preferred each episode to have been pared down to an hour, though the latter admired the way they were written, 'in a packed, dense dialogue which always implies more than it says; and they are acted with rare truthfulness by the whole cast. Mr Hopkins makes us free of the world he has conjured up. Even the simplest of these people seem important, and the truth about them important too.'

Philip Purser was also unsure about the length justifying itself and added a question mark to his headline in the *Sunday Telegraph* – DRAMA OF THE YEAR? Gillian Grant expressed no such doubts in the Sheffield *Morning Telegraph* about 'what must be considered one of the outstanding television drama achievements of the year'.

Kenneth Eastaugh went right over the top in the *Daily Mirror*. 'The most promising actresses, like Miss Dench, go on improving with each play. Then . . . Pow! With the right encouragement and the right degree of experience they turn in a performance, like the one this week, better than our most optimistic prophecies. I believe that with this performance Miss Dench, for the first time, showed that she is going to be capable of really great things.' Her fellow-professionals thought so too, and she won the BAFTA Best Actress Award for her portrayal of Terry.

It is a tribute to the indelible imprint the series made that the BBC decided, very unusually, to repeat it twenty-three years later, and that it again excited as much attention. Only the most truthful and high-quality work can have the same impact when re-viewed so long afterwards. (The contractual complications alone are normally enough to preclude repeats so long after the first transmission – the BBC eventually paid the actors sixty-five times their original fee.)

Most of Judi's best screen work has been for television rather than the cinema, until very recently, and she has chosen her vehicles with care, usually fitted around her commitments to the stage. Frank Hauser now enticed her back to Oxford with the offer of two very different plays from the European repertoire he championed for so long. This provided her next great springboard into a major new departure.

seven

1966–68

The Rules of the Game,
The Promise and *Cabaret*

In her first ten years on the stage Judi appeared in more than thirty productions, for the great majority of which she wore period costume, her modern-dress roles could be counted on one hand. A casual follower of her progress could be forgiven for thinking that she thought contemporary clothes were only for television parts. But now three very different twentieth-century authors claimed her attention in succession, for the last two of whom she scored her longest runs yet.

The first was also a critical success, but only had its regulation run at Oxford and a brief regional tour. This was Pirandello's *The Rules of the Game*, another fascinating European play, a popular favourite in its native Italy, rescued from obscurity in Britain by Frank Hauser. She played a provincial *femme fatale* in 1920s Italy, who has left her husband and gone to live with her lover. Her husband agrees to all her demands, and keeps turning up to ask if he can bring her anything, to the great irritation of her lover. When she is insulted by a drunken young man, she insists that her husband challenge him to a duel. He agrees, but at the last minute refuses to go. The rules of the game demand that his second takes his place and it is the lover who is killed. Hauser cast the two leads imaginatively: 'Judi played the Sophia Loren part, got up to look like Sophia Loren, and got away with it again.' Opposite her he cast Leonard Rossiter, famous later for his manic energy on stage and television, but here required to show no emotion at all until the very end.

With those two in place Hauser then invited a young actor in the Oxford Company, James Grout, to complete the casting and direct the production. James had admired Judi's recent performance in *Talking to a Stranger*, and he was appearing with Rossiter in *Volpone* at the Playhouse, but for the first week of rehearsals he doubted if he was ever going to be able to get his two leading players to act in harness. 'Leonard was a great technician and had worked out exactly what he was planning to do; Judi on the other hand was all "What do I do?" She wasn't as sure of herself as she is now and wanted a lot of reassurance from me as to what she should be doing in playing the part. Judi was desperate to like him, so she could work with him, and he was slightly handing her off, to use a rugby term. I reached a point where I was thinking, "This isn't working. How the devil am I going to get these two to change their way of working so much that they can work together?"'

That kind of conflicting approach from a couple playing man and wife can sometimes defeat the most experienced directors, let alone one with only a single previous production under his belt. But to James Grout's intense relief these two professional players solved the dilemma for him. 'Suddenly Leonard's defences against Judi fell, and they liked each other. One evening they got together for a drink and a chat. Leonard suddenly thought, "God, what a lovely lady", and Judi said, "This is a very clever man; I can work with him." The whole of the rehearsal the following day was a revelation – they suddenly all hit it; it was a great moment. I was totally speechless and I thought, "Oh gosh, this is going to be good."'

The play was in repertory with *Volpone*, which Judi was not in, but quite often at the end of those performances James and Leonard would look out of their dressing-room windows, onto the little alleyway between the stage door and the Gloucester Arms, to see Judi shouting up, 'What do you want to drink?' She had their glasses ready and waiting when they came into the pub gasping for a drink. Her keen company feeling extended even beyond her own performances.

James Grout was another who concluded that Judi was a natural leader in the company, 'because she was always concerned with others and what they had to offer. She would come up to me and say, "What about that lady, isn't she wonderful?" and she was talking about somebody who had no lines to say, but who walked on in a scene, and this was a rare thing I think.'

Rarer still was her behaviour on the first night. On the previous day she met James's friends, the director Bill Hays and his wife Jill, who had a two-month-old baby and consequently felt she could not attend the opening. Judi insisted that she should come.

'Well, what do we do about the baby?'

'Oh, I'll have him in my dressing-room.'

Her director laughs in astonishment at this impulsive act. 'A first night is not the best time to have a totally strange baby in your dressing-room with you, but she looked after the baby and did the play. That probably illustrates the woman more than anything else I can say.'

The backstage presence clearly did not inhibit her performance. Ian Donaldson in the *Guardian* thought that she caught perfectly 'the quality of Silia that really matters, namely, her volatility: by turns she is petulant, childish, feline, gloatingly triumphant, then suddenly dashed.' In the *Financial Times*, B. A. Young expressed surprise as well as admiration: 'As Silia Judi Dench produces a fund of sophisticated comedy that I had no idea she was capable of. She slinks about in her delicious 1919 fashions like a man-eating panther, posing herself in the elegant attitudes of the fashionable "vamp" of the days before youth-worship put elegance out of circulation; or turning at will into a little girl if that happens to be her mood.'

The regular local critic for the *Oxford Mail*, Don Chapman, was less surprised but just as admiring of the central partnership. 'It is the conflict of Judi Dench and Leonard Rossiter as Leone and Silia that gives the evening its power and comic impact. Miss Dench, exuding animal vitality and petulant wilfulness, watches him with minatory eye and ready claw like a caged cheetah. Mr Rossiter, breathing the calm, mannered confidence of the compulsive melancholic, handles her with the self-amused fatalism of a bomb-disposal expert.'

As soon as the Pirandello opened, Judi was plunged into rehearsals for a new play by Aleksei Arbuzov. He never admitted as much, but Frank Hauser is convinced that he wrote *The Promise* for Judi after seeing her in *The Twelfth Hour* two years earlier. This one opened during the Siege of Leningrad in 1942 and followed the changing relationship between three young people thrown together then, and over the next seventeen years.

Act I shows the three teenagers sharing their hopes against the hardships of the siege, before the young men go off to enlist. In Act

II they are reunited in 1946; Marat the would-be engineer is now a Hero of the Soviet Union; Leonidik the would-be poet has lost an arm in the war. Lika has to choose between them and, like Shaw's Candida, she chooses the weaker. Act III is set thirteen years later, when Leonidik sends for Marat, whom she should have married, and finally leaves them together so all three can make a fresh start, hoping to rekindle their youthful ambitions.

The two boys were played by Ian McKellen and Ian McShane, both of whom thought that the production was better than the actual play – a subjective judgement possibly confirmed by the fact that it has never had a major revival since.

Ian McKellen's main reason for accepting the part was his desire to work with Judi: 'She was a bit of a role model for me, because I'd seen her as Juliet at the Vic, and I knew of her work at Nottingham and Oxford, but I hadn't seen it. The idea that if you were going to act seriously you would not be too careful about where you did it, but you'd be careful about the company you did it in, seemed to me was what Judi was doing, and that was what I decided to do myself, so she was a bit of a special person.'

Ian McShane looks back on those first weeks as 'probably the most enjoyable rehearsals I've ever had. We're such different people, and we didn't live in each other's pockets; I don't remember being particularly close to each other outside the theatre, but those three hours on stage every night were three hours of concentration and exciting work.'

It was certainly hard work for all of them and Judi admits the truth of Frank Hauser's only complaint against her: 'I used to go to sleep all the time, during his notes to us. There was a big bed I used to curl up on, and Frank would say, "Is she awake? Is the pussy awake? Because I have a few notes."'

Ian McKellen worried that he was much slower than Judi in learning his lines, or understanding his character. 'My image of Judi rehearsing is of her tapping her toe, finishing off the *Telegraph* crossword, just waiting for everyone to catch up. "Come on, what's the problem?" She has a facility for acting which is bewildering, with a blazing sincerity and honesty; it wasn't a series of tricks she pulled out of the bag, it was all freshly minted in front of your eyes.'

But, despite their enjoyment of the rehearsals, none of the actors nor their director had the slightest inkling that this play would make any more of a mark than *The Rules of the Game*. The first indication of something special came after the first night performance. Unusually for such an occasion, none of the four of them had anyone they knew in the audience, so they all trooped off to an Italian restaurant just round the corner from the theatre. When they got downstairs Judi and the others were confronted with a potentially awkward situation. 'There was a huge table in the other half of the restaurant, taken up by every single critic. So we rather sheepishly looked at them, and they looked at us, and looked away, and *then* they all said, "Will you come and join us for coffee?" That's when we knew it was going to be the success it was, and I don't remember that happening before or since.'

Peter Lewis set the bandwagon of critical acclamation rolling by proclaiming in the *Daily Mail* that it was 'an obvious knock-me-down West End success'; picked up and quoted by Harold Hobson in the *Sunday Times*, who praised the production, the performances of the two Ians, and 'as for Miss Dench, I have never seen her so good and so resilient ... For once in a lifetime I ask managers to believe someone else rather than me; in this instance Peter Lewis. Bring the play to London. If money is lost on it, it will be lost honourably.'

The result was a cheering example of how a critical response can positively influence the course of events in the theatre. At the end of its Oxford run the production transferred to the Fortune Theatre in London, where it ran for ten months (though Judi relinquished the part of Lika to Prunella Scales in August). This success led directly to her next, surprising one, but it also, unknowingly to the parties concerned, delayed a major development in her personal life.

Just before that encounter with the press, Judi received a visitor from Stratford – a new young director named Trevor Nunn. He wanted her to come back there to play, amongst other things, Kate in *The Taming of the Shrew*. He enthused her with his idea of producing it as an Elizabethan *Billy Liar*; and mentioned that the Petruchio would be a young actor he knew called Michael Williams. 'She was very, very intrigued by the idea and said she'd love to come to Stratford. However, she said she was contracted to go to the West End with *The Promise* if it went in. "Between you and me," she said,

"I don't think there's a chance, but if you can hang on until we know I'm fairly certain that I'll be free." Of course it was adulated by critics far and wide and shot into the West End, and that was the end of any thought of having Judi at Stratford that season.'

So she was delayed in working with her future husband, though when Janet Suzman unexpectedly became available to go to Stratford in her stead, Trevor Nunn did meet his future wife. Happily for all concerned, Trevor was more successful in his next approach to Judi, which led to her longest association with the RSC.

Not that she had much time to waste pondering on might-have-beens, as they all prepared for the opening in London. Even now, they were not expecting a long West End run until Frank Hauser wandered into the box office on the opening day. 'The manager was on the phone and I heard her say, "Complimentaries? Oh no, no complimentaries, we're a hit you know." She was right, but it scared the pants off me.'

The actors were too busy to get scared. Now playing six evenings and two matinées a week, even Judi found it hard going. 'It ran nearly three and a half hours, and our dressing-rooms were up all those stairs at the Fortune. I had a huge change in both intervals – of wigs, costumes and make-up. As we came down at the matinées, it was something like the half for the evening', (the half-hour call before curtain-up). 'Oh, it was hard.'

But they had fun, too. At the opening of the third act, after Lika has married Leonidik and both have realised it was a mistake, Judi and Ian McKellen entered muffled up in fur hats and coats and took a long time shedding them without speaking to each other. Such a stage silence can have pitfalls, as Judi discovered at one performance. 'Neither of us spoke; it said a lot about the marriage. Then we heard absolutely clearly this woman say, "Oh, all them furs. Anyone would think they were in Russia!" '

The beginning of that third act had another trap that caught the actors out one night. The stage door sent a letter up to Judi in the second interval from an elderly friend of hers in York. 'I said to Ian, "She says in her letter she's a huge fan of yours, and she's coming round to see me. Please come round to my dressing-room to meet her." He said, "What's her name?" I said, "Mrs Bytheway", and Ian said, "What a strange name." We went on for the third act, quite

forgetting that the very first line of the third act was: "By the way . . . "
We were speechless!'

The critics who came to the Fortune were far from speechless.
Peter Lewis and Harold Hobson added further superlatives to their
first reactions at Oxford; W. A. Darlington in the *Daily Telegraph*
thought it was the best thing he had seen Judi do; Felix Barker in the
Evening News judged it 'the best performance by a young actress now
to be seen in London', and J. C. Trewin joined that chorus in
the *Illustrated London News*, saying she gave 'what I hold to be the
performance of her career'.

B. A. Young in the *Financial Times* was uncharacteristically swept
away: 'In the first and last acts especially, Miss Dench comes as near
to perfection as we need look for in this imperfect world; each
movement, each mannerism, each inflection of the voice is exactly
right. When, near the end, she stands right downstage, facing the house, and her eyes fill with tears as she realises what a
mess she's made of her life, I wept too – a weakness I'm not given
to.'

That desolating sadness is my own abiding memory of her performance in what I thought, and still think, was the most perfect three-
hander I have ever seen. Until then she had given many scintillating
performances in a wide range of parts, but this was the first one which
seemed truly brushed with greatness.

Ian McShane says that production was very special and rewarding,
but not just for the actors: 'You could feel the audience expectancy
each night before the curtain went up; they knew they were going
to have a good night out.'

Ian McKellen remembers the excitement the night that Richard
Chamberlain came to see it. 'At the time he was the most famous
actor in the world as Dr Kildare on TV and Judi and I were terribly
excited; I suppose we both fancied him. We could see where he was
sitting in that small theatre and wondered if he'd come round. During
that show there was a lot of singing the Dr Kildare signature tune
under our breath.'

But for Judi he was not the most significant American to visit *The
Promise*. That position was reserved for someone she never knew was
present in the Fortune Theatre until much later – Hal Prince. He had
directed the musical *Cabaret* on Broadway, where it was a smash hit

and was still running after eighteen months, and now he came over to cast the London production. He had a deservedly high reputation as the best director of musicals in the business and there was keen competition to work for him. The line-up for the leading role of Sally Bowles was impressive; as he says, 'It was a very heady day to audition, because I auditioned Vanessa Redgrave, Dorothy Tutin' (who had already played Sally in the straight play, *I am a Camera*) 'and Judi. All three auditions were good, but when Judi came in it *was* Sally Bowles – it was extraordinary, all that energy. Sally shouldn't be a great singer, or a comfortable performer, she's a show-off and she's edgy, she is a little hysterical, she's irresistible and she's very sexy. Judi had all that stuff, and she's got great looks, that girl. It was fun to have her audition, and it was just about two seconds later that everybody said, "Well, do you think she'll do this thing? If she'll do it we'll have to have her." '

That conviction of her rightness for the part was not universally shared. When Barbara Leigh-Hunt had seen the show on Broadway she was so enthralled by it that she even refused to leave her seat in the interval; she bought two copies of the record of the show and sent one to Judi. When Barbara returned from the Old Vic tour of the States and rang her at the theatre Judi said, 'Guess what I'm doing next.'

'Having a sleep?'

'No, no, I mean after this play.'

'Do you mean tonight, or do you mean professionally?'

'Yes, professionally.'

'Oh God, Jude, the world's your oyster. You're going to make a film?'

'No, no, no.'

'You're doing a play in the West End?'

'No.'

'Well I don't know what you are doing.'

'Well, *what record* did you send me from America?'

'*Cabaret*.'

'*Well?*'

'Well?'

'I'm playing *Sally Bowles*!'

'But you don't sing!'

'I *know*! And I haven't been able to listen to the bloody record since I knew I was going to do it.'

Barbara made very sure she was at the first night, 'because I said I wouldn't miss it for worlds'.

Judi's dressing-room at the Palace was in a half-basement, so she could see the legs of passers-by from the knee down, and also hear their conversation. Just before the show opened, she saw two pairs of trouser legs stop to study the posters outside and overheard a voice exclaim: 'Judi Dench in *Cabaret*? No one will go to see that, dear, no one!'

But the combination of Hal Prince and Judi had a few surprises in store for the sceptics. Her first preparation was to take the measure of the large auditorium of the Palace Theatre by going to see the current show there – *The Desert Song*. She went with her close friend James Cairncross. 'In the interval he handed me a beautifully wrapped box – his presents were always immaculate – and inside was some cotton-wool and a date and a card saying, 'This is the date that we're keeping tonight.'

James did not need to hint about her dietary regime. Judi took herself off to a health farm and lost a stone in weight before starting work on this new challenge; a preparation she has had to make more than once in her career as, to her undying regret, she says she can put on pounds just by looking at a plate of food. It is one problem that really worries her, as the assistant stage manager for *Cabaret*, Chris Cooper, noticed: 'If anyone so much as implied she was putting on weight, you were in serious trouble. She was so sexy and voluptuous and vulnerable in this part. There were bits of Judi that would have quite liked to be Sally Bowles; there was a raunchy side of her character that she could expose in that part, which was lovely to see from the prompt corner when it happened.'

When rehearsals began, Hal Prince quickly showed his command. 'In the Sailors' Dance, there was a moment when I jumped and they all caught me, and Hal said, "Oh no, cut that musical crap, everybody does that, don't do that." He had very fresh ideas about it, and he was good fun.' Those last two words are a mark of high approval in Judi's judgement of directors.

He observed how 'she can spot a falsehood in her own performance instantly. I remember watching her in rehearsal trying something and almost editing it, out of some shame, because it was too easy, calculated, adroit, crafty. What's worth mentioning about Dench is her thing about telling the truth; when you know you're working with somebody who just plain says what's on their mind all the time, you don't go home and worry about them. "Are they thinking something; are they percolating; have I got a problem on my hands that I don't know about?" She's cheerful and she enjoys it; I like to have a good time and so does she. Some of my colleagues like chassis; I hate it. I think they think it creates an atmosphere of creativity.'

However, Judi soon indicated that her responsiveness and adaptability should not be mistaken for weakness. She was apprehensive about the singing demands placed on her and went off for lessons in technique in how to put a song over from the singing tutor, Gwen Catley. The old musical hands in the company also did their best to help her, with the exception of Lila Kedrova early on. 'All the cast used to come to my room, which was next door to Lila's, to give me tips. She got it into her head that we were ganging up on her, so I just walked into her room and said, "Lila, what's this?" So she pretended she didn't understand what I meant, but then we were friends, though not like I was with Thelma Ruby, who took over from her later; we were great friends.'

Judi was happy to work with Peter Sallis again after their first disastrous foray in the West End together in *A Shot in the Dark*. They went out for a meal after rehearsals once or twice, 'and she wanted to know about the crew. She took a lot of trouble to memorise their names – the Berts, the Harrys and the Joes etc.'

The producers worried about the audience reaction to a musical set in a Berlin nightclub as the Nazis were coming into power and there were some grounds for their apprehension. Two rebukes Judi heard through her dressing-room window were, 'Arthur, you told me it was all about nuns and children!' And, since this was the time when Frankie Vaughan always sang a number called 'Come to the Cabaret' as part of his television act – 'Well, where was Frankie Vaughan? I was waiting for Frankie to come on!'

Some of the critics also seem to have been affected by misplaced expectations. Peter Lewis, who had so raved about *The Promise* in the *Daily Mail*, began his review by saying, '*Cabaret* is a disappointment', and he extended this from the production to the star – 'Judi Dench plays her with a funny little cracked voice and a determination to go to the bad, but she lacks the touch of one of Nature's butterflies ... Her opening number, "Don't tell Mama", is a delight, and she moves and dances with grace as a straight vaudeville charmer. But when the going gets rough, she looks too nice not to care.'

Jeremy Kingston in *Punch* found it 'schmaltzy and pallid' and only grudgingly conceded that 'Judi Dench deserves great credit for doing as well in such a feebly drawn role.'

But in the *Daily Telegraph* Eric Shorter predicted, 'The success of *Cabaret* at the Palace seems assured ... it is easy to see why it will be popular. It is brash. It is colourful. It is staged with brilliance and performed with uncommon verve and feeling ... Brilliantly miscast and spiritedly playing against her nature as an actress, Miss Dench sings and prances with engaging spirit and a quite surprising force.'

That verve stopped the show three times on the opening night, as the audience rose to its feet in roaring acclaim, and at the end demanded seven curtain calls before they would let the company go.

Judi tried very hard before the opening night not to have one at all. 'I loathe taking curtain calls, I loathe it. It embarrasses the hell out of me. I begged Hal Prince not to have one in *Cabaret*, because I thought it would be so wonderful to have that train going away.' But she has succumbed to the gentle arguments of her directors over the years, from Frank Hauser to Richard Eyre, that it is a courtesy the actor cannot deny to the audience.

Judi has always taken great care over her first night presents and for Hal Prince she found a Staffordshire figure of Hamlet doing the 'Alas, poor Yorick' speech, which stands on his desk in New York today. He managed to surprise Judi even more. 'He stole my watch when I was having a costume fitting and I didn't notice, and then I thought, "Oh dash, my watch." It had a leather strap and he took it to Asprey's and bought a beautiful gold strap for it – that was my first night present from Hal.'

One of the skills that has kept him ahead of the game as a director of musicals has been his ability to introduce the latest technical innovations, which he makes light of: 'I really don't care a helluva lot about spectacle, and this wasn't a spectacle; it was a big black velour stage with a mirror and some lights that came in. But the timing of the show was very specific, and in those days we had winches, eight-inch high plates that bring on scenery. We started with a sound system for cueing, and the poor people in the first few rows could hear the fly-floor, "Warning on 6 ... bring in 6." Then we went on to more sophisticated stuff and light cues.'

Today audiences take hugely mobile stage machinery for granted, but in 1968 the theatre crew found these technical demands stretched the capacities of the old Palace stage sometimes beyond breaking point. As ASM Chris Cooper noted, 'Half of the reason for people being nervous was that they didn't know whether or not they were going to be run over by the scenery. There were huge bits of scenery rolling all over this small stage, and many times it ground to a halt, and we'd have to wait for fifteen minutes or so to get the whole thing back on tracks again.'

The first time this happened, Peter Sallis went on and improvised for about twenty minutes, telling jokes, and then did his number while the chorus came on and sat around like his audience; another time he went on and read out some invented telegrams. Judi soon found this was a trick she, too, had to acquire, 'especially in the last scene where she has to tell Cliff she's had the abortion. That was wildly exciting, suddenly having to do that on a bare stage, and make it up.'

She did get fed up with audiences expressing concern about her voice, so much so that at one point she asked the management to put up a notice in the foyer saying, 'Miss Judi Dench does not have a cold, this is her normal speaking voice.' But their fear of the wrath of the Palace's owner, Emile Littler, stopped them complying with her request.

The show continued to pull in packed houses for nine months – Judi's longest run on her best salary yet. A friend of hers, the theatre publicist Theo Cowan, urged her to buy a house he had seen in Hampstead. She had no intention of doing so and the price of £14,400 seemed a fortune to her then, but he insisted, so she went to view it with him and Marty Feldman. 'I can't imagine what this lady thought was coming. It was such a rum three people – great big, tall Theo, Marty with his bulging eyes, and this dwarf beside them.'

She immediately fell in love with its eighteenth-century charm and its many tiny rooms, and bought it at the asking price. It has an almost rural feel, tucked away down a narrow lane, overlooking

Hampstead parish churchyard. This first home of her own has remained special to her, even though her main home is now in Surrey.

She said at the outset that she would not play Sally Bowles for longer than nine months and in August 1968 she confirmed that intention, saying she had no idea what she would do next. 'I'll have to see what's offered. I may even have a stretch out of work.'

Then, as so often at such moments for her, two invitations came hot on each other's heels, and the second was nearly jeopardised by the first.

James Cairncross was invited by the British Council to return to West Africa and take an actress with him for a two-handed recital tour, so he asked Judi to join him and she said, 'Of course I will.'

Shortly after that, Trevor Nunn went to see her in *Cabaret* and went round to her dressing-room afterwards, with fingers crossed that this journey would prove more productive than his first one to see her in Oxford. He had just taken over from Peter Hall as the Director of RSC and wanted to take a leaf out of his predecessor's book. Peter Hall had wooed Peggy Ashcroft to lead his first company at Stratford and the Aldwych, and Trevor Nunn was desperately keen that Judi should lead the next generation for his first season at the helm in 1969.

Before he could say more than, 'Hello', she told him she had had a visit the previous night from an old schoolfriend, Christopher Malcolmson, who had brought his wife. He said, 'I've brought you this letter to read.' She recognised her own handwriting as a fifteen-year-old – it was a letter to a boy with the message that they could go out together no longer, 'because on the walls last night you touched my coat'. He had been carrying it around ever since. Judi was full of mortified laughter that she could ever have been so prudish.

Then Trevor Nunn took her out to dinner and at last managed to ask, 'Will you come to Stratford for a season and begin by playing Hermione in *The Winter's Tale*?' She was keen to accept and her agent Julian Belfrage thought she had no option but to cancel her West African trip, but Judi said, 'No, no, I've promised James. He's a dear friend. I'm going to do it.' Happily the dates could just be accommodated, so she was able to do both.

What is more remarkable about her determination not to let a friend down was a premonition which she refused to divulge to him until after their return. When they did, he asked her what it was. 'Well, I was quite convinced we weren't going to return. I thought we were both going to be killed on the tour.'

James Cairncross shakes his head in wonderment. 'We were never in danger, either by land, sea or air, but it is quite amazing that she said that, and still went.'

Before she embarked on that trip she prepared to say farewell to the company of *Cabaret* with a last-night party given for her, before Elizabeth Seal took over the part of Sally Bowles. 'Then Emile Littler did the dirty on us. He wanted to bring in other shows. It was nothing to do with the bookings falling off; Liz Seal was a huge star; she'd done *Irma La Douce*. The last-night party they arranged for me turned out to be the last night for everyone. He brought in three shows and they all folded. I thought, "Serve him right; that'll teach him to laugh in church."'

diary entry two

10–15 December 1996

As Time Goes By – Episode 1, Series 6
Location – BBC Rehearsal Studios, Acton,
and Studio 8, TV Centre

Tuesday

Arrived at 10 a.m. Met Valerie Letley, Philip Jones and Andrew Wiltshire, of the production team. Judi arrived shortly after, in black sweater and trousers, which is her usual rehearsal gear, and introduced me to Moira Brooker who plays her daughter, then took me up to the canteen for coffee and a doughnut. We joined Geoffrey Palmer, who greeted Judi warmly, and we chatted briefly about the Wilton filming for *Mrs Brown*, where we had last met.

10.30. Rejoined everyone in the rehearsal room for the read-through, and the director Sydney Lotterby got up to greet me. When he asked Judi if she wanted to mark up her script now or later, she said, 'Oh, later', and then sightread it (brilliantly), with several giggles from the others on her occasional fluff. It is a standing joke that Judi has never looked at the script before the first read-through, unlike every other cast member.

11.10. After the reading there was a flurry of activity and then champagne and two trays of glasses were carried in to mark Judi's sixty-second birthday yesterday. Judi had brought in a chocolate cake for assistant producer Julia Thomas's birthday the previous Saturday, and it was also Philip Jones's on the Friday. Syd joked that this was always done on the first day of rehearsal. Annie Rayment, Judi's make-up artist, gave her a present of long black rubber evening gloves, with yellow gauntlets, and a rubber bunch of grapes attached to the wrist. Judi roared with laughter when she opened them and immediately tried them on. The cake was cut, and the champagne quickly swallowed, to allow the rehearsal to continue.

11.45. The director started blocking the moves from the beginning. After the first bedroom scene Geoffrey and Judi stayed on the bed, rehearsing that scene through again quietly on their own, while Jenny and Moira were put through their moves in the next scene.

12.45. Scene 8. A big discussion between cast and director over whether Lionel would drink tea or coffee.

Geoffrey: 'During the war we drank things all the time.'

Judi: 'Well, Geoffrey, I'm too young to remember the war!'

1.10. Break for lunch. Everyone went to a long table in the canteen. Conversation turned to the latest BBC reorganisation, and the abolition of the Costume Department. Judi said she wrote to John Birt to protest and was outraged that he did not reply personally, but passed it on to some spokesman in the Corporate Affairs Department. A mention of the new charges by the Pronunciation Unit of £25 per query, which meant programmes would guess instead (often wrongly), led to a shriek from Judi, 'Did you hear Nick Ross on Radio 4 this morning pronounce Nemesis as Knee-mee-sis? I shouted at the radio in the car!'

2.00. The remaining scenes were blocked.

3.00. Judi had to leave for Oxford, where she was giving a reading for one of the charities of which she is President (Down's Syndrome children). The rest of us stayed to watch the edited film sequences for all the episodes in the series, including this one. Geoffrey made some suggestions about tightening up a couple of cuts.

Wednesday

10.50 a.m. I arrived a little late, after a traffic hold-up, to find the cast sitting round the table reading-through for lines, minus Jenny. Her father had died in hospital overnight, and at the break they all discussed where to send her flowers, finally deciding on the stage door of the Orange Tree at Richmond, where she was about to open in an Ayckbourn play. Judi quietly took charge of the operation, saying casually, 'I've got a blank card here', and producing one from her capacious file. She seems to be equipped for any emergency.

Before rehearsal proper started again, Judi asked if anyone could find out whether her brother Jeffery was rehearsing next door today (as *The Brittas Empire* is chalked up on the board outside the adjoining rehearsal room). Andrew Wiltshire, the AFM, went off to find out.

12.20. Jeffery came in quietly, but immediately the rehearsal stopped for ten minutes, while the Denches embraced and talked about their respective current TV shows. Jeffery had also just had an offer from Vienna to go and play Sir in *The Dresser*. They parted, saying, 'We must have lunch together tomorrow.'

12.30. Big debate about how intense the row between Lionel and Jean should be in Scene 5, in the bedroom.

12.45. Judi mimed carrying a bag of plums, with an empty paper bag. She did the comedian's trick of throwing something imaginary into the air, and catching it in the bag, which twitched as if it were real. 'Eric Morecambe showed me how to do that', she said, and then kept doing demonstrations of it, to general laughter. (Much later, the business with the plums got cut, to get the time down to length).

1.30. Kitchen scene with the actor playing the tough bodyguard, known as 'Nails'.

Judi: 'I must do something, it's driving me mad not doing anything in this scene.' (She frequently shows the actor's need for some convincing business to counterpoint with the lines.)

Thursday

10.20 a.m. Judi arrived, having lost a contact lens, so she could not read her script in the car, and had to use her spectacles for today's rehearsal. She spent all the scenes she was not in, going over her lines, as they needed to be virtually word perfect for tomorrow's technical run in front of the studio technicians.

Lunch break. Judi and I collected Jeffery from the Green Room, and we all went off to lunch in the canteen together.

Friday

Jenny was late arriving, and had not rehearsed since Tuesday. Before she arrived Judi said, 'Shouldn't we be doing something when she gets here?'

Syd: 'Good thinking. Let's do the second bedroom scene.'

Jenny arrived looking pale and a little trembly. Rehearsal did not stop, but as each actor exited they all went to give her a hug.

The kitchen scene with Nails. Big discussion about the desired number of Jean's 'looks' – for laugh-lines. Syd and Judi agreed to settle for the first, and not the second.

11.30. The tech run. (Eleven extra crew arrive to watch.) First scene with Nails in hall. Judi's double-hop and quick turn when he does not follow her, got a laugh from the crew. Her line about 'Mr Two-Buckets' raised another. Big laugh on Lionel's '... with either a cup of tea or a cup of coffee'. Very big laugh at the end when Sandy succeeded in opening the jar of pickled onions, Jean's 'Oh dear', and Lionel's slow-burn look.

Lunch break for cast while Syd talked to the crew.

1.45 p.m. One complete run-through, to try and fix lines.

Saturday

Not attended by me. Two rapid run-throughs in morning only, before the long Sunday camera rehearsal and recording.

Sunday. Studio day.
10.30 a.m. Camera rehearsal started promptly.

12.10 p.m. In a break Judi showed me a framed family snap on a table in the living-room. It was only set-dressing and would never be seen in close-up; and is of Princess Elizabeth holding the baby Prince Charles, flanked by Queen Elizabeth and Queen Mary. Judi said it was put there by Francis (the props buyer) because of her recent filming as Queen Victoria. The private joke was much appreciated by the subject of it, and she said they are always playing jokes like this – obviously responding to Judi's own love of practical jokes on- and off-set.

When Scene 8 was first blocked for cameras, Judi was immediately worried that the cutaway to the phone was dwarfed by the bread bin, so that it could seem to the viewer at home that she was looking at the bin instead. While the director pondered this thought, Judi hastens to assure him, 'Of course, Syd, it's none of my business really.' But he just said, 'Don't be silly', and instructed that the bin be moved out of the close-up shot.

1.00. Lunch break. We all went to the canteen, and then Judi and Geoffrey both went for a lie-down in their dressing-rooms.

4.30. Make-up for the dress-run. Judi closed her eyes and rested through most of this process, remarking to the others in the room, 'I can't believe we've got to face that live audience again tonight!'

5.50. Judi said sharply, 'Is this iron going to be hot or not? Because if so, I've got to rehearse with it hot.'

6.30. Supper break. Began with twenty minutes of notes for cast. Hardly any of the cast then ate anything before the show.

7.40. Warm-up of the audience by the programme's regular warm-up man, Denny Hodge. As he introduced the VT clips from previous series the cast watched them on the monitor in the make-up room. Jenny, Philip and Moira were then all called in to take a bow. Geoffrey was introduced by Denny Hodge and he took over the radio mike to speak to the audience.

'It's nice to be back, with this lovely crowd.' He made a reference to Christmas and panto, then, 'Talking of panto, we've got a treat for you. Is it Bruce Forsyth, is it Lionel Blair, is it Jimmy Tarbuck? No, it's our very own Dame – Judi Dench!'

Judi doubled up in agony during all this, groaning, 'Why do we do this?'

But then she swept out to great applause, took the mike from Geoffrey and chatted to the audience as if it were her favourite activity.

8.00. The recording began.

There was the occasional retake after each scene, until they reached Scene 13 in the hall. Jean admits Alistair, but then Judi dissolved into giggles, saying, 'I can't shut the door.' The audience exploded with sympathetic laughter, the door was eased, and the next take went without a hitch. (Studio audiences always seem pleased if something goes wrong, as if they are now privy to the creative process, in a way denied to the home viewer.)

The kitchen scene at the end, that caused most camera problems in rehearsal, required several retakes before the director was satisfied. The cast took this in their stride, and reproduced their performances exactly; later the director will intercut the various takes in editing for maximum laughs. The audience have a little more difficulty in reproducing their level of surprised laughter from Take 1.

9.30. Recording ended on schedule, and everyone dispersed rapidly.

eight

1969–70

With Shakespeare to Africa, the Avon, Japan and Australia

James Cairncross was blissfully unaware of Judi's dire premonition of their demise as they fastened their seatbelts on 20 January 1969, but he could hardly fail to register her lack of enthusiasm for flying – as the plane picked up speed on the Heathrow runway she uttered her regular prayer on take-off, 'We are in God's hands, brother, not in theirs.'

Arrival in West Africa was not much happier. Their plane was delayed, so instead of having a rest day their first performance in Ghana was that very evening at the university. As they got ready, all the electric power in the hotel failed. It was as well they had been blooded by their earlier tour, or the American professor who greeted them might have been as crushed as he deserved. Asked politely if there would be many people in the audience, he drawled, 'Well, who knows? Who can dance to the rhythm of the student?'

In fact they played to audiences as crowded and enthusiastic as five years earlier. The British Council provided helpful fact sheets to brief their hosts, though a Nigerian nun seriously strained their composure when she attempted to introduce them from memory: 'Now we're most pleased this morning to have two famous British actors, Miss Judi Dench and Mr James Cairncross. Miss Dench is always winning the prizes for performing at Stratford-upon-Shakespeare, where she played the part of Isabella in *Two Gentlemen of Verona*, and the much coveted part of Hecate in *Twelfth Night*; Mr Cairncross is also winning the prizes for playing the Duke of Norfolk in *Salad Days* and the Army.'

Again they played mostly in the open air, where they grew used to people arriving late and animals wandering around, though Judi did have a particular fright one night. 'There was an open door at the back and the audience was very dark in silhouette in front of it, and I glanced up at one point and thought, "Oh the Devil's here!" because there were two heads and a third with horns. It was a goat standing between two people watching us.'

Their programme consisted mostly of scenes from different Shakespeare plays, but they did slip in the confrontation between Creon and Antigone from the Anouilh play, which was very effective. They had lively discussion sessions after the performances, particularly with the student audiences, though it was difficult for them always to keep a straight face here too. In Ghana the British Council representative said, 'Well that's enough for the morning. Miss Dench and Mr Cairncross have to go to lunch now, and they're appearing again this evening. There'll be just one more question.' A young man said politely to James, 'I merely wish to state that having seen you and Miss Dench acting for us, I have come to the conclusion that we ourselves are not so bad.'

In Nigeria they gave one performance in front of General Gowon and his entourage; when they were presented to him afterwards he said, 'Ah, Miss Dench, "All the world's a stage, and all the men and women merely players." Have I got it right?'

'Oh yes.'

(This appeared to be his favourite quotation. After he was deposed as President and came to England, he was asked by a radio interviewer if he was at all embittered by his experiences – 'No, no, all the world's a stage.')

After a hectic, seven-week tour of West Africa the two actors flew home on 7 March. Her relief and pleasure at her safe return were not entirely reciprocated by Trevor Nunn, who took one look at her very dark tropical tan and exclaimed, 'No, absolutely not, totally unlike the part, it simply won't do.'

Judi was beginning to have second thoughts about playing Hermione and sent her director one of her postcards saying, 'Is it mother's parts already?' About three weeks later she got one in reply, saying, 'Would you double Hermione and Perdita?'

During his research into the history of *The Winter's Tale* he had come across a Victorian poster advertising the fact that in 1887 one actress, Mary Anderson, was going to play both mother and daughter, the only time this had ever previously been attempted. The only difficult scene from a staging point of view was the final one, when Perdita is reunited with her mother after gazing on what everyone thinks is her statue, but this was surmountable by some trickery with doubles and cutting Perdita's very last line, 'So long I could stand by, a looker on.'

Before he worked it out in detail, he went to discuss the whole idea with Judi, to find her initial reaction was a very cautious one: 'Are you absolutely sure that that will work?' There was no question of agreeing just because it doubled the size of her part.

After he explained how he planned to do it, he got his first glimmer of the way in which Judi is prepared to take a major gamble with a director she has decided to trust. 'Well, if you think it can work, then I'll do it. It's not a necessity, but if you are telling me that you think it can work, of course it sounds a wonderful challenge.'

The huge advantage was that this Perdita did not have to struggle to appear to be Hermione's daughter and therefore really a princess in disguise, but could play the shepherdess with the same rustic accent as those with whom she has been reared since they found her as a baby. For the actress, the problem was the reverse of the usual one – she had to make mother and daughter convincingly different. The director's solution was to rehearse their scenes in quite separate chunks, several days with just Hermione, then a period just with Perdita and her fellows.

Polixenes, with whom Leontes is convinced his wife has cuckolded him, was played by Richard Pasco. He had known Judi socially for some time, ever since he had first courted and then married Barbara Leigh-Hunt, but this was the first time they had acted together. He wondered how on earth she was going to do it, 'because each part standing on its own is pretty substantial. They're both wonderful parts and I thought, "How in God's name is she going to manage this?" But she did it brilliantly.'

At the end, the audience looked at the recognisable features of Judi in the 'statue' of Hermione, aware that Judi herself was present on stage as Perdita; as the statue revolved out of sight Perdita ran behind to go on looking at it. In what appeared as one continuous movement Judi's double ran out the other side into the view of the audience, while Judi assumed the place of the statue. There is a very fine line between audience belief and disbelief in this kind of stage trickery, but to the director's great relief it worked triumphantly. 'They had all touched the glass, and the incarceration of the sculpture of Hermione in this glass object was incontrovertible. Then it moved, and not only moved, it passed straight through the glass. The responses at that moment in the theatre at Stratford were unlike anything I've ever come across. People did gasp, people did call out, people questioned each other: 'It's completely impossible, it can't be her'; it's the most sensational moment I've experienced in Shakespeare, with just those three syllables of Leontes' – 'O, she's warm.'

The Shakespearean authority Stanley Wells was one who was less convinced that the trickery at the end worked, but thought that Judi beautifully distinguished between mother and daughter earlier. 'I shall never forget the way she danced as Perdita in the pastoral scene. Florizel has those lines: "When you dance, I wish you/A wave o' the sea, that might ever do/Nothing but that." She conveyed that physically in an extraordinarily rapt way, a raptness she showed again movingly in *Twelfth Night* later that season.'

Some of the critics had reservations about the hippie-style costumes for Bohemia, the pop music songs, or the strobe lighting used in the opening scene of jealousy, but their doubts about the doubling of mother and daughter were soon stilled. In the *Observer* Ronald Bryden, unknowingly echoing John Hurt's comparison, thought she had never been better or looked better: 'radiantly dignified, transparent in heavy-eyed love, she generates a quality which makes you wonder if it isn't time we stopped lamenting the lack of an English Simone Signoret'.

J. C. Trewin praised the performances of Richard Pasco, Derek Smith as Autolycus, and Brenda Bruce as Paulina, in his review for the *Lady*, though 'for me Judi Dench carries the night ... I have seldom known anything more impressive than the appearance of Hermione, the wronged Queen, to answer the indictment in the court of Sicilia. The actress, almost dwarfed by the vast bare set, appears at the back of the stage and walks slowly down to face the King: no more than that, yet in those few silent seconds we are made aware of all that Hermione has suffered and the steadiness of her fixed resolve. It hardly needs to be put into speech. Later, the actress is a near-perfect Perdita, fresh and eager without a trace of skittishness, and deeply in love ... I do not like the permanent set, and the costumes can distract. Never mind: Shakespeare defies these minor griefs, and I felt that the dramatist might applaud the undeniable triumph of Judi Dench.'

In the *Guardian*, Gareth Lloyd-Evans felt her doubling achieved, especially as Hermione, 'a presence which touches greatness'. He also commended 'little Jeremy Richardson who makes Mamillius utterly natural, and makes us completely forget how embarrassing Shakespeare's children can be'. He was the son of Ian Richardson, who gives at least part of the credit to how Judi, playing his mother, brought him out. When it was televised later, the eight-year-old boy hated watching himself on screen and Judi had to jolly him out of his despair at the next performance in the theatre.

She very nearly despaired herself in the next production – *Women Beware Women* – but she was not alone in that. Richard Pasco found it 'the most fiendishly difficult text to learn. I didn't think I'd ever learn it; it's one of those texts where if you don't go over it at least once every two days it'll never come back to you. We were often doing it after a break of eight or ten days, without even a word-run sometimes, so Jude and I endured that together.'

Terry Hands was directing it and he lays the blame on the author. 'I think why Middleton will never be a truly great writer is that he keeps writing to plan; whereas Shakespeare you always feel does four acts, then throws away his plan and just writes where the characters are leading him. So Judi's role, which promises so much at the beginning, dies away at the end when Middleton goes on a kind of classical punishment for everybody in a masque of a chess-game.'

Judi was Bianca, married to Leantio, a lowly factor played by Richard Pasco, and seduced away from him by Brewster Mason as the lecherous Duke of Florence. All the sexual machinations were aided by Elizabeth Spriggs who, as the procuress Livia, stole most of the notices.

Judi felt that she let the director down in what she regarded as a marvellous production, a belief that he is quick to deny. 'I thought she did extraordinarily well, but if you put together the combination of an unsatisfactory plot, a too-young director,' (of twenty-eight) 'and an unsatisfactory role, the fact that she kept so cheerful and committed throughout the rehearsals is a great tribute to her basic nature. That she should look back on it and say, "Maybe I let Terry down", is typical of Judi.'

What is equally typical of her is the way she found of sustaining herself through this catalogue of lust and murder, up to the bloody sequence of revenge killings at the end. Midway through there was a lavish banquet, for which the food was supplied by Pargeter's in Stratford, with a lot of chicken in breadcrumbs. By this stage of the play Bianca had been seduced by the Duke and revealed her baser nature. 'I didn't have anything to say and I used to think, "Am I going out to dinner tonight? No, nobody's here that I know", so sometimes, when Lizzie Spriggs, for instance, was talking, I would get up and lean right across, take her chicken leg off her plate and sit and eat it. I had the most incredible time, just tucking into everything.'

The giant chessboard at the finale, through which the murder victims fell to their deaths, was visually very effective but complicated to operate and the technical run did not finish until gone 3 a.m., after which Judi and Brewster Mason unwound by finishing a bottle of champagne in the summer moonlight.

The opening night went smoothly; J. C. Trewin lauded Elizabeth Spriggs's Livia in the *Birmingham Post*, 'and the names of Judi Dench and Richard Pasco speak for themselves as the lovers so soon parted'. John Barber was cooler about the pair and gave the palm in the *Daily Telegraph* to the Duke and Livia; but Judi and Richard were singled out again by Jeremy Kingston in *Punch*, in what he thought 'a good play but not a great one'.

Terry Hands awaited the verdict with more than a little trepidation and noted in his diary, 'We've got better reviews than we deserve.' He tried to be philosophical about it and promised to remind himself of this if ever in the future he did a good production for which he got bad reviews.

Despite the mostly encouraging notices, the gloomy nature of the play did not attract the same audiences as *The Winter's Tale* and *The Merry Wives of Windsor*, which were both packing them in. But the following month, in August, Judi opened in one of her favourite plays, *Twelfth Night*, playing Viola again in a production that was so popular it stayed in the repertoire for three years.

John Barton only took it on reluctantly, because he feared he could never match Peter Hall's brilliant 1958 production with Dorothy

Tutin and Geraldine McEwan, but Trevor Nunn persuaded him to have a go and offered him 'just about the best cast I ever had'. A Shakespearean scholar with great insight into the text, he had one or two odd habits that Judi took some time to adjust to – he would sit on the back of a chair chewing razor blades, drinking great pints of milk out of a beer tankard. 'On the very first night he came up onto the stage to give some notes to Lisa Harrow and me. The whole stage was wood-slatted with great candles on both sides. He got up after the notes to walk across the stage, tripped on the top step and threw a whole pint of milk all over the stage.'

Judi was unhappy that most of the time he hardly gave her any notes at all, but he thought her instincts were so sure that she needed very few. That he was right was underlined by J. W. Lambert in a long and rapturous review in the *Sunday Times*: 'Viola comes stumbling out of the mist, held up by her sea-captain, sinks to the ground; and within a few minutes, long before her more famous moments, it is blessedly clear that Judi Dench has the measure of the part.'

Jeremy Kingston was captivated from the same moment, emphasising in *Punch* how 'she shows touchingly her understanding of love's sorrows, whirling the poignancy away by following a catch in her throat with a light laugh – smiling at grief, something this actress has always been able to do perfectly. Tender comedy sparkles between her and Lisa Harrow's gravely charming Olivia.'

The critics echoed the director's praise for his cast – Emrys James's melancholy Feste, Barrie Ingham's Scottish Aguecheek, Charles Thomas's Orsino, and especially Donald Sinden's self-important and outraged Malvolio. B. A. Young proclaimed in the *Financial Times*, 'There are no reins on this performance; Mr Sinden is capable of making us laugh with any bare monosyllable he chooses, and indeed does so with his first word, which is "Yes".'

Judi's keen professional eye noted how he could get a laugh without even saying a word: 'Donald invented a wonderful piece of business on his entrance in cross-garters, when he walked forward and looked at the sundial, then he looked at the sun, then he took out his watch, then he moved the sundial.'

This was her first encounter with his comic invention and their partnership was to gain even greater plaudits later on. Another great joker also now made her acquaintance in *Twelfth Night*. Roger Rees was playing the small part of Curio and he and Judi very quickly got onto the same wavelength. When he found a pack of children's playing cards in the Green Room, with pictures of animals on them, the two of them invented a game they called 'Ferret in the foot', also known as 'Badger in the boot', or 'Rabbit in the ruff', which had to be indicated with the appropriate action by different members of the cast. Judi claims, 'I don't think anyone in the audience saw, but it was very exciting, and it didn't half get you through that interminable last scene.'

Each credits the other with the idea, but they quite clearly egged each other on, and the games these two invented to enliven a long run became ever more elaborate when they appeared on the same stage. This game did get cut short one night, when the production transferred to the Aldwych and there was a power blackout all over central London, which hit *Twelfth Night* about twenty minutes into the fifth act. The audience yelled out, 'Oh please, please continue the play in the dark, you have to finish it!' But by that time, Roger says, 'Judi and the rest of us were in the pub next door. It was such a pleasure not to have to do the rest of it.'

Judi marked the occasion of Regatta Day on the Avon by initiating the 'Regatta game'. On everyone's first entrance they had to accompany their speech with a rowing action of the arms, without the audience registering what they were doing. She insisted that everyone had to do it, whether they were playing a messenger or King Lear.

Roger Rees's most vivid memory of the jokes in *Twelfth Night* was of one they all played against Judi on the tour of Australia. 'She developed a big spot on the end of her chin, which she couldn't cover up with make-up, and in the fifth act everybody came on with a spot; Donald Sinden came on last as Malvolio from the dungeon, with a *very* big spot, because Donald always went too far. It was glorious.'

Sinden was the target of one of her mystery walk-ons, when he was playing Henry VIII in that 1969 season. The director was Trevor Nunn and one night when he was in the audience he was mystified by the presence of an extra cardinal on-stage, ' a very short cardinal I didn't recognise, with a huge cardinal's hat. Just at the last moment, as the cardinal exited, I recognised it was Judi.'

She hotly denies this story, just a little too specifically: 'That is not true. I never was a cardinal in *Henry VIII*, never, that has been attributed to me, but I can give you my word I was never a cardinal.' Since Roger Rees, amongst others, confirms Trevor Nunn's observation, one is forced to assume that her borrowed costume was possibly a bishop's and not actually a full cardinal's rig.

What is harder for her to dispute is what Trevor heard her say as Viola protesting to Olivia about her virginity. 'Judi noticed that she had potentially a very funny line – "Nor never none shall be mistress of it." She recognised that "Never none" was a close relative of mine and one night actually said –"Nor Trevor Nunn shall be mistress of it", in front of a paying public! She's very outrageous.'

But none of this larking about seems ever to have affected the general appreciation of her performances. Roger Rees, one of her partners in the crime of corpsing, insists it is not because she succeeds in hiding it: 'not at all, she's the one who invented laughing openly at the audience'.

This worked with audiences at home, who had by now taken Judi to their hearts, but how would she, and the RSC as a whole, go down in Japan, which was the first leg of a major foreign tour the company embarked on in the winter of 1969–70?

Unlike western audiences, they watched in a rapt silence throughout – the lack of reaction convincing the actors that the performance was not going down well. It was only the explosion of applause at the end, which they learnt was the Japanese custom, that persuaded them otherwise.

The company also had to adjust to a Japanese stage crew, few of whom understood English. At the first walk-through of *The Winter's Tale* the follow-spot operator at the back of the gallery was briefed by the stage manager via the Japanese interpreter for Hermione's walk across the stage – 'Tell him when Miss Dench appears to follow her.' Judi entered, the spotlight came on, but when she moved it failed to move with her. They tried again, and again, with lots of shouting in Japanese, and still they could not get the follow-spot to move. Eventually it was discovered that 'a Denchi' is Japanese for a torch battery, and he was waiting for a torch battery to come on.

The second play here was *The Merry Wives of Windsor*, which Judi was not in, so she soaked up the local culture, visiting lots of temples and other sights and attending performances of both the Noh and the

Kabuki theatres. The latter made a great impression on her. 'We talked to a tiny, round little man with glasses, a bit like Michael MacLiammóir. Then they said, "You must go, and you mustn't say anything because the ground is all blessed where they are"; and when they're making up a young actor comes along and bows down and makes a long speech. I asked, "What's he saying?" Apparently the gist was, "You must forgive me because I know I'm not worthy to do this scene with you." I thought, "Hello, I can see this going down well at home!" In the auditorium the Hanamichi, the Seven Steps to Heaven, came right down beside us, and quite suddenly this just exquisite creature came walking down very slowly, and this beautiful young woman was the middle-aged man we'd met earlier. It was wonderful.'

After three weeks in Japan the company moved to Australia, substituting *Twelfth Night* for *The Merry Wives of Windsor*, to be played in three cities – Melbourne, Adelaide and Sydney. Here, tragedy struck.

Orsino was played by a talented young actor called Charles Thomas, who had made a considerable impression on Stratford audiences, looking like the Hilliard miniature of Sir Walter Raleigh. The passion underlying his scenes with Viola continued for him off-stage and his devotion to Judi became close to infatuation. The depressive side of his nature led him to drink too much too often; Judi did her best to cure him of this by refusing to let him come near her whenever he was the worse for drink. For much of the time her firmness worked, but in Melbourne his self-control cracked. A group including the two of them went down to the beach, which had a bar on it, and he was rapidly in his cups. True to her resolve, Judi left him there and went back to the hotel. He later followed and tried to ring his wife, who had instructed their children that if he sounded remotely intoxicated on the phone they were to hang up. In the morning, he was found dead in his room.

Judi was naturally devastated and so was everyone else. When Barbara Penney and Judi discovered that neither of them was sleeping, the two of them moved into one room together. Her brother Jeffery gave them a huge jigsaw and they stayed up late doing that and talking the whole sad business out.

The tour had to go on and Richard Pasco stepped into the breach at Trevor Nunn's request, on condition that he did not have to wear his dead predecessor's clothes as Orsino, taking over the part with just a few days' rehearsal.

The tragic accident at the opening of the eleven-week tour cast a shadow over most of it, but one unexpected arrival did much to lift the spirits of the company, and especially Judi's.

Michael Williams had joined the RSC in 1963, the year after her first season, but they were never in the same half of the company, so their paths had only crossed infrequently. During the London run of *The Promise*, Michael had bumped into her when he was appearing in *The Representative* nearby at the Aldwych and they had rather a gloomy cup of coffee together, commiserating with each other about the break-up of their recent romances.

It was another two years before their casual acquaintanceship was transformed into something much deeper. Playing football for the RSC, Michael damaged his knee and a cartilage operation laid him up for several weeks while he recuperated in his cottage near Stratford. 'One night I decided to go and see *Twelfth Night* at the theatre, in which Judi was starring. I went round to see her afterwards with some mutual chums, and we went for dinner at the Dirty Duck. That's how it all began really.'

When he finished playing in *Troilus and Cressida* he decided almost on the spur of the moment to fly out to Australia and surprise Judi. At Heathrow airport he met Trevor Nunn returning, who broke the news to him about Charlie Thomas's death and its impact on the company. 'I was only supposed to be there a week, but I kept going to the airport, and then thinking I didn't want to go back yet, so I'd be in the hotel when they all came in. I did that for six weeks; I resold my return ticket to have something to live on and hitched a lift back with the RSC. I did appear once on the stage in Melbourne, dressed as a village idiot in *The Winter's Tale* with my teeth blacked-out. Jude dried in mid-air during her dance, when she finally recognised me under all those spots and a terrible old fright-wig.'

After five weeks in Melbourne, the tour moved on to Adelaide and then to Sydney. In Adelaide, Michael proposed to Judi for the first time, but she said, 'No, it's far too romantic, with all this sun and the beaches. Ask me again one rainy night in Battersea.' Which was what he virtually did, except it was in his flat on the other side of the river from Battersea, but it was raining.

So Australia, which had begun so unhappily, ended by opening up a new and happy chapter in Judi's private life, in a year in which she and her future husband at last acted opposite each other in one of the great surprise hits for the RSC.

nine

1970–72

Marriage and Motherhood

The Royal Shakespeare Company had embarked on its long tour to raise money and returned to the news that the Arts Council grant would not be increased, meaning a cut in real terms. So the Aldwych arm of the company was under severe threat unless the new production of *London Assurance* became a smash hit.

It had been written by the nineteen-year-old Irish actor and playwright Dion Boucicault, and received its first performance in 1841, when it scored a resounding success. It became a regular fixture in the Victorian repertoire, but its last run was in 1895 and it had been dismissed by most theatre historians as a thin version of the town-versus-country plot. The ageing fortune-hunter, Sir Harcourt Courtly, goes down to Gloucestershire to snap up the young heiress Grace Harkaway, only to find his own son has beaten him to it, and he is then diverted into pursuit of a married lady mad on hunting.

Ronald Eyre adapted and produced it as a high comedy of manners and allowed full rein to the inventiveness of his gifted cast. As the foppish sixty-three-year-old baronet, Donald Sinden modelled his appearance on the actor Michael MacLiammóir, with an over-heightened make-up, rouged cheeks, and too-black wig. He and Judi, as the target of his attentions, worried a bit in rehearsal over the implausibility of the father failing to recognise his own son immediately, on the line, 'How d'you do. Good God, that's my son.' The solution was to make him distracted by his infatuation. 'Judi and I loved this moment, which we stretched as far as the elastic would go. "How d'you do", looking him straight in the eyes, then looking back at her, then walking slowly upstage before, "Good God, that's my son." We did the longest double-take you've ever seen in your life.'

They had enormous fun in rehearsal, but nobody really guessed what a triumph it would be until it opened. Great care went into the production. The designer, Alan Tagg, sat in on the rehearsals and when he saw Judi snipping the thorns off the roses at the beginning he gave her roses that she could really snip at every night. This attention to detail on the set, and in the late Regency costumes, combined with the high comic style of the playing to make it one of the big hits of the London season.

The rest of the strong cast included Michael Williams as the son who wins the girl, Judi's brother Jeffery playing her uncle, Elizabeth Spriggs as the horsy Lady Gay Spanker, Barrie Ingham and Derek Smith. Irving Wardle hailed it in *The Times* as 'a memorably enjoyable opening' to the RSC's new season, particularly admiring Donald Sinden's 'manner of impregnable vanity, pained and exasperated during the longueurs of hunting chat, and rising to climaxes of fruitily baroque ardour when Lady Gay Spanker shows signs of succumbing … Judi Dench, in the play's most original part of the heiress – at once independent-minded and virginally unawakened – brings out the character's intrinsic comic qualities and those (like her rural poeticisms) that only appear to a modern audience: and allows neither to overcast the girl's real strength.'

Harold Hobson predicted in the *Sunday Times* that it would become one of the RSC's outstanding successes, saying he left the theatre filled with happiness, and conveyed his delight through some vivid analogies: 'Judi Dench's formidably unusual heroine looks as innocent as a bowl of cream, and as powerfully self-protective as a bed of nettles. Elizabeth Spriggs's … eyes sparkle, her teeth glitter, and she hurls her legs about as if she were throwing the hammer over a five-barred gate. This exhilarating performance is matched by Donald Sinden's Sir Harcourt, who resembles Oscar Wilde simultaneously playing George IV and the Apollo Belvedere.'

The production played to such packed houses that it stayed in the repertoire well into the following year, saving the Aldwych operation in the process, and eventually transferring to the New Theatre for a continuous run.

Michael Williams' courtship of Judi continued on-stage and off. That summer he was making a film in Yugoslavia with John Gielgud and Ralph Richardson – *Eagle in a Cage*, about Napoleon's last years on St Helena. He asked Judi to join him when she had a week off between performances. Kenneth Haigh was playing Napoleon and when she arrived he invited her and Michael, and several members of the cast, to dine with him at the villa he had rented near Split. Michael soon found he was not alone in competing for Judi's attention. As they were having a drink on the sofa prior to dinner, Ralph Richardson leant over and bit her very gently on the ear. Judi exclaimed: 'Oh, oh, Sir Ralph you bit me!'

'What's a bite between friends?'

Despite this unorthodox greeting, she came to share Michael's admiration of the great actor and enjoyed working with him later on a couple of radio productions. More importantly, the week did much to cement her relationship with Michael.

London Assurance was joined by *Major Barbara* at the Aldwych, in which Judi repeated the title role with the same Undershaft as she had had in the TV production eight years before – Brewster Mason. Other leading players in this cast were now all old friends – Elizabeth Spriggs, Richard Pasco, and Roger Rees – so the director Clifford Williams should have been less surprised than he was by how easily it all went. 'We never had a cross word during that production, which was most unusual. It seemed too easy a part for Judi, not too much to wrestle with in performance; I think she was able just to cruise through it.'

That is higher praise than it seems from such an experienced Shavian director, since Shaw really did give 'the devil all the best tunes' in this play. Brewster Mason made the most of them and Irving Wardle asserted in *The Times* that 'Judi Dench's Barbara is no match for this opposition.' But J. C. Trewin recognised in the *Illustrated London News* how the author had stacked the odds against her: 'we can feel, as we should, for Judi Dench's Barbara, though Shaw has given her a desperately difficult final speech.'

Philip Hope-Wallace's response to her in the *Guardian* began with an injunction and ended with a confession: 'If she will keep her voice up a little more she need fear no comparison, not even with Sybil herself who was lovely, or with Wendy Hillier in that film. It is a peach of a part: Vivie Warren, St Joan, both Mrs Pankhurst's daughters rolled into one, the do-gooder, the tough, the vulnerable suffragette finding her courage after losing out on "hope"; enough to make strong men or even this weak one brush away a tear.'

The winter of 1970/71 was a busy one for Judi, when these two new productions were joined in the Aldwych repertoire by *The Winter's Tale* and *Twelfth Night*, both of which had gained in depth and polish since Stratford and the subsequent tour. But plans were afoot for an additional special performance before a glittering, invited audience. The chosen date was 5 February 1971 and the venue was the Catholic church just round the corner from Judi's house in Hampstead.

Michael Williams had been brought up as a Catholic and his marriage to a Quaker caused some complications with the Church that took some unravelling before the ceremony could go ahead. The local priest, Father Morrell, later became a good friend to them both, but he insisted on the usual stipulation that any children must be brought up in the Roman Catholic faith. Judi told Michael, 'I want to have a look at the script', and when she read the marriage service she was unhappy that she would not be permitted to take communion when he and his family did.

So she said No, and Michael got very despondent. 'We had a great chum who was the parish priest of St Mary-le-Bow, Joseph McCulloch, and I said, "Joe, you've got to help me, I'm in trouble." So he invited us to dinner with Tom Corbishley, who was a great Jesuit, and Edward Carpenter, the Dean of Westminster Abbey. The three of them had a fascinating theological conversation, most of which went over our heads, and then at the end of dinner Tom Corbishley said to me, "What's the problem?" So I told him.'

He advised them to go ahead with the marriage service at St Mary's, and to call on him a couple of days earlier at Farm Street, where he gave them a private nuptial mass and a blessing. The public service at St Mary's was ecumenical, conducted by a Dominican monk who was a friend of Michael's, the parish priest assisted by Father Corbishley, and the address was given by the Anglican Joseph McCulloch. Only later did the bridal pair discover that Father Corbishley had exceeded his powers and was hauled over the coals by Cardinal Heenan, who reportedly told him, 'Tom, you have now finally gone mad.'

No such clouds appeared to mar the happy day. The church was crowded with their friends from the RSC, the Old Vic, and else-where, including many of the names who have already appeared in the preceding pages. Over 250 guests packed the church and the music was provided by the Royal Shakespeare Company Wind Band. The ushers were Ian Richardson and Alec McCowen; Alec had been instructed to give the signal when the bride arrived at the church. 'This huge limousine drew up and very rashly I gave the signal, the organist struck up the Bridal March, and it turned out to be Danny La Rue. He thought it was a practical joke, and was quite startled to hear "Hear comes the Bride".'

Judi in fact walked to the church, since it was less than a hundred yards from Prospect Place, to be given away by her eldest brother, Peter, and observed the bride's prerogative of arriving ten minutes late. She wore a long white coat with a big fur hood over a silk dress and blue boots, and carried a spray of lily-of-the-valley. Terry Hands almost forgot where he was: 'Judi and Michael had one of the most beautiful weddings I've ever been to. She looked so stunning; she glowed; she was just – what am I saying? I was in the congregation and I was about to say she gave another great performance! But it had a serenity which I'd never seen in her earlier performances – it was the ceremony itself, everything about it was just perfect.'

James Cairncross was to give a reading and eventually had to speak quite firmly to the leading players in this production. 'I was rehearsing at Leatherhead for a play and she kept ringing me up and saying, "Darling, we've found a wonderful bit of Thomas Traherne for you to do", and I said, "Judi Dench, your wedding is rapidly degenerating into my audition for the Royal Shakespeare Company, and I bet I don't get in." And I didn't.' (But it was a lovely passage, beginning, 'You are as prone to love as the sun is to shine.')

For all her planning, Judi was surprised by one charming revelation on the day. The critic John Trewin had followed her career from the beginning and was a hugely knowledgeable historian of the profession. He discovered that Mary Anderson, the only other actress to have doubled Hermione and Perdita, had also been married at that very same church during the run of *The Winter's Tale*, so he slipped a little sepia picture of her in with the wedding present he and his wife Wendy had chosen. The long arm of coincidence has frequently reached out and tapped Judi on the shoulder, in ways that no scriptwriter would ever dare, though not always as such a happy augury.

After the ceremony the wedding party all drove down the hill for the reception at London Zoo. Judi had been a frequent visitor when she lived in Regent's Park Terrace and found it so relaxing that she went nearly as frequently after she moved to Hampstead. She admitted that 'perhaps I do get a bit upset about seeing certain animals in a rather confined space, but they seem rather happy and in good condition in that zoo'. It now offered a suitably exotic background for a marriage to which both partners had come quite late; Judi was thirty-six and Michael was thirty-five. No one could accuse them of rushing into it, after knowing each other for nine years, and both of them had had a number of those fleeting romances that are common in the nomadic actor's life, as well as a few deeper attachments which had eventually ended unhappily. Now the two of them were ready to settle down. Their mutual decision not to spend months apart filming or touring abroad may have affected both their careers, when they rejected such offers, but it has done much to preserve the stability of their marriage to the present day.

That all lay ahead. For now, they could enjoy only the briefest of honeymoons. They flew to Dublin and had just two days in Galway. Michael was refused a hire car because he had an endorsement on his licence for speeding, and Judi had still not taken her driving test, so they ended up on bicycles. On Monday Judi was back on-stage at the Aldwych. For someone who refuses to stand on ceremony herself, she retains a curious attachment to the formality of address that was the custom in her early days at the Old Vic, and once expressed a hankering for the Victorian practice of prefacing the name in the programme with the actor's status. So she was pleasantly surprised by the stage management that Monday, when the calls came over the tannoy for 'Mr Sinden' and 'Mrs Williams'.

Shortly afterwards, she and Michael went up to Stratford to begin rehearsals for *The Merchant of Venice*, which was to open the new season, with Judi as Portia, Michael as Bassanio, and Emrys James as Shylock. At first she resisted playing it, until Trevor Nunn talked her into it, though the casting had been done by Terry Hands. 'I worshipped Judi. I thought she was so exciting to watch on the stage – the intelligence and the ferocious attention to detail. Here was Portia, who is famous for her intelligence, sense of fairness, justice, deep mercy; for me she was Portia, and therefore I very much wanted to work with her on it. It was a good rehearsal period, but sometimes a very sharp rehearsal period. Judi wasn't happy, and she didn't seem to get any happier.'

Judi underlines that perception much more pungently, saying she loathed the play and could make no sense of it. 'Terry got very cross with me and there was a tremendous antagonism between Emrys and me. When Shylock raised the knife I would say, "Tarry, Jew", and was told, "Don't say it yet." I had to wait until his hand was coming down to stab him and then say, "Tarry, Jew." I thought it was false. How could you leave it until the knife was actually coming down on him? She would have died of fright; she wouldn't have left it that long. At one point Terry sent everyone out of the rehearsal room and jumped on a table, I'll never forget it, and said, "You're not to be unkind to Emrys; his father was a miner." I wasn't being unkind; I was trying to make sense of something. I think I drove Terry mad, but I couldn't do it and I never want to see the play again. I wouldn't cross the road to see it; it's the only play of Shakespeare's I dislike; everyone behaves so frightfully badly.'

Terry Hands believes that it is very difficult to stage the play in the second half of this century because, since the Holocaust, the whole issue of anti-Semitism is almost impossible to handle; but although he shares her view about the nature of the characters, he makes an exception in the case of Portia. 'It is about a world obsessed by money, where the problems of sexuality, and greed, and possessiveness, are fought out by a woman who is pretty well alone. So she wasn't happy, which I was sad about.'

But one of the marks of her commanding self-control as an actress was that no hint of her unhappiness in the role escaped to the audience, though she suspected that someone who knew her particularly well had seen behind the actor's mask. 'I had this idea of a wig with lots of curls, and Johnny Neville came over to see it. I hadn't seen him for years, and he knocked at the door and said, "Hello Bubbles" – that's all he said to me, and quite right too.'

He was right to be tactfully silent. Apart from Colin Frame, who enthused in the *Evening News* that he found the production 'richly satisfying', and that Judi 'bubbles her way through the part', the critics generally savaged both production and players. Even Harold Hobson, usually the most generous of critics, was deeply disappointed in the *Sunday Times* at 'an evening in which the overall conception is clearly superior to its execution. Apart from Mr Church' (as Antonio) 'and David Calder's straightforward Lorenzo, the company is as yet either inappropriate or inadequate. Judi Dench brings to a Belmont hung with jewels the healthy heartiness of a medieval dance round the Maypole.'

After a dismissal like that, an actor has just got to swallow hard and carry on through the run hoping things will improve. But on one notable occasion the play very nearly ground to a complete halt, and it was Judi's fault. Portia has a speech to Bassanio in the Caskets scene: 'I speak too long, but 'tis to peise the time,/To eke it out, and to draw it out in length,/To stay you from election.'

The two of them were framed by the Wind Band playing softly on stage and several other actors, as Portia launched into her speech, 'and I said, "To stay you from erection", absolutely boldly and out front. Well, the wind band left the stage. My brother Jeffery was playing a monk, with Bernard Lloyd and Peter Geddes. They all left; nobody could stay. And I laughed. Michael had a great long speech as Bassanio. I've never seen him use his hands so much, and turn his back to the audience; oh, it was terrible.'

In July another difficult play – *The Duchess of Malfi* – joined the repertoire, with several of the same actors. The director Clifford Williams quickly observed the continuing clash of personalities. 'She didn't get on with Emrys. He was a very talented actor, but he got at cross-purposes with most people.'

More happily, she was joined by Richard Pasco, but he caused her a different problem. 'As the Duchess's disfigured lover Antonio, I had this terrible thing on my face. The first time it appeared Jude just collapsed, of course, she couldn't stop laughing. I could move it, too, and then she'd be in agony.'

Despite these various strains and the difficulty in learning Webster's lines, Judi loved the part and found it 'thrilling' to play, even if she now says she cannot remember a single line of it, not even the famous one, 'I am Duchess of Malfi still.'

Michael was playing her wolfish brother Ferdinand and he shared her enjoyment of the production, once he had surmounted what turned out to be a fraught opening night for him. 'After the first scene I had a quick change to go into the boudoir scene with the Duchess and Antonio, when I had to stab Dickie; but my lovely aged dresser had taken my costume and my dagger up to the dressing-room, which was too far to go. I was also playing Henry V at the time, so I raced round to the prompt side and grabbed my dagger from Henry V and went on with that. So it wasn't a very auspicious opening night for me, but it was a wonderful production. I used to wear spurs, which struck sparks from the wire-mesh floor in the scene we played in the dark.'

He also had to wear silver lurex tights, which showed off his legs to advantage. Judi remarked, 'Those tights are strangely attractive', so one night he wore them home and got into bed still wearing them to give his wife a thrilling surprise.

The critics were less thrilled with what they saw on-stage. John Barber in the *Daily Telegraph* found the whole evening prosaic: 'This is a sane production of a mad play, and it will not do', though he did express admiration for Judi's performance in the title role, 'always at her best as a virtuous wronged lady. The actress has never looked more beautiful or gracious as, robed in crimson like a Holbein portrait, her peerless forehead held high, she proposes marriage to the man she loves.'

Irving Wardle was equally dismissive of the production in *The Times*, though conceding that Judi's Duchess 'has all the necessary qualities of serenity, authority and charm'.

J. C. Trewin challenged these criticisms with his praise for Clifford Williams's production in the *Lady*: 'The Duchess may not be everybody's revival on a summer night; but it is mine and I am glad to say so.' Unlike his fellows, he thought it both well cast and well spoken: 'It is hard indeed not to suffer with Judi Dench, and the death scene has a memorable strength and simplicity. To the last, in Webster's most famous phrase, she is Duchess of Malfi still (and when have those words been better said?) Michael Williams, too, can fix the Duke for us in a performance that is as quiveringly sensitive as it is finely spoken. With Richard Pasco's entirely realised lover – nobody who cares for acting can miss the quality of his ultimate scenes – and with Geoffrey Hutchings, another imaginative speaker, as Webster's enigmatic Bosola, the text is closely guarded.'

After her gloomy time with Portia, and the more enjoyable but doom-ridden days with the Duchess of Malfi, it was a huge relief at the end of the season when Trevor Nunn called everyone in to announce that the Christmas romp would be *Toad of Toad Hall*. The title role was played by Peter Woodthorpe, Rat by Jeffery Dench, Mole by Michael Williams, Badger by Tony Church, and Judi was given three parts – the First Fieldmouse, a brave Stoat, and Mother Rabbit. Euan Smith's lively production delighted the mostly young audience; there were lots of school matinées, and the cast soon learnt not to change out of the animal costumes before the children came round afterwards. When Judi was stricken with a violent bilious attack, she was still dressed as Stoat with a tail and a brown slouch hat when the doctor came and found her being sick into a bucket – that was one call he never forgot.

Her Mother Rabbit was played as visibly very pregnant, and the actress herself was soon to follow suit. In February the company set off for another tour of Japan, this time with *Twelfth Night*, *Henry V* and *Othello*. When Judi discovered her condition, she cabled home to give advance notice that she would now be unable to complete the run of *London Assurance* when she returned. For the first few months the wardrobe progressively let out her costumes, until even the high-waisted Empire line could not conceal that Grace Harkaway was no longer the virgin she was supposed to be. Just before she relinquished the part, Judi had an unexpected visitor backstage. 'I had a lovely friend in Nottingham called Brian Smedley, who's a judge, and he'd asked me to marry him. I'd said, "I'll have to think about it Brian." I never got in touch with him; the next time he saw me I was about five months' pregnant. He just put his head round the door and said, "I take it the answer's no?"'

On her last night in the part, Janet Whiteside's line to her, 'Do you feel nothing stirring?' got a huge laugh from an audience which knew by now why she was leaving. One lady sitting behind Burt Lancaster, who was not in the know and was puzzled by the laugh, enquired of her neighbour, 'Do you think she's pregnant?' When the actor went round afterwards he told Judi, 'I was able to reassure her that you were.' Sinead Cusack took over Grace Harkaway for the remainder of the run.

Michael and Judi were both convinced the baby was going to be a boy, and settled on the name Finn. In late September Judi was taken into the Avenue Clinic in north London. Michael was present when the baby was born on 24 September 1972. It was a girl, promptly referred to by her parents as Finty. She was christened Tara Cressida Frances, but the name Finty stuck with others too. When she went to her first school, St Mary's Convent in Hampstead, Judi had to order Cash's name tapes for her uniform and rang up the nuns. 'They said, "Oh we think she has beautiful names but we shall be calling her Finty." So I said, "Right, that's it, that's what we shall do." And it's stuck.'

Finty's godparents were chosen not just for the baby's sake. Barbara Leigh-Hunt was touched by Judi's reason for asking her, 'because she knew that it was unlikely I was going to have children, and she said, "Well, you can share Finty", and I thought that was such a loving and generous thing to do.' James Cairncross was one godfather, another was Professor Stanley Wells from the Shakespeare Institute at Stratford, who had also become a close friend; he only married quite late, when he was forty-four (to the novelist Susan Hill). 'I think Judi probably thought I was always going to be a bachelor, and she'd provide me with a surrogate child, as it were.' Those decisions were not all initiated by the baby's parents. Judi's first director at the Old Vic, Michael Benthall, came with Robert Helpmann to see *London Assurance*, and went round afterwards to tell her how much he had enjoyed it. When he discovered she was pregnant he asked, 'Can I be a godfather?' Without hesitation Judi replied, 'You certainly can.' Sadly for Finty, she never knew him, as he died only a couple of years later.

With the birth of her child, for the first time in her career Judi was quite happy to stay at home instead of setting off for the theatre every night. 'I was prepared to give up work altogether, but Mike didn't want me to do it. In fact what I did was theatre when she was tiny, so I was going to the theatre when she was going to bed, then later I did television during the day while she was at school, and had the evenings off, so I didn't miss out on anything.'

Michael and Judi wanted Finty to have as normal an upbringing as possible, so they made a pact from when she was tiny not to discuss work at home. There was a natural expectation that she would follow her parents into the theatre, but they were anxious she should not feel pressured to do so. They showed her all the different sides of being an actress, hoping it would put her off. But she responded eagerly to certain lines and speeches; if one of them said, 'I'll put a girdle round about the earth . . .' she would leap in, 'in forty minutes.' When asked 'What does King Lear say?' she answered 'Never, Never – FIVE times!'

This infant knowledge disconcerted other actors. Her nanny was waiting for Judi at the end of one matinée, holding Finty in her arms. Dudley Jones came upstairs with Judi, and when he first set eyes on the baby he said, 'Oh! Shall I compare thee . . .', and when the tiny figure completed the line 'to a summer's day?', Judi said, 'He was so shaken he nearly had a heart attack.' This aptitude blossomed into an enthusiasm for acting in her school plays, and Judi often made her costumes. Once, she played the inn-keeper's wife in a Nativity play, and when Richard Warwick asked her what it was about, she replied, 'It's about this inn-keeper's wife, of course.' Judi says, 'It was, too.'

Her first career ambition was to be an acrobatic nurse, swinging round the ward upside down to take the temperature of patients. Judi encouraged her in this, just as she delighted in teaching her imaginative new games. Pet cats and goldfish were part of the household from the beginning, and when the first hamster arrived Michael said sternly, 'That hamster is not allowed on the table.' But while Judi was giving Finty breakfast, before taking her to school at St Mary's, he would hear shrieks of laughter coming from downstairs; 'Fidget in New York' was the name of a game Judi invented, with cereal boxes all over the table as skyscrapers, and he knew that the hamster was on the table.

As soon as she was old enough Finty was taken to see her parents acting in the theatre, and it is hardly surprising that their enjoyment in their work should have influenced her own choice of career.

When she later asked if she could follow in her mother's footsteps to the Central School of Speech and Drama, her parents accepted the inevitable and supported her in that decision. But that was eighteen years ahead; it was a few years yet before Finty even saw either of them on-stage.

The months just after her birth were the longest break Judi had taken from the theatre since she first joined the Old Vic but, despite her airy talk of giving it up altogether, Michael knew her own nature better than she did – she could not live without acting.

Her very first work after Finty was born was a few days in the television film of *Luther,* and her return to the stage was in April the following year, when she jumped at the chance to appear in her home town of York, for the first time since she played the Virgin Mary in the Mystery Plays in 1957.

ten

1973–75

Return to York, farewell to Oxford, and mixed fortunes in London

The Director of the Theatre Royal in York, Richard Digby-Day, had tried once before to tempt Judi back to her home town, suggesting the part of Rebecca West in Ibsen's moodily powerful *Rosmersholm*. It was a pity that he only succeeded with a play that was nowhere in that league. The novel *La Lumière Noire* had been adapted for the stage by Claude-Andre Puget and Pierre Bost, and this English adaptation was by Alan Melville under the title of *Content to Whisper*.

After an abortive assassination attempt on the Austrian Governor of Torina in Northern Italy in 1842, a Swiss watchmaker and an actress in a tatty touring company are thrown into adjoining cells in the police station for interrogation. They can talk through a hole in the wall, but not see each other, and they fall, improbably, in love.

Judi and Michael were playing the two prisoners and she soon realised they had made an awful mistake. 'It was the most terrible play known to man, and the terrible thing was that Richard Digby-Day knew it too; it was dreadful. The police chief was that divine actor, Sidney Tafler, but he's the worst laugher I've ever been with; he just couldn't get the words out sometimes. The only good thing about it was that we were in York with Mummy, which was wonderful; the day that Finty was six months old, we got home and there were two Union Jacks on the door – Finty had cut two teeth.'

When it opened in March 1973 the local *Yorkshire Evening Press* was so glad to welcome Judi back with her husband that its critic, T. S. Williams, only hinted at the shortcomings of the vehicle, concluding that 'for many playgoers, it was a most welcome return to the solid, old-style play. It was like the theatre used to be.'

But Merete Bates did not mince word in the *Guardian*, finding the script empty and the details inaccurate or improbable: 'throughout, the dominant sense was of a demeaning waste of potential talent'. In the case of the three leading players, the adjective 'potential' was insulting enough in itself, at this stage of their careers.

Judi has regularly been back to York since that theatrical disaster, but mostly to see her family, or to receive dental treatment from her nephew Simon, and although she has given charity recitals she has never appeared in a play there again. However, that visit planted a seed in Michael's mind about the family living arrangements. His parents and Judi's mother all seemed to get on well with each other when they came to stay every Christmas and Easter, so over dinner one night at the Dirty Duck Michael caught Judi by surprise. 'He said, "Wouldn't it be wonderful if we could all just live together?" That was absolutely my idea of heaven; it's like a proper Quaker community, both for bringing up a child, and the whole idea of looking after your parents. It appals me more than anything else in this country, how they are shot off somewhere where they sit like zombies in a room, and they're there to die.'

Elizabeth and Len Williams and Olave Dench were just as enthusiastic about moving from Liverpool and York respectively to somewhere near Stratford. It took Judi and Michael a while to find a place big and adaptable enough, but eventually they found a converted stable with eleven rooms at Charlecote, about six miles outside Stratford. Olave moved in early in 1974, and Elizabeth and Len a little later. While they were playing in London, Judi and Michael stayed in Hampstead, drove up to Stratford after the Saturday night performance, and Judi cooked Sunday lunch for them all. As one might expect, there were some strains in the arrangement, but Judi has no regrets about the decision. 'I wouldn't say for a second that it was an easy thing to do; I was in tears some of the time, but the good times far outweighed the bad.' The most visible problem appeared to be electrical: 'We had to buy a toaster every single year we were there, and they were there for twelve years. Every Easter they got a new toaster. They used to break it; I don't know how.'

Both the mothers lived the rest of their lives at Charlecote and when Len Williams was widowed, his other son Paul and his wife moved in to help look after him.

Ironically, having decided to buy the house near Stratford, Judi's next three theatre engagements were not with the RSC at all, which she did not rejoin until the autumn of 1975. The first offer was one she was unlikely to refuse, since it came from her trusted and admired friend Frank Hauser, and reunited her with her jokey sparring partner Edward Woodward. The play was another little-seen European classic, *The Wolf* by the Hungarian Ferenc Molnar: written in 1911, this was its British première.

Edward played her ex-lover, met by chance in a restaurant when she is dining with her ageing and insanely jealous husband, played by Leo McKern. In the middle act she dreams of her old suitor wooing her again, as a soldier, a diplomat, an opera singer, and finally as a waiter; in the last act he visits them in reality, as the diffident lawyer's clerk he has in fact become.

Frank Hauser waited for two years to get his ideal cast. 'Judi was having a baby; Leo had given up the stage and gone back to Australia, and Teddy was in fact free and wanted to do it. Then Judi had her baby; Leo came back from Australia deeply disillusioned about his roots, and we did it. They were exactly the right three; I couldn't possibly have done it without them.'

At the time, Edward Woodward was in the throes of both a personal and professional crisis. His marriage was breaking up, he felt his career was stalled, and he feared he might be having a nervous breakdown. 'I think I would have gone right under if it hadn't been for Judi. She was marvellous; it was far better than going to a psychiatrist or a doctor; she helped me enormously just by being her, really. In the end I think it was certainly in the top three of my most wonderful times in the theatre.'

When it opened in Oxford, most of the national critics made the same clarion call for its transfer. Frank Marcus welcomed in the *Sunday Telegraph* 'an evening of sheer delight: an exhilarating experience which must not be withheld from London audiences'. Robert Cushman urged in the *Observer*, 'the sooner this Oxford Playhouse production comes to town the brighter town will be'; and Irving Wardle concluded a paean of praise for 'an evening of major acting and copious directorial verve' with the unequivocal assertion that 'this show would make a luxuriant oasis in the present West End desert'.

The only flaw in that metaphor is that an oasis is a fixed point, whereas *The Wolf* ended up playing in three different theatres in London – the Apollo, the Queen's and finally the New London – so that the cast called themselves 'the only touring show in the West End'.

The reviews and the audiences were ecstatic, but there is always one exception. After husband and wife had their row in the first act, Leo McKern had a line: 'I'm so happy'. A man shouted out, 'Well, I'm glad you are!' This could not mar Judi's enjoyment of a play in which they all had so much fun. 'Teddy, Leo and I had to drink in one scene, and one night Teddy knocked the bottom of the glass and it broke off, so I handed him mine. Leo said, "What good's that going to do us?" thinking of the business we had later on in the play.'

It could have had a long run, but Judi would not do more than six months and she only did that because it was Frank Hauser's swansong production after seventeen years at the Oxford Playhouse. She had such faith in him as a director that she once said, 'If Frank asked me to step in front of a bus, I'd do it. I'd know he had some good reason.'

When yet another funding crisis broke over him he decided to call it a day at Oxford, rather than lower his standards. His track record there had been phenomenal, mounting brilliant productions of the classics, many of them unfamiliar foreign masterpieces, with casts that read today like a *Who's Who* of the English theatre. When the news of his departure was announced in the *Oxford Mail* in January 1974, Judi was quoted commenting sharply, 'Well, it's Oxford's loss of course. But in a sense it's the theatre's gain. In my view he's been too loyal to the Playhouse. It's time he shared himself around a little more.'

That long line of distinguished actors who had been brought on by Frank Hauser were all determined to demonstrate their loyalty to him; Judi was a moving force in getting so many of them to come back and stage a gala performance of previous triumphs under his baton. It was planned as a surprise for him one Sunday night, and it certainly was. 'When I arrived at the theatre, having been taken out to dinner, the auditorium doors were flung open, Richard Cottrell threw his arms wide and clapped, and 700 people rose and clapped too. I thought, "Oh shit!" and then I thought that was possibly not the kindest and most graceful response.'

The show was entitled *Pussies Galore*, since he habitually called all his actors 'pussy'. It overran so much that the scene from *The Wolf*, scheduled for the end, was cut at the unanimous suggestion of its three protagonists.

After the security of working for a man who always gave her the most precise and helpful notes – 'When he's directing you feel that there's always somebody on the bridge' – Judi found herself a bit adrift with her next stage director. But between the two she slipped in another small part in a film. Tony Richardson was directing her husband in Dick Francis' racing mystery *Dead Cert* and persuaded her to come along and play the trainer's wife. She quite liked the rough-cut of the movie, but found the cutting in the final version a bit strange.

Then she tackled her second musical, but this was very different from *Cabaret*, both in the direction and the whole rehearsal process. Hal Prince had ironed out all the kinks in the score and the plot in his Broadway production, so the London production of *Cabaret* had been not dissimilar from rehearsing a straight play. Judi had never done a musical from the beginning before, until she embarked on *The Good Companions* adapted by Ronald Harwood from J. B. Priestley's play, with music by André Previn, and lyrics by Johnny Mercer. 'I didn't know that it was all rewritten in rehearsal. J. B. Priestley saw a run-through and he wasn't impressed with me at all; then he saw me dressed up and said, "Oh that's much better." Well, he saw me in a marcelled wig, looking a bit more like Miss Trant.'

John Mills was one of the stars of the show and, like Judi, he was a bit nonplussed by the approach of the director, Braham Murray. 'He seemed to be a very intelligent, brilliant young man and he talked to us about *Good Companions* for an hour before we started. Judi and I were frightfully impressed. We thought, "We've really got something here." Then somehow when it started we looked at each other, and nothing seemed to be happening in the way that we thought it might happen. He was wonderful in talking about *Good Companions*, but that's about where it finished.'

Judi thought he was 'all over the shop', and when he tore her off a strip he got more than he bargained for. Celia Bannerman was originally cast as Susie, but was unhappy and left the production at short notice, so her understudy had to go on in her place. 'We worked so hard that night with the understudy in front of an audience, you can imagine, and we got such a dressing-down the next day from Braham Murray. I was so angry that I said, "You must be joking if you think any of us wouldn't be working hard, you must be *joking*, Braham, if you think that we were all pulling back and not doing our best, with an understudy on playing the lead!" '

Judi and John Mills found they were forced largely to direct themselves, and did this so successfully that they stole most of the notices. The essence of her characterisation of Miss Trant was captured by Jeremy Kingston in *Punch*: 'the young spinster whose ache for adventure is indicated by Judi Dench with her incomparable skill. She finds a neat character touch in blurting out an inmost wish then covering her face with an outspread hand. But the strong foundation of her comic technique is her power to suggest, by voice, expression, gesture, that her hold on happiness is tenuous, that every happy moment, merry incident or kind word is the rarest treasure. Her quality is such that she can make us suspect our hold on happiness is no less fragile.'

That quality is one that several of her more perceptive colleagues have observed. Where other actors can often remind us of people we know, friends or neighbours, Judi's truthfulness is such that we can relate her feelings and behaviour directly to ourselves. John Mills compares her truthfulness of emotion to that of another of his co-stars, Celia Johnson.

There was quite a lot of corpsing in rehearsal and some practical jokes in performance. They put stage weights in the suitcase of one difficult member of the cast, who suddenly found he could not lift it in the scene when the concert party is changing trains, though the two culprits each give the other the credit for the idea. They also pulled surprises on each other. When Mary and John Mills were taking Judi and Michael for supper at Overton's after the show, their orders had to be telephoned through in advance to the restaurant. So Judi marked up the menu and attached it to the front of her clipboard in the luggage-checking scene; when she handed it to her supper host on-stage, it produced an unscripted double-take from him.

Despite its uncertain and unhappy genesis, the cast had a happy time during the run and the show filled the cavernous auditorium of Her Majesty's Theatre well into 1975. John Mills says it was just like a party: 'Judi has this wonderful personality backstage too; I mean nobody dreamt of going out between the shows, because there were all these tea-parties with Judi.'

During a long run she has to occupy herself with other activities. One of her favourites is to transform the look of rooms in the house, preferably while her husband is away. While she was at Her Majesty's, Michael went off to Switzerland, taking Finty with him. Judi invited an actor friend from *Good Companions*, John Bardon, to come and stay and they redecorated the main bedroom and bathroom and changed the carpets and curtains. She arranged a children's party to celebrate Finty's second birthday on the day they returned, without warning Michael about either event. He went upstairs and she heard a shout, 'Christ, where is everything?'

He should not have been too surprised, since she pulled this trick on him just after she came out of *London Assurance*. He went off to do the matinée and evening shows and with her mother's help Judi decorated the whole of the kitchen of Prospect Place. When he came home at night and poured himself a drink, he nearly choked over it as he glanced up and suddenly went, 'Good God.' Life is never dull in the Williams household.

Good Companions marked a milestone in Judi's career that has only become apparent in retrospect – this show was the last one for which she had to audition. Ever since, she has been offered her parts unconditionally; indeed the boot has often been on the other foot, with directors having to use all their persuasive powers to get her to accept certain roles.

Her expectations for her next play were very high, since it was being directed by one of her great heroes – John Gielgud. *The Gay Lord Quex* by Arthur Wing Pinero had been a success in the early years of this century, with Irene Vanbrugh as the manicurist Sophy Fullgarney. Gielgud's mother had seen it several times and passed on her enthusiasm to her son, though it had not been seen for over half a century. He had wanted to produce it for years and when the impresario Eddie Kulukundis offered him the chance and a generous budget, 'I stupidly became obsessed with the idea that I must do it exactly as it was written. We did it very elaborately, spent an awful lot of money, and I miscast several parts in it. I was so thrilled to be working with Judi, who was so easy and played so well, and Siân Phillips too, they were both very good'.

Judi played the Irene Vanbrugh part of the manicurist; Siân Phillips was the Duchess of Strood, the old flame of Lord Quex (Daniel Massey), 'the wickedest man in London'. The big scene in Act III was the confrontation between manicurist and marquess, when she attempts to prevent his marriage to her foster-sister, and virtue triumphs in the end. The plot carried little plausibility to a 1975 audience, which the director tried to overcome with period detail and stylish manners.

The rehearsals had some memorable moments for Judi. 'We were in the crypt at St James's Piccadilly and we'd been rehearsing for about an hour and a half one morning. Suddenly out of the men's loo ran a man carrying a pair of trousers, followed by another without any, and John laughed so much he gave us the day off, he couldn't go on rehearsing.'

Judi and Siân Phillips were kindred spirits and sought refuge in laughter from the problems of rehearsing the play. Siân was impressed by this first experience of working with Judi and observed her approach to her work keenly. 'I've worked with a lot of wonderful actors and actresses, but I thought that Judi, of all of them, had the most acute actor's intelligence – you know the way a footballer thinks with his feet, well Judi thinks with her acting ability. Now she says she is not a technical actress, but her technique is in fact impeccable; it's a technique that people would kill for.'

At one difficult point in rehearsals Judi went home, reread the whole play through from beginning to end and came in the next morning to tell Siân she thought she suddenly knew how to solve the problem. 'She talked about it like a crossword puzzle, as though she'd got the first bit of a clue, which she then pulled, so that she could make sense of her part. The play still didn't work, but she did make sense of what she was doing, and I was impressed because she didn't panic, she didn't run around, she just worked it out.'

Her director, too, was grateful for that indomitable spirit: 'We were not happy in the rehearsals at all, but Judi was marvellously gallant, and didn't show it at all. I remember the dress rehearsal, knowing absolutely certainly that it would be a complete flop, and it was.'

That was when she displayed her resilience. She came on in her nightgown costume to be met with an anguished cry from the darkened stalls: 'Oh no, no, no, God, Judi, you look just like Richard

III.' Siân Phillips had her tribulations too, when he told her to change the move on her entrance and come on and sit down. She said that her appearance in this scene was so brief that 'if I sit down in the train, the tiara, the feathers, it's going to take for ever'. Actress and director argued for a few moments, until she gave in with an audible sigh. 'Then John said, "I know it's dreadful, I know it's dreadful, but you're so terribly tall when you're standing up!" So it was *that* kind of dress rehearsal. It was a nightmare.'

It was no wonder she had so little patience when Judi told her she would like to be very, very tall. 'I said to her, "You must be quite mad." I think she's exactly the right size for a Dench.'

Daniel Massey was unhappy with the part of Quex, and it was only later that Gielgud wondered why he had not tried to play it himself: 'I might have been rather amusing in it, but it never occurred to me.' That was probably as well, since he was playing in Pinter's *No Man's Land* at the time, a much better play which was packing them in next door at Wyndham's Theatre.

At the Albery the Pinero met with a curiously sharp division of opinion. Jeremy Kingston attacked it in *The Times* for striking false notes at all the crisis points, and 'the reason for choosing this play to revive is baffling'. John Barber was equally dismissive in the *Daily Telegraph*: 'Pinero betrays his reputation as a master of dramatic construction, and fails to persuade us that his people are anything other than vapid nobodies.'

But at least three critics went out of their way to say they disagreed with their colleagues. Sheridan Morley justified the revival in *Punch* as 'the theatrical equivalent of a folly, but a highly stylish one ... if you want boulevard acting at its very best and you happen to have Judi Dench, Daniel Massey and the exquisite Siân Phillips around then it's hard to think of a more suitable vehicle though that doesn't seem to have occurred to anyone except the director, Sir John Gielgud.'

J. C. Trewin offered another dissenting voice in the *Illustrated London News*, politely advising his fellow-critics 'to read the play before cavilling at Sir John Gielgud's production, which is at once sure, affectionate, and detailed', and praising Judi's playing of Sophy 'with an enchanting, alert assurance, a feeling for every flick of comedy'.

Frank Marcus also argued in the *Sunday Telegraph* that direction and playing overcame the weaknesses in the writing; 'as for Judi Dench, she has the enviable talent of bestowing truth and poignancy on everything she touches. Surely she is everybody's favourite actress?'

Even if all his readers answered that question in the affirmative, there were not enough of them to save the play, which only ran for a few weeks. Judi's last memory of it is told with a huge and indulgent laugh: 'We were going into the Albery stage door and John was going into Wyndham's; he called out, "Hello, Dan, I hear your show's coming off. No good? Oh my God, I directed it!"'

After a run of four shows, of which only *The Wolf* could be described unequivocally as both a critical and commercial success, Judi now returned to the RSC, where she had four great hits in a row, before stubbing her toe in the final play of the season.

eleven

1975–76

A triumphant season with the RSC

1976 was a golden Shakespearean year at Stratford, for the company as a whole and for Judi in particular; and as a harbinger of one of her most famous partnerships she was reunited with Ian McKellen in a Shavian curiosity at the Aldwych the previous autumn. *Too True to be Good* is often dismissed as one of Shaw's inconsequential political extravaganzas, which had failed at its première in 1932, despite a powerful performance by Ralph Richardson.

It is difficult for an audience to take it seriously, with an actor playing a Microbe in Act I and a parodied T. E. Lawrence arriving on his motor bike in Act II, but Clifford Williams drew performances from a talented cast that won plaudits all round.

Judi suspects that Shaw is more fun to be in that it is to watch, and she certainly thought that 'it was absolutely heavenly to do'. She was originally asked to play the part of Mops, who is transformed from a hypochondriac into a social ball of fire, but for once she read the play in advance and decided that playing Sweetie Simpkins would be even more fun, as the Cockney nurse who masquerades as a French Countess, so Anna Calder-Marshall played Mops.

Ian McKellen was Pops, the burglar turned preacher; he was well aware that the play was not easy to bring off, and thought that many people underestimated how good Judi was in it. 'Shaw wants fully rounded acting, and he doesn't always get it, but Judi embodied this person and brought her totally to life, not as someone with a lot of bright things to say, but someone with passion, and once you bring passion to Shaw he's revealed as being a great playwright – he doesn't get the performances he deserves, I think.'

G. B. S. would surely have smiled on this production and its reception, especially Frank Marcus's judgement in the *Sunday Telegraph* that Clifford Williams had wrought a miracle in rescuing the play from neglect, 'bestowing on it the status of a classic. Even the most ardent Shavians, of which I am one, will be amazed.' B. A. Young thought it 'altogether a very good evening indeed' in the *Financial Times*, and Michael Billington added his voice to the welcome in the *Guardian* for 'a feast of good acting . . . Judi Dench as the sex-loving quondam chambermaid whose gravelly accent constantly breaks through her elaborate Garboesque façade is richly funny.' Billington reserved his highest praise for the performance of Ian McKellen, culminating in his final speech in which 'he achieves a piercing unaffected simplicity that hits an audience straight between the eyes'.

During the run the actor was hit straight between the ears. He overheard two actors tearing his performance to shreds and tried to shrug it off, but the next night during Act II, in the scene on the beach, 'I was facing out front, and I thought every single one of the people in the audience thinks what that man said last night, and I couldn't carry on. It must have been very odd for Judi, because I just turned my back on the audience and had one of the very few attacks of stage fright that I've ever had, and she just carried me through the scene. I explained myself to her at the interval, and at the end of the show there was a little note pushed under my door, just saying, "You were wonderful, and those people were wrong, just carry on", and to know that she was there for the rest of the run. She was totally supportive when I was climbing back to some kind of self-confidence, and that's the closest I've ever got to Judi, I think.'

The rapport between the two of them was multiplied about twenty-fold in the 1976 Stratford company, most of whose members look back on it as the happiest of their RSC careers. It included Donald Sinden, Francesca Annis, Bob Peck, John Woodvine, Greg Hicks, Roger Rees, Barbara Leigh-Hunt, Michael Pennington, Nickolas Grace, Robin Ellis, Richard Griffiths, Ian McDiarmid, Griffith Jones, Mike Gwilym, and Michael Williams; this assembly of gifted talents was forged into an ensemble that enriched the experience of players and audiences alike.

The plays themselves were the subject of some negotiation between actors and management. Donald Sinden agreed to play Benedick if he could play Lear, and Ian McKellen was similarly reluctant to come just for Romeo, holding out for Macbeth as well, with Judi as his first choice to play his wife. She ended up with a sharply contrasting quartet of Beatrice, Lady Macbeth, Regan, and Adriana in *The Comedy of Errors*.

She was very happy to be back with all of her family from the three generations now living together at Charlecote, and the season was helped off to a flying start by one of those fortuitous quirks of casting for the first two productions. While the Sinden/Dench team were rehearsing *Much Ado*, the McKellen/Annis duo were already at work on *Romeo and Juliet*; everyone else was common to both plays, so the complete casts had six weeks' rehearsal, but the two pairs of leads had the luxury of twelve weeks to work on their parts, which Donald Sinden says was longer than he has ever had for one play. He and Judi and the director John Barton had deep discussions on what exactly had been the previous relationship between Benedick and Beatrice, that has made them so wary of each other as the play opens. Eventually their director stopped them, saying it was much better to leave the audience guessing about what had gone wrong.

The setting was brilliantly original – the British Raj in 1880s India – which John Barton explained was the most recent time in history when a cavalry regiment could have been billeted on a civilian establishment. One inspired touch was to have John Woodvine play Dogberry as a turbanned Sikh, which made perfect sense of him not quite understanding the language; another actor with a mischievous sense of humour, he made the Watch corpse nearly every night.

Donald Sinden's great appetite for theatrical research led him to sound out John Gielgud over lunch at the Garrick Club. 'When I saw your production in 1952 you persuaded me that Benedick was a witty man, and now we're doing it I don't find him witty at all. She's the witty one.' His enquiry was rewarded with what he hugs to himself as 'my very own perfect Gielgudism'. Sir John was quick to agree with him: 'Oh you're perfectly right. I made a great mistake there. Benedick is a very boorish fellow; you'll be much better than I was.'

Judi was also following in the footsteps of a line of famous Beatrices, from Ellen Terry to Peggy Ashcroft, and her assumption of the part was soon talked of in the same breath as theirs. Her co-star thought it one of the best things she has ever done, though he confesses that he did not always make it easy for her. 'I used to strum on a guitar before she came on, then rest it against the table. There was a moment as we were sitting there when our hands just sneaked across the table and we held hands. One night the guitar slipped and fell down with a b'doinggg, and I said, "I'm suffering from guitar." The audience laughed and Judi practically went under the table, she was a goner – how could anyone do that in the middle of Shakespeare?'

One laugh that the two of them were determined to head off was on the famously difficult line of Beatrice's, 'Kill Claudio', and they succeeded on every occasion bar one – the opening night at Stratford, when so many of the audience knew the play well and were accustomed to laughing at that point. But that did not prevent them winning a first-night ovation.

J. C. Trewin said it was many years since he had seen a Beatrice and Benedick to approach this pair and reached for superlatives in the *Birmingham Post*: 'This is high comedy, and no Beatrice in memory has been more firmly based in truth. Donald Sinden has always been able to speak a line as though it had just occurred to him; and he does not try to persuade us aimlessly that Benedick is the nonpareil of wits.' (The Gielgud advice had been taken to heart.) 'He and his Beatrice, in the tangle of misapprehensions, bring style to style, humanity to humanity. I think they might have pleased those conflicting critics, Walkley and Shaw.'

He was also taken with John Woodvine's Babu Dogberry, and so was Michael Billington in the *Guardian*, who thought the whole piece 'exhilaratingly took off', praising Barton, Benedick and Beatrice.

Robert Cushman gave full credit to the first two in the *Observer*, but devoted most of his column to the latter. 'When she melts, the effect is breathtaking. Miss Dench is always inspiring sentences like that, but her means for doing so seem simple enough; she merely injects into a hush a few lines denoting surrender and spoken with an unquestioning directness that inspires kindred feeling in the audience. But I wish I knew how she created a hush in the first place; can there be more to it than concentration? I know, though, that while her spark and bubble make her a fine comic actress, it is these moments that silently proclaim her great.'

Her Benedick has shared the stage with great actors of an earlier generation, and makes an interesting comparison from that vantage-point: 'Peggy Ashcroft for instance fined everything down, while Ralph Richardson, I noticed, built everything up; but Judi seems to have a pretty good idea of where she's going from the word go.'

He based that observation on her Viola as well as her Beatrice, but there have been occasions when she worried that things were not gelling in rehearsal, and this was the case with her next play in the season, *Macbeth*. Trevor Nunn had produced it in the main house only two years earlier with Nicol Williamson and Helen Mirren, so he would only stage it in the small auditorium of the Other Place, with a cast of just sixteen and much doubling of the smaller parts.

The action was played in a circle and the cast sat outside it on upended beer crates when they were not involved in a scene, and these silent watchful figures concentrated the focus on the acting-area. The audience of about 150 sat in three rows on three sides of a square and in the upper gallery, so everyone was far closer to the actors than even the occupants of the front stalls in the main house.

The bare simplicity of the setting worried the actors in the beginning and after only a couple of weeks Judi voiced this to Trevor Nunn as they walked back to rehearsal. Twice she expressed her fears, and each time she tripped and fell over as she spoke, which she thought was ominous, 'but it came right in just the last few days'.

Few people were aware that Judi had played the part in West Africa and even her friends expressed a little surprise at the casting. John Gielgud remarked to Coral Browne, 'You know, Coral, Judi Dench is going to play Lady Macbeth.' Her characteristic response, 'Oh, then I suppose we shall have the postcard scene!' soon became famous, not least because when it got back to her, Judi repeated it gleefully to all her friends.

Seeking an insight into his own character, Ian McKellen asked Trevor Nunn, 'He's Nixon isn't he, Macbeth?'

'No, no, he's not Nixon, he's Kennedy. It's the golden couple; everyone loves the Macbeths.'

The two of them also conveyed a very strong sense of the physical attraction between them. John Woodvine, who played Banquo this time, has appeared in half a dozen different productions of the play and played Macbeth himself twice; he thinks that this was the best production of it he has ever seen. 'Ian and Judi mined stuff in that play that had just never been seen before. I thought that was a terrific achievement, and doing it in that small space was a huge bonus.'

The claustrophobic atmosphere was intensified by the doors clanging shut at the beginning, and by the decision to play it straight through without an interval, so nobody could leave before the end. Some schoolboys who were skulking in the men's lavatory were almost scared out of their wits by Marie Kean suddenly appearing in front of them dressed as the First Witch and hissing, '*Get back* in there!' They turned and fled.

But it was not just schoolchildren who were fearful. In that confined space, cast and audience were equally conscious of each other and the actors came to recognise the same priest, Nevile Boundy, sitting in the front row night after night holding up his crucifix to protect them, because he said the sense of evil was so overpowering he feared for their safety. Judi says, 'He was a very theatrical priest.'

She is no more immune than other actors to the superstitions that surround this play and established her own rituals to fend off the traditional bad luck. She wore a simple, one-piece black smock that zipped up at the back. At the first preview Bob Peck happened to be nearest when she needed zipping up at the last minute, so he did it, 'but once that had been established she needed me to do it every night, because she had this routine, and I did it throughout the long run'.

When it opened, praise was heaped on both conception and execution. Robert Cushman devoted his entire column in the *Observer* to it, making a point of saying, 'the supporting playing is the best all round at Stratford for years', that the Macbeth of Ian McKellen was the best he had seen, and 'Judi Dench . . . edges her ring of confidence with steel; murder, as she counsels it, sounds the most sensible thing in the world . . . the triumph of both protagonists is that their passions live up to the claims made for them in the text.'

One of the revelations of the production was how 'the golden couple' traced his descent into evil and hers into madness. Both of them became convinced that those who argued, like Edith Evans, that there was a scene missing for Lady Macbeth, were quite wrong.

Judi insists that the line of development is quite clear in the text: 'Just before he speaks to the murderers Macbeth says, "We will keep

Amanda with Edward Woodward as Elyot in
Private Lives, directed by Ronald Magill,
Nottingham Playhouse 1965.

'Sometimes the two of them corpsed each
other so much that one of them would actually
have to walk off the stage to recover.'

Isabella with Edward Woodward as Lucio in
Measure for Measure, directed by John Neville,
Nottingham Playhouse 1965.

'Though it is a very pretty production,
Mr Neville, you must not call it altogether
Shakespeare.'

With John Neville on the West African tour, 1964.

'I would not have missed the whole experience of that tour for worlds.'

On location in Putney for *Four in the Morning*, 1965, with Joe Melia, Norman Rodway and director Anthony Simmons.

"That must be the noisiest location in the whole of London – on the flight path to Heathrow, by a railway bridge, by a road bridge and opposite where all the river-tankers come and dump their rubbish.

Frank Hauser, Artistic Director of the Oxford Playhouse Company, 1956–74.

'If Frank asked me to step in front of a bus I'd do it. I'd know he had some good reason.'

Irina with James Cairncross as Solyony in *The Three Sisters*, directed by Frank Hauser, Oxford Playhouse 1964.

'Her sense of excitement for three acts that she alone might get away from this awful town makes the final realisation that she too is trapped all the more poignant.'

Silia in *The Rules of the Game*, directed by James Grout, Oxford Playhouse 1966. 'By turns she is petulant, childish, feline, gloatingly triumphant, then suddenly dashed.'

Lika with Ian McKellen as Leonidik and Ian McShane as Marat in *The Promise*, directed by Frank Hauser, Oxford Playhouse 1966, Fortune Theatre 1967.

'She has a facility for acting which is bewildering, with a blazing sincerity and honesty.'

Sally Bowles in *Cabaret*, directed by Hal Prince, Palace Theatre, 1968.

'Brilliantly miscast and spiritedly playing against her nature as an actress, Miss Dench sings and prances with engaging spirit and a quite surprising force.'

Hermione in *The Winter's Tale*, directed by Trevor Nunn, RSC 1969.

'In a few silent seconds we are made aware of all that Hermione has suffered and the steadiness of her fixed resolve. It hardly needs to be put into speech.'

Madame Ranevskaya in *The Cherry Orchard*, directed by Richard Eyre, BBC TV 1980.

'She was just heart-stoppingly beautiful.'

Viola in *Twelfth Night*, directed by John Barton, RSC 1969. 'Long before her more famous moments, it is blessedly clear that Judi Dench has the measure of the part.'

Juno in *Juno and the Paycock*, directed by Trevor Nunn, RSC 1980. 'A wonderful blend of exhaustion and despair.'

Grace Harkaway with Donald Sinden as Sir Harcourt Courtly in *London Assurance*, directed by Ronald Eyre, RSC 1970.

'We did the longest double-take you've ever seen in your life.'

Beatrice with Donald Sinden as Benedick in *Much Ado About Nothing*, directed by John Barton, RSC 1976.

'When she melts, the effect is breathtaking.'

Madame Ranevskaya with Michael Gough as Firs in *The Cherry Orchard*, directed by Sam Mendes, Aldwych 1989.

'Vladimir Ashkenazy is out without his coat again.'

Mr and Mrs Michael Williams – 5 February 1971.
'I want to have a look at the script.'

ourself/Till supper-time alone: while then, God be with you!" and she leaves him. After he has seen them, and before the two of them meet again her soliloquy says it all: "Naught's had, all's spent,/Where our desire is got without content:/'Tis safer to be that which we destroy,/Than by destruction, dwell in doubtful joy."

'It charts every bit of his breakdown. Then you see the beginning of the banquet, when she's trying to make this tremendous effort and suddenly the whole thing just cracks into thousands of pieces. She can't go on; she answers in one-lines from then on. That's why it's so important at the beginning that it's not a person who could do it on her own; I'm always against those Lady Macbeths who are so strong and evil at the beginning. If they can do it on their own, why do they invoke the spirits to help them? When she says, "You lack the season of all natures, sleep", it tells absolutely what's been happening to them. He starts to preclude her from everything, and obviously paces around alone at night. So it's right that she disappears from view, and suddenly you see her with her mind completely gone. I don't see where there could have been another scene, what it would say that isn't said already in the play. I remember saying to Trevor one day, "We must do it so that any schoolchildren who come to see it and don't know it, will think that they may not do the murder." We all take so many things for granted.'

The conviction in the performances quelled any impulse to laughter at the unexpected from the audience, though it was sometimes not so easy for the actors. The costumes were all monochrome, mostly black, with Duncan in a white robe and Malcolm in a white sweater, but when Roger Rees as the latter broke his foot, he had to come on in a bright blue wheelchair, as there were no understudies at the Other Place. It was nearly too much for Judi: 'At the beginning when we all took our seats one of the Witches came on stooped and dribbling; Griffith Jones as Duncan was helped on by two people, and when Malcolm came forward in his wheelchair, Marie Kean passed me and said, "It's the Lourdes production!"'

On another night, when Macbeth and Banquo leapt into the circle to meet the Witches, a bit of wire on John Woodvine's beer crate caught on his sword-belt and it entered with him, 'so we played our first scene with the witches with Banquo having a beer crate hanging off my breeches. Judi was hysterical, sitting on her beer crate shaking.'

She tested everyone's self-control by inventing a game with some pink fluorescent dots she found in the stationery cupboard, that everyone had to wear and show to all the rest of the cast without the audience knowing. She wore hers on her earring, Ian McKellen his on the pommel of his sword, John Woodvine's was on the sole of his shoe as he knelt, Ian McDiarmid's as the Porter on the end of his nose, and Griffith Jones' under his beard, which he flipped up. Ian McKellen does not really approve of such pranks, 'but I joined in and loved it'.

The demand for tickets was so overwhelming that the theatre was swamped by letters protesting that they could not get in, so reluctantly Trevor Nunn scheduled a three-week run in the main house, which pacified the keen theatre-goers but not the players, who hated suddenly having to blow up this intense chamber performance into something much more expansive. They tried to preserve its ensemble spirit by refusing to occupy the much more splendid individual dressing-rooms now available to them, and insisted on using a single big chorus-room with just a partition between the men's and women's dressing spaces, to replicate the atmosphere of the Other Place. The only member of the cast who actually seems to have enjoyed these larger audiences was Bob Peck, despite the fact that the adjustments to the fight at the end caused Macbeth to slice Macduff's ear in half one night, necessitating emergency repairs at Leamington hospital.

Any long-running production can slow down a bit after a while, but whenever that began to happen to this keen troupe someone would say, 'Right, tonight we'll do a speed-run.' This is a rehearsal technique to tighten up the running-time, but one that is only rarely exercised in performance. John Woodvine says, 'We used to fly around. Every entrance and exit was made at a run; we'd be in a state of hysteria all night, but the audience was never aware of this and it always worked and pulled the show together.'

The life of the production continued well beyond Stratford. The following year it was revived at the Donmar Warehouse, then the RSC's small theatre base in London, went on to the Young Vic and was finally recorded by Thames Television. The reception was rapturous on each occasion.

Michael Billington was even more bowled over than he had been at Stratford. 'McKellen and Judi Dench as his Lady, in fact, usher us into the hair-raising, unmistakeable presence of great acting and both are at their finest in the Banquet scene ... It is one of the few occasions in the theatre when I have felt that combination of pity and terror one is supposed to feel in tragedy: these are not monsters but recognisable human beings willing themselves to evil and dis-integrating in the process.'

Robert Cushman went even further than he had done at Stratford, now saying, 'It is the best Shakespeare production I have ever seen'; and Irving Wardle thought it 'the RSC's finest Shakespearean achievement since Brook's *A Midsummer Night's Dream* ... a reminder that the test of great acting is not impersonation but revelation'. After all these eulogies few were surprised when Judi won the first of her Best Actress Awards from the Society of West End Theatres, nor that Ian McKellen and Trevor Nunn picked up a matching pair for Best Actor and Best Director.

Frank Marcus urged the RSC to retain it in the repertoire 'to give as many people as possible a chance to experience what must be accounted one of the pivotal interpretations of our time. I do not think that the actors will tire of playing it.'

His supposition was correct and few tragedies can ever have had so many comic stories associated with them, both voluntary and involuntary. The worst of the latter happened at the Young Vic in the Banquet scene when the intercom got caught up with a taxi service at Waterloo station and everyone heard, 'Two for Basingstoke, if you're ready, Fred', just as Lady Macbeth was saying, 'Pray you, keep seat; the fit is momentary.'

The most challenging of the former was when Judi made a birthday cake for Roger Rees, representing the set, with little icing figures on top, of all of them sitting in a circle of liquorice. She took it to the Young Vic in a taxi, 'and it was on my knee so they got rocked about a bit. Roger said, "How lovely," and then John Woodvine said, "We've all got to sit at the matinée like we are on the cake." I don't know how we got through sometimes.' Roger Rees kept the figures and had them mounted in a glass frame as his memento of that time.

The best memento for the fans of great Shakespearean acting is the video, which was imaginatively shot in pools of light and more big close-ups than usual on television. This enabled the viewer to see how, in the sleepwalking scene, Lady Macbeth stared fixedly throughout it without blinking once. After her line 'all the perfumes of Arabia will not sweeten this little hand', she gave a strangled endless scream, underscoring how she had now gone completely over the edge. Trevor Nunn and his television director Philip Casson used one particularly dramatic electronic effect – they took all the colour saturation out of the picture except for the blood after the murders, thereby heightening the shock for the viewer.

Sean Day-Lewis compared it favourably in the *Daily Telegraph* with the expensive naturalism of the BBC Shakespeare series which was then underway. Peter Fiddick also commended it in the *Guardian* for eschewing pseudo-realism and capturing the spirit of the original: 'Ian McKellen's Macbeth and Judi Dench as Lady Macbeth, came to the screen with all the weight of experience behind them and it showed from the first word to the last.'

Most of us would echo that verdict, but not the Lady concerned, when she watched it at Trevor Nunn's house with the rest of the company. 'I was terribly disappointed in my own performance when I saw it on TV, because I thought I was doing something better than that, and I vowed I'd never watch myself again.' Nor has she until very recently. She has seen none of her television series nor most of her films; she was only prevailed upon to break this self-imposed rule for the premières of the Bond films and *Mrs Brown*.

The television broadcast was shown in January 1979, by which time the actors had lived with *Macbeth* for nearly two and half years, but they did much else besides in that period. Many of them were also in *The Comedy of Errors*, opening only a month after it in Stratford, which for Trevor Nunn was a particular bonus, as he said that 'there was no company formation left to be done, they trusted and admired each other, and everybody decided that they were immensely fortunate to have each other. So it was deliriously happy.'

He had decided to produce it as a musical, keeping the Shakespearean text, but adding some lyrics of his own, set to music by Guy Woolfenden. To help him stage the song and dance routines he called in the choreographer Gillian Lynne. For her the job satisfaction fortunately far exceeded the remuneration (£375 in total for ten weeks' work, and accommodation found), but she made one important stipulation. 'My condition for the lousy money was that *everybody*, regardless of status, had to come to class at the start of every day, otherwise I couldn't get what I wanted. Judi was wonderfully supportive; she was there and doing it, and they all got mad about it in the end. Eventually I even managed to get Trevor into it. The joy of working with actors is that they are so thrilled when they can do an exercise on Wednesday that they couldn't do on Monday, and Judi was like the leader of the pack. I made the Dr Pinch number go very wild at one point, absolutely crazy, and when Trevor saw it he rolled about. "How did you get them to do that?" I said, "Because Judi was right there with me, leading the wildness." '

Roger Rees was open-mouthed in astonishment at one particular movement Judi invented as she warmed to her task. As Antipholus of Syracuse, his line on first sighting Judi as Adriana was, 'But soft! who wafts us yonder?' She was up on the balcony, 'doing this extraordinary low bend, as if she was wearing Little Tich's boots, because she bent over sideways completely from the ankles, to indicate that I should come to the bedroom. When I ignored that she came on and did this long, long speech, beginning: "Ay, ay, Antipholus, look strange and frown", and she did it again in the middle of the stage. It was the most extraordinary bit of ballet. I don't know how she ever stood upright really doing it; it was as though she was on a wire.'

Gillian Lynne's class exercises began at 9.30 a.m. and went on for an hour. Even her trained dancers find them hard, so they were quite a shock to the system for the actors until they got into the rhythm and saw what was happening to them. Judi says that all of them were never so fit as they were during that run.

Michael Williams was both rueful and admiring of the way Gillian put them through their paces. 'I nearly threw a chair at her once, but I restrained myself, thank God. She asked you to do things that you think are physically impossible, but she gets it out of you.'

Unlike *Macbeth* this show seemed to go like a dream from the very beginning. When John Napier showed them the model of his set, with its open-air taverna and the walls hung with shawls, tea trays and hats, like something straight out of a holiday brochure for Greece, everyone burst into spontaneous applause. Trevor Nunn looks back on it as the most enjoyable rehearsal period he has experienced to date.

The performances were even more fun. At the beginning the cast swarmed onto the stage, waving to the audience, and at the end invited them up onto the stage to join in the dance. This became so popular that by the last night it carried on for nearly half an hour, until the cast had to say politely, 'I think you'd better go home now.' Judi has never had so many letters from schoolchildren, 'because they couldn't believe it was just so immediate, like a place they might go on holiday'.

Most of the critics welcomed it as a wonderfully entertaining evening. After admiring several of the leading performances, Irving Wardle expressed a tiny reservation in *The Times*: 'At present there are moments when the company are having too much of a good time but the comic centre is already strong enough to survive the raw edges. We are unlikely ever to see a funnier Adriana than Judi Dench, a peremptory odalisque downing her terrified servants with flying trays and point-blank bursts from the soda syphon and relapsing into voluptuous submission with her supposed spouse.'

John Barber struck the only really sour note in the *Daily Telegraph*, complaining 'this is a comedy and I did not laugh once' and attacking the production for betraying Shakespeare's intentions; a view firmly rebutted by B. A. Young in the *Financial Times*. 'To argue that what Mr Nunn has done is un-Shakespearean is to my mind to miss the point of what Shakespeare intended; which was to set the audience laughing as constantly as possible . . . I thought the evening an exceedingly joyous one.'

Anthony Everitt argued in the *Birmingham Post* that 'Oddly, this irreverent treatment does more justice to the play than a straight-forward approach. We leave the theatre with a sense that the young Shakespeare wrote better than we knew.'

Several of the cast said that it was one of those shows where they almost ran to the theatre every night to get into costume and get on-stage, it was such fun. The last night at Stratford was a near-riot. John Woodvine had taken over from Robin Ellis as Dr Pinch, and this night he started adding more lines of his own. As he made his entrance from the audience he called out to his wife, 'Is the seat all right, Aphrodite?' Then he sent Judi over the edge by topping her greeting, 'Good doctor', with, 'I'm not a very good doctor, I haven't the patients.'

Trevor Nunn said to them afterwards, 'I couldn't believe it was going on in my theatre, in a play by Shakespeare.'

Thames Television also recorded this production but this time in the theatre before an invited audience, and the video has some imaginative moments. When Antipholus removes Luciana's spectacles, there is an out-of-focus subjective shot of him from Francesca Annis' viewpoint. When both sets of twins are brought together at the end, the laugh at Judi's glee on 'I see two husbands' is only exceeded by the one on her double-take as she says, 'Which of you two did dine with me today?' Delight and horror chase each other across her face on the dawning realisation that she took the wrong brother to bed.

After these three major triumphs in succession, which thrust her unmistakably into the front rank of classical actresses, Judi's impulsive desire to be one of the company led her into a request that she came to regret bitterly. The final play of the season was *King Lear*, and when Michael Pennington suggested casually to her that she ought to play Regan the temptation to ask to be in that also was too great. Trevor Nunn agreed, but that was virtually Judi's last happy moment in the production. It was in the hands of not one but three directors – Trevor Nunn, John Barton, and Barry Kyle – who had individually directed all the other plays that season. In their eyes this collaboration flowed naturally from the group approach to most things within the RSC, but it does not seem to have achieved a single coherent vision of this most demanding play.

At the first rehearsal the costume designs were put out round the room for the actors to see. Barbara Leigh-Hunt was playing the other evil sister, Goneril. 'I found Judi transfixed in front of hers for the scene where she travels to Goneril's castle. The costume was a long grey fur coat with a very high collar, and a huge flat grey fur hat, and she was frozen in horror in front of this design. She looked up and said, "If I run on in that they'll shoot me." '

She buckled down to the rehearsals and one improvisational exercise with Donald Sinden produced an interesting psychological insight into Regan's relationship with her father. In the early scenes with him she would stutter until the King slammed his fist down on the table, establishing her fear of him. The stutter only disappeared when the power relationship was reversed.

It was the physical cruelty in the character that Judi found hardest to stomach, not made any easier by a bright idea of John Woodvine's at the dress rehearsal. He was her husband, the Duke of Cornwall, and at the blinding of Gloucester he slipped a false eye out of a concealed bag as he said, 'Out, vile jelly!' and flung it at the wall, where it stuck. This was too much for Judi, and for Trevor Nunn too. 'John Woodvine looks sepulchral in appearance and likes to encourage the idea that he really works as an undertaker, but of course it's nowhere near the truth; he's every bit as mischievous as Judi, and it is an almost impossible combination. It was rather like having to separate the children in a classroom, and send one to the back of the room. Anything would set them off.'

So the eye-throwing business was outlawed, to John Woodvine's regret, but Judi never got any happier with her performance. The only part she really enjoyed was making an off-stage effect. When Lear arrived at his daughter's house with his hunting dogs the animals were not seen on-stage but their presence was conveyed by Bob Peck and Judi standing in the wings barking. He thought 'it was probably the only pleasure she got out of the show'.

The late nineteenth-century setting did not endear itself to many of the critics, who liked some of the performances, such as Sinden's King and Michael Williams' senile busker of a Fool, but not the production as a whole. J. C. Trewin wrote regretfully in the *Birmingham Post*: 'This is not for me; it may be for others.' It was not for Irving Wardle of *The Times* either, who felt that 'in this production one is led step by step up the garden path and then plunged into the abyss, with no further pretence to consistent interpretation'. Frank Marcus was more encouraging in the *Sunday Telegraph*, believing that it showed 'the seeds from which something remarkable will surely grow'.

But it would have to grow without Judi, who pleaded to be let out of it when it transferred to the Aldwych. Regan remains one of the two Shakespearean characters, which, like Portia, she positively hated playing, and regrets that it cast a slight shadow for her over the end of a phenomenally successful season. But Beatrice, Lady Macbeth and Adriana went on to set London by the ears, and it is a pity that we do not have a permanent record of the first as well as the other two.

twelve

1977–80

From Congreve to O'Casey at the Aldwych,
and Pinter to Mitford on Television

The end of 1976 saw the first visit of the RSC to Newcastle, which has now become a popular annual event. Trevor Nunn saw it as an opportunity to fill the short period between the end of the Stratford season and going to the Aldwych, by running in new productions. He was also keen that the company should express itself in a way not possible at either of those places, by doing community work and some short experimental pieces. Cicely Berry devised some performances for the actors, and Judi volunteered her services in a hitherto unseen capacity.

One of the actors in the company, John Bown, wrote a short play about two characters loosely based on Gielgud and Richardson sharing a dressing-room on tour, and what happened in the half-hour before curtain-up. It was directed by Clyde Pollitt, and the author took the small part of the dresser; the two stars were played by Paul Brooke and Paul Moriarty. Judi said she would love to design the set for it and created one with make-up tables but no mirrors, so that the actors looked straight out at the audience as they made up (exactly as Judi herself did in the last act of *Amy's View* over twenty years later).

Paul Moriarty thought it was 'typical of her work in that it was exactly right and yet not drawing attention to itself. There was great detail and exactitude, and yet everything was so right that you didn't really notice it. You could see it was an undernourished part of her life in a way.' He laughs that 'her design was a lot subtler than the acting, I would say.' It was given only a couple of late-night performances, but established a tradition of such events in Newcastle.

Judi had few opportunities for such extracurricular work, as she was soon plunged into the transfers of the 1976 Stratford plays at the Aldwych, and then the rehearsals for a new London production of *Pillars of the Community*.

It was exactly a century since its première, and it was the first of Ibsen's naturalistic rather than poetic dramas. It had not been seen in London for fifty years and John Barton cut it and reshaped it quite severely. Ian McKellen played the hypocritical shipowner Karsten Bernick, whose respectability has been sustained by allowing his brother-in-law Johan to take the blame for his own youthful escapades. Judi was Lona Hessel, thrown over by Bernick so that he could make a financially advantageous marriage with her stepsister. The truth comes out when Johan and Lona return from fifteen years' exile in America.

Ian McKellen thought it was very generous of her to take what was a smallish part. They only had three scenes together, but Lona is crucial to the plot and Judi had some effective moments, with a flamboyant entrance after being caught up in a circus parade. Robert Cushman noted in the *Observer*, 'no actress could more efficiently dispense the "fresh air" which Lona declares to be her new gift to her home town', and he was impressed by 'her superb watchfulness'.

Juggling plays and players into the right combination is a necessary skill if one is running a company the size of the RSC, and one that Trevor Nunn was required to exercise towards the end of 1977, when a planned production of Schnitzler's *La Ronde* suddenly foundered over the rights clearance. He and John Barton rapidly read about forty plays, searching for something to suit the group of actors available to them, which included Judi, Michael Pennington, John Woodvine, Bob Peck, Roger Rees and Nickolas Grace. They only found it with *The Way of the World*, though the prospect terrified even such a scholarly director as John Barton. 'I could never understand the plot, but it just happened that it fitted that very strong group. We were all debating and arguing about the plot for weeks in rehearsals; people had different views about what had actually happened in the play, and never quite agreed about it.'

Gillian Lynne was working with him as assistant director. One morning in Floral Street *en route* to the Covent Garden rehearsal room, she saw Judi running towards her calling out urgently, 'Gillie,

Gillie, can you stall for time?' It was already three minutes to ten, so she said, 'Judi darling, what do you mean?'

'Talk to John, do anything, stall for time for about ten minutes.'

'Why?'

'I've been reading this damn thing again and again and again. I just can't get the hang of it, and I've heard there's a child's version, a Lamb's Version with a précis-ed breakdown. I've got to go and get it and read it in the loo.'

So Gillian stalled for time, ever more anxiously as John Barton began to get angry with her for delaying the start, until she saw Judi slip unobtrusively into the rehearsal room.

The cast never did unravel Congreve's elaborately complicated plot, either in rehearsal or performance, but after two years together as a company they revelled in what became virtually an end-of-season romp. Mirabell was Michael Pennington's first leading part with the RSC and he was thrilled to be playing opposite Judi's Millamant. 'She's got a fantastically mercurial swift quality, terrific speed of thought and emotional change. You don't half give your best shot opposite Judi; she raises your game tremendously. If that sounds like a competitive thing it isn't really, but the standard that she sets from the moment she comes on is such that you'd better keep up. I felt very lucky.'

The critics affirmed that he did more than just 'keep up'. John Peter recognised in the *Sunday Times* that from the first sight of Mirabell you knew you were in the presence of a hunter. 'In his famous proposal scene with Millamant he stands, courtly but watchful, head thrust slightly forward, his thoughts clearly focusing both on her body and her dowry. There's not a trace of affection in the air. Judi Dench's Millamant is a dainty preying mantis, sensual but controlled. Under her arch, venomous wit lurks, just perceptibly, a sense of brittle insecurity. Their duet is also a duel. These two performances are among the best I've seen in this theatre.'

Michael Billington was not happy with the production in the *Guardian*, but he also admired the central partnership, although he saw them 'as people genuinely in love'.

For *The Times*, Irving Wardle thought it 'by far the best production I have seen', and drew favourable comparisons with an earlier brilliant exponent of Congreve, especially in the marriage scene, 'the high point of Judi Dench's wonderful Millamant, a piece of high-precision sexual engineering constructed from languishing cries, bubbling laughs, instantaneous mood transitions, always in motion with a train like a matador's cloak, designed at once to exert invincible attraction and evade capture. One masterstroke among many is her final compliance with Mirabell: "I hate your odious provisos." Even Edith Evans delivered this skittishly; Miss Dench lingers caressingly over it.'

J. C. Trewin struck a similar chord in the *Lady*, expressing his astonishment, 'because at last, after more than half a century, we find that Dame Edith Evans does not stand alone: her Millamant had appeared to be unsurpassable, but Judi Dench has re-created the part for our stage ... It is the living Millamant, not for one moment the self-conscious exercise in coquetry we have often had as a substitute.'

After these eulogies it was a disappointment to many that the demands of the new season made it impossible to present more than a couple of dozen performances of *The Way of the World*. There were just enough for John Woodvine to lay one trap for Judi, based on her nickname for his character, Fainall. In his grey costume she said he could not be King Rat, but he was possibly King Mouse. So he cut out some cardboard whiskers and, on his exit, he turned upstage and stuck these cartoon mouse-whiskers up his nose, 'which was very unfair because I was leaving the stage and she had to continue'.

Finty was now five years old and just starting school, so for the next twelve months Judi changed her work pattern by making five television films so she could be home with her daughter much more in the evenings. This proved to be easier with the recordings of *Macbeth* and *The Comedy of Errors* than with the others.

Langrishe Go Down was adapted by Harold Pinter from the novel by Aidan Higgins and directed by David Jones, who had just taken charge of the BBC's Play of the Month series. The script contained nine nude scenes and David Jones had to talk Judi and Michael through all of them, until they were both satisfied that they were integral to the story. Several of them were only seen fleetingly or in long-shot, but one scene with Jeremy Irons as the German student was very full-frontal. The problem for the director was not his star's excessive modesty. 'She had no inhibitions in the nude scenes. When she had to daub the cream off the meringues on her breasts she just broke up, because she said she looked up and saw the five men on the crew all averting their eyes.'

She played Imogen, an Irish girl who has an affair with the ageing perpetual student and is eventually left on her own with his letters; in the early part of the film we see Annette Crosbie, as the elder sister Helen, rereading the letters from her fiancé, killed in the First World War. At the end, as Otto cycles away, Imogen fires a shotgun after him. Helen dies, and Imogen sees a *Times* headline: 'Germany invades Austria'. So the story comes full circle, as we presume the younger sister will lose her love in the new war.

Judi loved being back in Ireland and playing this flirtatious Irish spinster, but not everyone was happy with the ambience. Harold Pinter arrived to play one short scene, some way into the filming and David Jones suddenly saw a different side of Judi. 'She and I and Jeremy and Annette had dinner together every night before Harold arrived. That night, dinner was rather slow in coming and he was getting a bit impatient. Judi said to him, "You're not in London now, Mr Pinter, you'll just have to go at the Irish pace." '

Not that she was content to work at the Irish pace. David Jones found that she was so quick on the uptake that she kept saying to him, 'Don't tell me, I know exactly what you're going to say.' He was deeply impressed by her immediate tuning in to his wavelength. 'It's the closest rapport I've ever had with an actor. Judi has such inner truth and economy of effort. She has an ability to see how she is going during a take and to adjust it accordingly. On film she is always open to the mood of the moment – the sun suddenly coming out, or the rain. It's one of the pieces of work I'm proudest of.'

Judi was proud of it, too, but she refused to let her small daughter watch it then, or ever since on the video she has on her shelves. Nor would she tell Finty why she was forbidden to see it, though several million viewers at the time saw Judi in the buff. This may have surprised her fans, but it was her leading man who got the greatest boost to his career; for Jeremy Irons *Langrishe Go Down* led to him starring opposite Meryl Streep in *The French Lieutenant's Woman*, which also had a screenplay by Harold Pinter.

Judi's next screen role was opposite Richard Briers in Shaw's one-acter *A Village Wooing*, made by Yorkshire Television. Judi was unhappy with her own performance, but her affection for the play brought her back to it on-stage opposite her husband three years later.

Much more challenging, emotionally as well as dramatically, was her 1979 role for the BBC as the foster-mother of a thalidomide child in *On Giant's Shoulders*. Her director was Anthony Simmons, with whom she had first worked on *Four in the Morning*, and Bryan Pringle was playing her husband. They were portraying a real couple, the foster-parents of Terry Wiles, who played himself. He had never acted before and his voice had to be dubbed as it had now broken and he had to appear younger.

She agreed to do it before she had met the family and was feeling very apprehensive when she went up to meet them for the first time at Sandy in Bedfordshire. 'Driving up, we stopped the car and Bryan and I got a huge amount of sweets, because we were both very, very, nervous about it. Of course the moment we met him, this wonderfully cheeky attractive boy of seventeen, with no legs, just feet, and very short arms, he completely charmed us. He adored dancing and the only way I could dance with him was to carry him. Because he was so funny and jokey, I got really fond of him.'

But, despite her affection for him, she found the demands of the part a strain, and the Fens where the film was shot a depressing place to work in. 'I was so upset one morning I just went walking off and Bryan Pringle came marching after me. He said, "You can't care about the whole world." '

Judi knows that this is sensible advice, but she has always found it difficult to act on it, because of her deep compassion for the afflicted – physically and mentally.

I observed this involvement for myself, when one of our all-day conversations happened just after the horrific massacres in Rwanda in 1997, and there was much public concern about the fate of thousands of refugees who had fled into the Congo and then disappeared. When Judi and I broke for lunch I stayed in the room to make a telephone call. As I rejoined her in the kitchen she was listening to *The World at One* on the radio, and turned with shining eyes to say, 'Oh John, they've found those refugees.' It was as if she knew them all personally, and her genuinely heartfelt relief was indicative of that compassion for the troubled and oppressed which can overwhelm her so easily. It gives her an emotional depth which can be heart-wrenching for audiences, but can sometimes be almost too much for her to bear; and Bryan Pringle's sympathetic remonstrance failed to lift her spirits for long.

For her, the most unnerving moment of the filming was not acting with the real Terry, but coming out of her caravan on location the first morning and coming face-to-face with her own character, the real Hazel. But the truthfulness of the playing of the central trio never struck a false note and the transmission had a great impact on the television audience.

Before starting work on a much more light-hearted television series, she returned to Stratford for one of the most difficult plays in the Shakespearean canon – *Cymbeline*. The plot is implausible and has some notoriously tricky scenes where it can seem very difficult to make the audience suspend its disbelief. The part of Imogen offers a challenge that can only be conquered by a great actress; it is noteworthy that Ellen Terry and Peggy Ashcroft both rose to it magnificently. Those who placed Judi in the line of succession to those two great actresses eagerly awaited her assumption of that role.

Judi went to see Dame Peggy before she accepted the part and was not overly encouraged by her advice: 'It's an absolute pig of a part, I never got it right. You'll hate playing it each night, but on the last night you'll regret not being able to play it again.'

David Jones was the director and overall he was less satisfied with his achievement than he had been with *Langrishe Go Down*. The great hurdle is when Imogen wakes beside a headless corpse she mistakenly thinks is that of her love, Posthumus. David Jones argues plausibly that Imogen's speech at that moment is not exactly Shakespeare's best bit of writing:

> A headless man! The garments of Posthumus!
> I know the shape of's leg: this is his hand;
> His foot Mercurial; his Martial thigh;
> The brawns of Hercules: but his Jovial face –
> Murder in heaven? How! 'Tis gone.

Quite apart from the language, Judi was only too conscious of Shaw's comment that Shakespeare had done the most unkind gesture to any actress, having to wake up with a dead body beside her. She was not helped by the construction of the dummy of Bob Peck, whose knees used to bend the wrong way, and giggles uncontrollably at the memory. 'Unless I was very, very careful it used to get a belter.' One of Judi's catch-phrases is, 'Oh! you're early today, butcher!' if someone bumps into the back of her, but it also popped out a few times when she woke up beside the headless corpse in rehearsals.

Christopher Morley designed a predominantly black-and-white set which was quite striking, but he was not well at the time, so the costumes arrived very late. The designs lacked any detail and were just washes of colour and, to the actors' dismay, when the actual costumes arrived that was what they still looked like. Roger Rees said, 'I was in pink, Judi was in beige, Bob Peck was in green. We all looked like those figures unearthed in that Chinese tomb, only in different colours.' Bob Peck thought they looked more like spacemen and he was 'a Jolly Green Giant'.

In desperation, he over-compensated by allowing his performance as Cloten to go 'totally over the top', and he corpsed more with Judi in this play than any other. 'We had confrontations on-stage and there was one dry that went on for ever. We just went on parading up and down laughing at each other, while she kept on hitting me on the chest with a rose.'

Roger Rees was not much more help to her when two large and inadequately secured rocks began moving up and down the stage of their own accord, during one of their scenes together, provoking some unrehearsed double-takes from Imogen and Posthumus.

Her brother Jeffery was now playing her father Cymbeline and he thought it was a much less successful production than the previous one at Stratford in which he had also appeared, with Sebastian Shaw in the title role, and Vanessa Redgrave as Imogen.

The critics did not much like the production, but even those who were not admirers of the play's construction thought it was saved by some incomparable verse. 'This verse is spoken nobly by Jeffery Dench (Cymbeline), Judi Dench (Imogen) and Roger Rees (Posthumus)', wrote Francis King in the *Sunday Telegraph* and he even approved of Bob Peck's over-the-top performance as the oafish Cloten, 'with the broad emphasis of an actor sensing – in this case rightly – that only thus can he galvanise the audience out of incipient torpor'.

Michael Billington's resistance to the production in the *Guardian* was also overcome by some of the performances, especially the 'constant mercurial humour' of Judi's Imogen, 'which belongs right up there with Ashcroft and Redgrave ... Blonde, impassioned and comely, Miss Dench is a divine Imogen.'

J. C. Trewin agreed with him in the *Lady*: 'At Stratford now we have, in Judi Dench, a beautiful and winning Imogen. She conquered me so surely at the première that, for an hour or two, I was in danger of imagining the general production to be better than it is.'

More work is usually put into a production if it misfires at the opening, but David Jones had to leave immediately afterwards to go and work in America. Judi made it very plain to him that she could not understand why he wanted to do that, and leave what was for her the centre of the theatrical world. As it happened, this play was her own last appearance at Stratford, though there were a few more non-Shakespearean plays to come at the RSC's London end.

Now she turned her attention to the Thames Television production of *Love in a Cold Climate*, adapted from Nancy Mitford's novel by Simon Raven and directed by Donald McWhinnie. This had several bonuses for Judi – not only was Michael in it with her, but so were her great friends Job Stewart and John Moffatt, in a strong cast that also included Michael Aldridge, Vivian Pickles, Adrienne Corri, Patience Collier, Lucy Gutteridge and Jean-Pierre Cassel. The filming was most uncharacteristically relaxed for the actors, since it was scheduled during the long union dispute between ITV and the ACTT. While there was a work-to-rule the cast were not called until about 11 a.m. and the wrap was called at about 4 p.m., as the crew had to allow time for travelling to and from base within normal working hours. When the dispute escalated into an all-out strike, the cast were all paid a retainer until shooting could be resumed.

Somehow none of this affected the continuity of performance when it was finally screened. The rehearsals were astonishingly brief and frequently ended after only about an hour and a half, as the director said he did not want them to get stale. When they said, 'Donald, don't you want to do it again?' he replied, 'No, I've cast it perfectly, why bother to go on?' Job Stewart claimed the record for the shortest rehearsal of all – of less than fifteen minutes before he was sent home.

Some of the most enjoyable times were when they did the advance filming of the exterior scenes, one of which was in the actual Mitford country, near the church where Nancy Mitford is buried. Many of the locals had known the family, and the originals on whom she based her characters, and came to watch. One formidable lady approached Judi and asked, 'What are you playing?'

'I'm playing Sadie, Lady Alconleigh.'

'Oh yes, I knew her very well. She was very, very tall and very, very pretty, but I suppose you'll do it with acting!'

Judi could hardly wait to tell the others of this encounter. The actors got so inside the characters and thirties period atmosphere that when John Moffatt arrived at the Cheltenham hotel he looked down from his window to see the others sitting outside, just to check if they had changed into formal evening dress for dinner.

As several of them were being driven to a location in costume in a pale grey vintage Daimler, by a chauffeur in a pale grey uniform, Judi felt that 'people must have thought they'd seen a ghost, as we were all in these beautiful thirties clothes, without a camera in sight'.

Because of all the union problems, the six episodes took ten months before everything was safely in the can. The series was a success not just in Britain, but also abroad, and it tickled Judi's sense of humour that the very first country to buy *Love in a Cold Climate* was Iceland.

1980 was the centenary of Sean O'Casey's birth and to mark it Trevor Nunn decided to present one of his masterpieces, *Juno and the Paycock*, set in 1924, just after the end of the Irish civil war. Later a rumour gained currency in the company that there might be a less respectful secondary motivation for the director's choice. This was that Terry Hands bet him that he could not direct a major classic on a big stage and do it naturalistically; that Trevor accepted the bet and decided to prove it with this play.

His first task was to recruit Judi and she agreed deceptively easily when he broached the idea: 'I've just read it again and I was so bowled over by it that I want to do it, and you should play Juno.'

The following day Judi came to him and said, 'Oh, that play you were talking about?'

'*Juno and the Paycock?*'

'Yes, that one, yes I'll do that, wonderful, thank you, goodbye.'

Three months later everyone assembled to talk about the play and read some passages of it for the first time. Judi tugged at Trevor Nunn's sleeve: 'You've made a terrible mistake.'

'What are you talking about?'

'Well, I read this last night. She's middle-aged, this woman!'

'Judi, what are you talking about? You read it before.'

'Well no, I trusted you completely, but I mean she's older than I am.'

'I know she's a bit older than you are, but that's the challenge.'

'Are you sure you don't want to change your mind now, because honestly I really understand, I shouldn't have agreed.'

More worrying for Judi was the fact that all the rest of the cast were Irish and, despite her mother's ancestry and her own recent portrayal of an Irishwoman in *Langrishe Go Down*, she was self-conscious about attempting an Irish brogue.

But she was not half as terrified as Dearbhla Molloy was of playing her daughter, until their first meeting in the ladies' loo just before rehearsals started. 'The first thing she said was that she absolutely hated the first day of rehearsal, and wasn't it awful. It was such a relief to hear that somebody like Judi Dench could be nervous of a first day of rehearsals.'

The two of them became very close during the rehearsal process, and soon Dearbhla was emboldened enough to say to Judi, who was still struggling for the absolutely correct accent, 'You're going to have to say it louder', and then she suddenly captured the right nasal intonation. Trevor Nunn thought that 'she was faultless as far as the idiom was concerned'.

He made them all undertake a research project into different aspects of the background of the play and produce a paper to read to the rest of the company. Judi's subject was the tenement buildings in Dublin at that time; Dearbhla's was women in trades unions in Ireland; Norman Rodway had to look at the value of money then; John Rogan at music-hall entertainment; and Gerard Murphy really went to town on the historical situation to date, relating the 1924 situation to the existing troubles and violence. He delivered quite the longest paper and talked for about two hours. Not everyone took this all-day seminar so seriously, but Dearbhla Molloy thought in retrospect that it was a brilliant idea, 'because it consolidated the context from which we all drew our characters and our background'.

Judi had never done anything quite like this before, but she warmed to the task like the others. 'We were permanently on the phone to Dublin.' Some of the advice was much nearer to hand. Marie Kean was playing Mrs Tancred this time, but had played Juno previously and was a great expert on O'Casey and his beliefs, so there were long discussions between as well as during rehearsals. In fact, according to Trevor Nunn, 'We had probably more talk about the circumstances and the background, more ratio of talk to rehearsal than anything else that I've done. But for all the political content of the play, the reason we adored it was for the humour.'

Norman Rodway was playing Juno's husband, the work-shy Captain Boyle, and was delighted to be working with Judi again, though he chided her in mock-aggravation, 'You're a bloody outrage, because you don't appear to have done any homework. You just learn it at rehearsal, whereas I have to go home and sweat over it', echoing the complaint of Ian McKellen and other of her leading men who envied her being such a phenomenally quick study.

In his search for naturalism the director put up four walls around them in rehearsal; at the first main dress rehearsal on-stage at the Aldwych he made them play it with the curtain down to act as the fourth wall, and repeated that after several previews, to pull the actors back into the very intimate relationship he was after. It was this technique which convinced them all about the bet, though Trevor Nunn says regretfully that the story is quite apocryphal, 'but it takes its place alongside many more'.

On the first night he manipulated them in a way that only a director with the utmost confidence in his cast would dare to try. He went to Dearbhla Molloy's dressing-room and said, 'I want you to do something to Charlie Bentham that's totally unexpected, and I don't want you to tell him that you're going to do it, or anybody on-stage that you're going to do it. I want it to be something that tells us Mary has gone overboard here, that she's stepped outside an imaginary boundary.' She thought, 'Oh my God!' She only found out afterwards that he had gone to each member of the cast and given them a similar personal note. As she says, 'It could have been a complete disaster, but what sheer chutzpah to do that. What it produced were all these little ping! ping! pings! of actors' reactions going off all over the stage on the first night. It was marvellous.'

It left all the critics gasping in admiration. Michael Billington hailed it in the *Guardian* as a magnificent production, 'a glowing realisation of a play steeped in a poetic, humorous despair'. He spotted the naturalism in the relationship between Norman Rodway's Paycock and John Rogan's Joxer, and that of mother and daughter. 'Judi Dench's Juno is a wonderful blend of exhaustion and despair. Tiny gestures like a cynical lift of the eyes when the Captain starts his seafaring nonsense speak volumes; yet there is also in the very way she plumps the cushions, stokes the fire, or makes the breakfast the suggestion of a woman who finds what she can in domestic routine.'

Robert Cushman also zeroed in on her 'immense practicality' in the *Observer*. 'As for her last familiar lament, I doubt any other actress could re-think or re-phrase it to greater effect. It is a reprise, remember, and Marie Kean who does it the first time is a hard act to follow. Between them they give the play some of the grandeur of *The Trojan Women*.'

J. C. Trewin though it 'a superb night' in the *Illustrated London News*, and that Judi gave 'the most telling performance of the part in my memory . . . In the past, famous Irish actresses I remember have set Juno's speech apart, affectingly, it is true, but making of it something inevitably theatrical. Judi Dench did not try to magnify a lament that rose from the heart of sorrow; and before then she had flashed up Juno with consistently affectionate truth.'

The other notices sang variants of this tune, but Trevor Nunn had no intention of letting his cast rest on their laurels. The day after the opening he took Judi to lunch at the Café au Jardin in Covent Garden and told her, 'We can celebrate just today, then we've got to forget it, and start getting it better.' Forgetting the chorus of acclaim was easier said than done, as over the next few months Judi swept the board of Best Actress Awards for Juno, from the Society of West End Theatres, the *Evening Standard*, *Plays and Players* magazine and the Variety Club.

The realism of Judi's performance was built on a mass of tiny details. At one point her daughter Mary came on in a new frock to sit on the arm of her mother's chair and, as they were talking, Judi fixed the collar of Dearbhla's frock in a natural maternal gesture. One night Bryan Murray, who was playing Mary's suitor Charlie Bentham, leant over and did something to her frock before Judi did it. Dearbhla wondered how Judi would react. 'When we came off she went up to him and said, "Bryan, that's my piece of business, which I have set up and have been doing for several days now, and you mustn't steal it." She didn't say any more and she was extremely nice about it. She didn't give him a lecture on why he shouldn't do it; but she was perfectly firm about it, and there was no argument. He didn't do it again. She hides her strength quite a lot, but in that tiny little example I suddenly saw this woman who is immensely powerful, who is very comfortable with her own strength, and only uses it when necessary.'

She would need all the strength she could muster to cope with the trials and tribulations of her next venture – the Trevor Nunn/Gillian Lynne production of Andrew Lloyd-Webber's new musical, *Cats*.

thirteen

1980–83

From *Cats* to *Year of the Cat*

Judi has made it a cardinal policy to try to move from a success in one dramatic form to a new challenge as different as possible from the last. Sometimes a chance remark has triggered the next offer. While she was still struggling in the early rehearsals to get Juno right, she sighed to Trevor Nunn, 'Oh why can't I play some mangy old cat in this thing you're doing?'

'This thing' was a musical he was planning with Andrew Lloyd-Webber based on T. S. Eliot's poems, *Old Possum's Book of Practical Cats*. After their successes together, particularly in *The Comedy of Errors*, this was hardly a request that the director was likely to turn down and he quickly offered her the two parts of the Gumbie Cat and Grizabella. Her leading man, or rather cat, was Brian Blessed.

Gillian Lynne was the choreographer and she developed some very demanding song and dance numbers. Most of the rest of the cast were dancers who could also sing, rather than the other way about, and in the early rehearsals Gillian was always calling out, 'Brian and Judi, don't do this.' As the Gumbie Cat, Judi had a dance number with the ballet dancer Wayne Sleep; at the end of one morning's rehearsal there was suddenly a crack like a pistol shot and Judi felt a searing stab of pain. 'It's just like a cart-horse kicking you in the back of the leg. Wayne Sleep just picked me up and carried me off. I don't know how he did it.'

The company manager, Roger Bruce, took her to the Remedial Dance Clinic to see Charlotte Arnold, who told her she had snapped her Achilles tendon. She had a bath at home with some difficulty. Then Roger drove her to see the surgeon Justin Howse, who took one look at her leg and said, 'You must come in tomorrow and have it operated on.'

When she asked how long she would have to be out of rehearsals he said, 'Six weeks.' Michael was away filming abroad, and she gave instructions that when he telephoned he was not to be told until after the operation. She was kept in the Fitzroy Nuffield Clinic in Bryanston Square for two weeks, where she was visited by Trevor Nunn and Andrew Lloyd-Webber. They said, 'We'll delay the opening. You obviously can't play the Gumbie Cat, but you can still play Grizabella, because she's meant to be clapped-out, so it doesn't matter.'

By the time she rejoined rehearsals, they had been moved into the New London Theatre and the set was represented by ramps. Judi brushed up her song with Trevor the day before but, when Gillian Lynne saw her standing with her crutches at the end of the ramps, she said in alarm, 'Trevor, please, don't let Judi go up that ramp. They're hard for the kids with all their swift-moving dexterity; it will be so hard for her. I think it's too dangerous.'

He said, 'No, no, she wants to do it.'

Judi attempted to walk up the ramp, but then fell off, with her crutches clattering behind her. She went to her dressing-room, called a taxi and went home to Hampstead, rang up and said, 'Trevor, we have to be practical, there's no way I can do this.'

So it was recast, and Elaine Paige took over as Grizabella. Michael was home briefly, but had to return to Paris to continue working on the film *Enigma*, whose director, Jeannot Szwarc, said to him, 'I think we ought to get Judi out of England for the opening of *Cats*. I don't think she should be around for that razzamatazz.' So she and Finty flew over to join Michael for a week or so, where she had to change the dressing on her leg every day. It was continuing to trouble her, so she was dismayed at the airport on her return to find that all the moving walkways had stopped and everyone had to walk long distances; fortunately another passenger spotted her distress and carried her suitcase for her.

Her leg began to fester, so she went to see Justin Howse, who said, 'Oh, something terrible's happening. I'll have to re-operate on it.' She went into the Nightingale Clinic in Lisson Grove for the operation, but the following day when the surgeon examined her wound, it had burst and all the pus had drained out of it. He said, 'In fact I'm not going to have to operate at all. Something extraordinary has happened to it. What you will have to do, though, is just lie there.' Which she did for a month and a day.

This unaccustomed inactivity was a great strain for her, 'and it was then I realised how tiring it is to lie in bed'. She had a stream of visitors and she read a lot, but the unexpected life-saver was the All England Tennis Championships on television. 'I was never interested in Wimbledon before, but that saved my life, and I've always loved it ever since.'

The news of Judi's injury and withdrawal from *Cats* spread quickly and when Hal Prince heard he rang the hospital from America. 'I'll tell you exactly what you're going to do after you come out of there. You and Finty and Mike are going to come and join us at our house in Majorca. We're going to be there for the summer. Come and have a holiday.' Because of their work schedules Michael and Judi had never had a summer holiday before then, but ever since they have insisted on doing so, 'because we realised that it's absolutely essential, to get the batteries going again'.

When they arrived to stay with Hal and Judy Prince there was another house-guest swimming in the pool, who was introduced just as Steve. Later he was playing the piano and Michael suddenly whispered to Judi, 'Hello, you know who Steve is, don't you?' It was Stephen Sondheim. They met up again fifteen years later when she starred in his show *A Little Night Music*.

By the time they returned from Majorca, *Cats* had established itself as a smash hit. Judi finally went to see it on 9 September 1981. She thought it was wonderful, and after all she had been through she found she could now be quite philosophical about it. 'I thought I was going to find watching it really awful, but I didn't have any regrets at all.'

She eased herself back into work with a show that was much less physically demanding. The little ninety-four-seater New End Theatre in Hampstead asked Michael and Judi if they would do a two-hander to help to keep it open, so she rang up Frank Hauser to ask his advice. He knew she had done *A Village Wooing* on television and he suggested they combine that with a series of readings from the year in which Shaw wrote the play – 1933. He wished afterwards that he had chosen Chekhov's *The Bear* for the other part of the double-bill instead, as his compilation was savaged by several of the critics. A short note in the *Observer* said tersely 'this was pasted up by Frank Hauser, and all three should be ashamed of themselves'. The merits of the play were more appreciated, 'especially when directed (as Frank Hauser does here) with style and precision', as Anthony Masters put it in *The Times*. Michael Coveney saw the same quality in the *Financial Times*: 'Dench and Williams find a wonderful pace in the lines and chart with fine precision the shifts in the relationship.'

In conversation with their director they both insisted on more than one occasion that, though they loved playing together, they were not a double-act – casting one of them did not mean having to cast the other as well. However, the public were about to see them teaming up more over the next four years than in any period before or since.

The first vehicle was a new and controversial departure for both of them – a television situation comedy. An earlier approach to Judi had met with the response, 'No, I don't think a sitcom is really me.' But one of the qualities that propelled Humphrey Barclay to the position of Head of Comedy at London Weekend Television was persistence. Bob Larbey had previously written the scripts for *Please Sir* and *The Good Life* with John Esmonde, before he came up with his first solo idea about middle-aged people who are terribly shy and fall in love. He took it to Humphrey Barclay, who said at once, 'I'll commission that.' When he read the first script he thought of Michael Williams to play Mike and said to Bob Larbey, 'In a dream-world, who would you like to play Laura?' Bob said, 'Judi Dench', and laughed. But Humphrey said, 'Well, we can send her a script. She can only say No.' He sent it via her agent and, to their astonished delight, Judi's response was, 'Well, I think it's rather nice and I think I might like to do it, but is there any chance that Michael could do the other part?'

She said she was frightened of the form, with a studio audience, so she would have to have a director she knew and trusted. 'What about Jimmy Cellan-Jones?' The latter agreed, provided it was an actress he approved of, saying, 'What about Judi Dench?' The ease with which all these components fell into place seemed a good augury, and so it proved. Susan Penhaligon was cast as Laura's younger married sister, with Richard Warwick as her husband.

The one early hiccup was known only to the writer, Bob Larbey. 'When Judi agreed, I then couldn't write for three weeks, the only time I've ever had writer's block, because it was Judi Dench. I just sat at home and froze.' Fortunately, he recovered his creative faculties.

The delight at LWT was not initially shared at the RSC. Trevor Nunn tried to dissuade Judi and Michael from doing it, as he did not believe TV sitcoms were quite the thing for classical actors from his company. But by now Judi was adamant. 'I think it's our business to do as many things as we can. My God, it teaches you something – people shouldn't demean situation comedy, because it's so difficult. You only get one go at it and you've got to make people laugh; it's very, very hard.'

The hardest thing for Judi was not the usual one of playing to the camera and the viewer at home whilst simultaneously responding to the laughter from the studio audience, but the prior requirement of having to come out as herself and say a few words to that studio audience before the recording started. She hated having to do that and still does, but accepts that it is something that has to be done, and it is only her fellow-actors who see her doubled up backstage groaning, 'Why are we doing this?' Michael would reply, 'The money, Jude, the money.' Her director used to come out with them, and observed how she then carried it off with total command. 'She would come on and say one sentence to introduce herself and they would be at her feet. We all used to do a little bow and go off, and I once did an imitation of hers, a weird amusing curtsy; then she imitated mine, and it was so cruelly funny I never did it again.' One of his other bright ideas was more successful, when he suggested that Judi sang the title song over the opening credits, from the original Jerome Kern number 'A Fine Romance'. The graphics on the credits featured, appropriately, a single rose. At about this time Michael had the inspiration for a birthday present of ordering a single rose to be delivered to Judi every Friday. At the end of a year he thought it would seem churlish to say, 'Well, that's it', so the Friday ritual has carried on now for about twenty years.

Most television companies hire a professional warm-up artiste for the studio audience, but Humphrey Barclay was so anxious to create the right atmosphere for this show that he always did the warm-up himself. He was impressed by how Judi took liberties with the conventions from the beginning. 'In the very first episode, when she and Mike met at a little drinks party given by her sister, Laura was handing round little sausages on sticks and she suddenly offered one to the camera and moved swiftly on, which broke all the rules. Jimmy said, "Keep it in", and I said, "Yes, lovely, let's keep it in." Normally you'd say, "Well, yes, if you're going to do that as a stylistic thing we must do it quite often in the series." But she only did it that once, a piece of impishness, probably because she wanted the camera crew to have as much fun as everybody else.'

They obviously did, because the director managed to retain the same crew throughout each of the eventual four series. The original plan was just to do six programmes but, before the end of the first run, Humphrey went to the pub with everyone in the lunch break and said, 'We're having a good time, aren't we? Shouldn't we be thinking about doing some more of these, what about that?' They all agreed, though Judi told him later that she was amazed that the actors should be consulted about such a decision.

The series was an instant success from the moment it hit the screen. The *Stage* predicted 'in the knowledge that the first episode can too often prove unreliable, I shall be very surprised if *A Fine Romance* does not prove to be the comedy show of 1981.' By the end of the first series Bill Grundy was saying in the *Guardian*, 'Mr Williams and Miss Dench have been perfection in this very amusing series, helped by a lovely script from Bill Larbey, and excellent direction by James Cellan-Jones, never the least bit afraid of playing a pause for all it was worth.' Philip Purser in the *Sunday Telegraph* put his finger on why '*A Fine Romance* is staying up very well. It is good to see solid actors and a solid drama director applying themselves to a comedy serial without either patronising the form or thinking they have to change their standards.'

Judi undertook this as just another acting job and was amazed by the audience response, the recognition in the street, and having champagne brought to her and Michael on an aeroplane; she said she didn't know things like that happened to television celebrities. Many of her new audience were quite unaware of her theatre experience and at one recording, when a group of American college students were in the studio, one of them asked, 'Oh Miss Dench, do you ever get a chance to do any classical theatre?' Judi replied unblushingly, 'Oh yes, once or twice.'

At the end of the first thirteen episodes, James Cellan-Jones declined to direct any more, thinking that there was nothing left to say about this relationship, and Don Leaver took over. It was another thirteen episodes before the rest of the team arrived at the same conclusion. Humphrey Barclay asked the writer, 'Does it end when they go to bed together?' Bob Larbey said, 'No, no, that only complicates things; it finishes when he says to her, "I love you."' So in the final episode Mike presented Laura with a huge floral tribute, with its back to the camera. Judi read the message out with a question mark: 'I ove You?' The reverse angle showed that the L had fallen off, which ended the series on a huge laugh.

It was not just the fourteen million viewers who were reluctant to see it go. Bob Larbey received a note from John Birt, LWT's Director of Programmes, which simply said, 'I hanker after another series of *A Fine Romance*.' His reply was even more succinct – 'I don't.' When John Birt pressed them all to do more, Judi made a counter-proposal: 'We said we wouldn't do more, but why didn't we make a feature-length film of it? No, that wasn't pursued.'

Her permanent reminders of the series are the two BAFTA Awards she won for her performance as Laura. In the years since it ended, their fans have frequently asked Judi and Michael when they are going to do *A Fine Romance* again, touching proof of how the characters were taken to people's hearts, but the line has been firmly drawn under it; although Judi was quick to work with both Humphrey Barclay and Bob Larbey again when the opportunity was offered.

Her happy memories of that show are only overcast by one wrenching bereavement which occurred during the run. Her mother's faculties began to fail in her last years – her sight went, and she had trouble with her legs, though even with those disabilities she still struggled in on the bus from Charlecote to Stratford to do the shopping. But her indomitable spirit began to give up in February 1983. Just before a recording at LWT Judi received a call from Warwickshire to say that her mother had gone into a coma. Somehow she got through the show and immediately afterwards Michael drove her up to Charlecote. Judi stayed with her to the end, which came on 20 February, and slept in the same bedroom the night before she died. Both her brothers were there, and her close friends rallied round. Barbara Leigh-Hunt was deeply fond of Olave and did her best to help Judi through her grief: 'Even by the time of the funeral she was still distraught; she came into church and she couldn't speak, she was awash.' Judi was also appearing at the National Theatre at this time, and was much comforted by the presence of her friend Susie Bodmer who, without being asked, just came and sat in her dressing-room night after night, to try and keep her from dwelling on her bereavement.

Michael says Judi grieved terribly at her mother's death and that she always tried not to think about mortality. 'Of course the older you get, the more you think about your mortality. Jude wants everything to stay as it is today; she doesn't want to think about tomorrow, or yesterday; today is the way it's always got to be.' It is one of the things that drives her to work so hard. Many people say we should always live each day as it if it might be the last, but Judi is one of the few who actually behaves as if it could be. According to Michael, 'Jude just doesn't want to know about things like wills, or pension funds.'

The early eighties were particularly busy for her and she became especially visible on the small screen. The first episode of *A Fine Romance* was shown on ITV just after the BBC transmitted *The Cherry Orchard*, directed by Richard Eyre. It was nearly twenty years since Judi had played Anya in her debut with the RSC; now she took on Ranevskaya, which Peggy Ashcroft had played in the earlier production. She said that even after two decades, 'I could hear Peg all the time; I still can hear Peg in it.'

Richard Eyre had watched Judi acting at Nottingham, and over the years since had often talked to her about the possibility of working together, but this was the first time he managed it. Anna Massey, playing Carlotta, watched them adjusting to each other. 'At the read-through Richard gave a speech, and Judi was all ready to go. The speech was quite long, about the Russian scene, and she was quite nervous. It was like being held in reins. You could see somebody just ready to fly, but then she flew.'

The director very quickly found that she was unlike some other actors he knew who liked to talk everything out in the rehearsal; she trusted her instinct about the character. 'We were filming the scene in the second act when Ranevskaya is sitting with Lopakhin, who is hopelessly in love with her and she's perfectly aware of it. He's hugely sexually and romantically attracted to her, and has been since he was a child. Billy Paterson was playing him beautifully and she said to me just as we were about to film her reaction, "She's a terrible old tart, isn't she?" What she meant was that this woman is sexually experienced; she really knows men and is able to tie them up in knots.'

Judi quoted to him, as she has to many people, the verdict on her very first screen test – 'Miss Dench, you have every single thing wrong with your face' – but that early judgement does not chime with his own experience. 'She's radiantly beautiful on-stage, and on screen that sort of luminosity probably didn't lend itself to the camera when young; but there is a photograph of her in *The Cherry Orchard* which I think is just heart-stoppingly beautiful. You should put that in your book.'

The question of whether the camera 'loved her', as the film world puts it, was also analysed by the director of her next television film in 1980, Stephen Frears. 'I suppose that someone like Garbo had some translucence in her skin, or some opaque quality, so that she could have been thinking of anything and it always looked rather interesting. Judi just seemed to be very, very alive, and to have an extraordinary interior life going on. There are parts of *Going Gently* where she was mesmerising to watch. If you could get the light in the right places, she was absolutely dazzling. But I wouldn't say that's because the camera loves her, I would just say it's because she's such a great actress. I don't know what she was like when she was young, but by the time I met her the feelings came from so deep inside her that she was fantastic.'

The story of *Going Gently* was about two terminally-ill cancer patients in the same ward, a salesman and an irascible professor, looked after by Judi as Sister Scarli. The young directors from the Royal Court Theatre, including Stephen Frears, had always had a deep resistance to using anyone from the RSC, but he had been very impressed with her performance in *On Giant's Shoulders* and now ironically found it much easier to cast her than either of the two men. One early thought had been Trevor Howard, but eventually he cast Norman Wisdom as the salesman and Fulton Mackay as the professor.

It was shot in a disused children's hospital just up the road from the BBC's Ealing Studios. Slightly to his surprise the director found it a very easy shoot. He found that the emphasis shifted in performance so that Sister Scarli became the emotional centre of the relationship between the three central characters. Like his predecessors, Stephen was impressed by Judi's ability to deliver an instant response. 'She would sleep a lot, until I woke her up and say, "It's time to do the take", and she'd just go and do it. There was no evidence that she'd even read the script before. I'd explain the continuity of what went before and after and she'd just do it. I've never met anyone else like that, except for John Hurt, completely reliant on their instincts. She was word-perfect, and very skilful with the text.'

Unfortunately she was not quite so skilful with the needle, even though she had taken advice from her nursing friend Susie Bodmer. 'I did a terrible thing to Norman. I had to give him an injection and I missed the wadding, and stuck the needle into him. I don't know who was the most frightened, him or me.'

The dramatic situation could have been simply depressing, but the truthfulness of the playing and the direction made *Going Gently* both wryly amusing and emotionally uplifting.

One member of the television audience who found it deeply affecting was the writer and director David Hare, who thought it was Judi's best film performance, until he saw her in *Mrs Brown* in 1997. 'I was in floods of tears and I couldn't work out why; although it's the men that are dying, it's Judi who makes you cry. She makes the bed after one of them has died and I don't know any other actress who could seem to be doing so little and yet be able to contain within her expression, her manner, her body, the whole experience of losing this man.'

When he watched that he had no idea that he was shortly to work with her for the first time. He had written a film script entitled *Saigon – Year of the Cat*, about the last days before the American evacuation of that city, which he sold to Thames Television. It was technically ambitious and turned out to be a logistical and creative nightmare; almost David Hare's only happy memory of that production was the experience of working with Judi, who played Barbara, an English employee in a bank who has an affair with an American CIA agent. That casting took some time to settle. Thames began by working through what the author thought was 'a ridiculous list of people who were going to play it; Julie Andrews was going to play it at one stage'. But when Stephen Frears came on board as director there was no question of who would play Barbara; after *Going Gently* he was, in David Hare's words, 'completely artistically in love with her'.

But if ever there was a project in which troubles came, not in single spies but in battalions, it was this one. After the Thames proposal that Vietnam should be recreated in Twickenham was vetoed, the film recce in Bangkok was held up when Stephen Frears caught pneumonia. When the actual shooting began, he discovered to his horror that the daily crewing rosters were being organised from London and, when all the Thames crews in England went on strike, they called out the Bangkok crew as well. Stephen used to watch his people on the telephone to London every evening trying to sort out the next day's arrangements.

As if that were not enough to contend with behind the camera, a major confrontation threatened what was supposed to be happening in front of it. The CIA agent who becomes Barbara's lover was played by Frederic Forrest, who had worked with Marlon Brando on another fraught shoot in *Apocalypse Now*. Brando told him never to say the lines he was given, that he must make up his own lines on the spot, as he did in that movie.

That may be the way to cope with unspeakable scripts from inferior screenwriters, but this approach was unlikely to appeal to a writer of David Hare's distinction. 'He showed me his copy of the script, in which he'd copied out my lines on one side of the page, and then he said, "Now here on the other side is what I'm intending to say." So the gauntlet was thrown down from the first day.'

His propensity to improvise bizarrely when the camera was rolling drove everyone to despair. At his first meeting with Barbara he suddenly said, 'Is that a gun in your pocket, or are you just pleased to see me?' which made absolutely no sense in this context at all. While director and writer were tearing their hair out over their American star, Judi was caught in the crossfire, but managed to retain her composure, saying patiently, 'Yes, Freddie, what are you trying to do? What are you trying to express?'

The eight-week shoot in Bangkok staggered from one crisis to another. The Thai army had promised to cooperate with the filmmakers, but consistently failed to turn up when required. The evacuation by helicopter for the climactic scene at the end frayed a lot of nerves, a tension from which the director tried to shield Judi. 'The day before we took off in the Chinook, there had been a huge air disaster between two Chinooks on that airfield, and Stephen hid the newspapers from me. I would in fact have taken comfort from that. I mean, if it's going to happen one day, it's not going to happen the next, is it?'

But there was always something else that happened the next day. As David Hare shudders, 'The whole thing was like every film nightmare you've ever lived through, and then we shut the film down half-finished.'

This was caused by a strike about sound technicians, and since it would have been prohibitively expensive to suspend shooting in Bangkok indefinitely, the Thames management called the union bluff, closed the film down and called everyone home. It was not completed until nine months later, with Shepperton Studios and Battersea Park standing in for Vietnam, as Thames had originally wanted. It was so ingeniously shot that it is impossible to tell in the finished film which scenes were shot later, though the leading actors had to go and lie on sunbeds to get brown again for their love scenes.

It is a tribute to the professionalism and sheer determination of the principal players in this whole horrific saga that the end result was so good; and the effort of surmounting all these obstacles forged a close bond in particular between the three Britons. Stephen Frears was appreciative, if surprised, that Judi never went to see the daily screening of the previous day's rushes: 'The truth is, she just decided to trust me for the two films we made together, which was very nice of her.'

For David Hare, this first experience of Judi's strength under pressure was to bear more fruit later on. 'It could not have been a more difficult shoot. It would have tried anybody and it showed her to be such an extraordinarily good character, as well as a wonderful actress, and she's terrific in the film. So we inevitably got to know each other rather well under those circumstances.'

Both the men were aware that Judi was also very homesick in Bangkok and deeply missed her family, so it was arranged for Finty to be brought out for the last couple of weeks to be with her mother, which helped.

There were fewer jokes on this location than usual with Judi, but one running gag was when they would be going to the town of

Phuket. This, together with the new problems each day, inspired Judi to embroider a cushion for David with 'Fuck 'em' all over it, in tiny stitching so his mother would not notice. She did another one for Stephen, though his message was embroidered in very large letters. Both cushions remain prized possessions.

The struggle for *Saigon – Year of the Cat* to succeed continued right up to its eventual transmission in 1982. Against it the BBC scheduled Alan Bennett's film about Guy Burgess, *An Englishman Abroad*, with Alan Bates and Coral Browne, directed by John Schlesinger. Since Alan Bennett's previous films had been directed by Stephen Frears, who turned this one down to direct the Hare script, the competition between the two dramas had an additional personal edge. The honours broke about even – ITV pulled a bigger audience, with around seven million, but the BBC offering garnered the better reviews. Fortunately the burgeoning number of domestic video recorders meant that connoisseurs of good writing, good acting and good direction could catch both broadcasts.

By now the great viewing public had begun to regard Judi as a television actress, but she had no intention of abandoning the stage, and in 1982 accepted Peter Hall's invitation to join the National Theatre, to play a part which sent a great frisson of surprise through her theatre-going supporters.

fourteen

1982–84

From *The Importance of Being
Earnest* to *Pack of Lies*

When Peter Hall asked Judi to play Lady Bracknell in *The Importance
of Being Earnest*, she agreed with considerable qualms. These were
increased when Peggy Ashcroft and George Rylands went round to
see her in Hampstead and both of them said, 'You mustn't do that.
That would be a dreadful mistake.'

Edith Evans had left such an indelible impression on the role,
from her first appearance in it in John Gielgud's brilliant 1939 stage
production, through the Anthony Asquith film in 1951, to her final
portrayal in 1960 on CBS Television, that many people had come to
accept her portrayal as definitive and to believe that the character
could only be played as a formidable old matriarch.

But Peter Hall always begins afresh, with the actual text, and
although Judi feared that she was too young he never accepted that
for a moment. 'Lady Bracknell is after all the mother of that young
girl, and the point is that she's in her early forties, and Judi reclaimed
the part in some ways. She was very, very good. I really felt that Lady
Bracknell was a mercantile agent, out for the best marriage.'

Judi took some reassuring in the early rehearsals and for the first
couple of weeks found it impossible to get hold of the character. She
kept saying, 'I can't do this', until the director finally put his foot
down and commanded, 'Just don't say that again, just get on and do
it.'

True to her new resolve to take a summer holiday, she asked Peter
Hall for two weeks off. He said that was no problem, 'as you're not
in Act II we'll set Act I and Act III, and then when I do Act II for
two weeks, you can go off to Scotland.'

He was only trying to accommodate her need for a holiday, but the break actually provided the sudden inspiration which had failed to come in the rehearsal room. 'I had *no idea* how to play it, no idea at all. We took the car up to Scotland and stopped at Inveraray for lunch on the way up. I looked at that Castle and I thought, "I know exactly how to play her. I'll play her like Margaret, Duchess of Argyll, with that very pale face, dark hair, and red mouth." I never knew her, but I thought there's also a quality in Lady Bracknell that could be quite predatory. She's so awful about Lord Bracknell, so I thought she was always dying to get round to Half Moon Street, to have her hand on Algy's knee.'

When Judi returned to rehearsals it was quickly apparent to everyone that she had found the missing key to her interpretation while she was away. Martin Jarvis was playing Jack Worthing and he noticed that, whereas before she had hardly projected at all, now 'she suddenly started to move into a gear that was not hugely loud, but a brilliant, cunning, witty, charming, and above all sexy approach, which came out early on in her relationship with her nephew Algy, which I'd never seen before. It was a completely new and original approach.'

A strong, well-balanced cast also included Nigel Havers as Algy, Zoë Wanamaker and Elizabeth Garvie as Gwendolen and Cecily, with Paul Rogers and Anna Massey as Chasuble and Miss Prism. The teamwork became very polished, despite the handicap of playing on what Martin Jarvis described as 'an atrocious, blue, shiny, forty-five-degree set', and Paul Rogers even more vehemently as 'that bloody hill. It was a swine, and anything that went wrong with that production I would blame on that.' The actors' problems with John Bury's set were successfully concealed from the critics, who only gave it a passing mention.

Judi was more concerned about his costume design for Lady Bracknell, 'that I thought was too dour, and too earthy, so I suggested we had a change of hat. I had a more coquettish one made, with a whole bird in it.'

Those who had expressed doubts in advance about her ability to convince as Sally Bowles or Lady Macbeth were far outnumbered by the sceptics who now gathered to see if she could cast off the shadow of Edith Evans that had dogged all Lady Bracknells since; a question that Robert Cushman reported in the *Observer* was 'a source at the première of quite remarkable tension. Everybody loves Miss Dench; nobody could quite see her in so unsympathetically formidable a role. We waited with bated breath for her solution, and our joy when she revealed it knew no bounds ... This is probably the best acted Lady Bracknell there has ever been. (Edith Evans's was a Happening.)'

Michael Billington in the *Guardian* responded warmly to all the individual performances, 'but the great merit of the production is that, instead of a lot of elegant people saying witty things, it offers genuine emotional reality. And nowhere is this better seen than in Judi Dench's superb Lady Bracknell.' He cited as just one example of her achievement the greatest hurdle of all in her inquisition of Mr Worthing as a possible son-in-law. 'The shattering news of his origins is greeted not with a sub-Evans swoop, but with a very slow, incredulous removal of her glasses and a *sotto voce* rendering of "A Handbag?" in thunderstruck disbelief. Ostentatiously tearing up her notes, she conducts the rest of the interrogation with the hurried politeness of someone anxious to catch a train.'

Michael Coveney in the *Financial Times* thought her performance was 'typical of the production's thoroughness in finding a rhythm that both belongs to the text and is true to itself'.

Anna Massey shared a dressing-room with Judi when they were on tour and was astonished to see how her instincts were so foolproof that she could sense things even when she was not on-stage. 'We were sitting in the dressing-room while the two girls were playing the tea-party scene, and Elizabeth Garvie put in five lumps of sugar. We couldn't see it; we were listening to the tannoy and Judi was doing her tapestry. She said, 'There should only be three', just like that. She knows without being there – she could give you a note from anywhere.'

But for all her sure-footedness, she tripped one night over her own major obstacle. Martin Jarvis was coming up to his line, 'I was found, Lady Bracknell', when Judi suddenly skipped half a page and he heard her say, 'In what locality did this Mr James, or Thomas, Cardew come across this ordinary handbag?'

He thought, 'Have I had a little blackout? We haven't got to that point; she hasn't asked me where I was found!' He only had a split second to decide whether to try to go back, or just carry on. Judi says, 'My God, I saw the whites of his eyes! It was terrible, I didn't know where I was.' They carried on to Lady Bracknell's exit line, 'Good morning, Mr Worthing' (where Oscar Wilde himself momentarily nodded, since they have just had afternoon tea).

Nigel Havers entered as Algy and looked at Martin with one eyebrow raised nearly into his hairline. The two of them had a ten-minute scene to the end of Act I and Judi normally returned to her dressing-room, but this night she was waiting in the wings as they came off, and wailed, 'Mart, oh Mart, what are we going to do?'

He said, 'Do you know, I don't think people noticed.'

They spent both intervals trying to work out whether the plot could now be unravelled sensibly or not at the end of Act III. The scene went as well as usual and the audience response was just as enthusiastic, and only a very few people did indeed seem to register the absence of 'A handbag?' Two members of the audience came up to Martin in the foyer bar of the Lyttelton Theatre afterwards to say they thought it was a very interesting idea to cut it altogether, assuming it had been deliberate.

Judi was not let off so easily, and that Boxing Day performance was seared into her memory by a vituperative letter from a Mrs Davies in Welwyn Garden City. She wrote to say, 'You have ruined my entire Christmas.' Judi was so mortified she wrote back, 'I'll tell you why I've ruined your Christmas. It's because just before the performance my shower-head suddenly burst with boiling water and flooded all the dressing-room. So I went on stage in a terrible state and cut all mention of the handbag.'

She recognises that it was no accident that it was the most famous line of the play that she cut. 'It is the great hurdle, that's why the dam burst at the weakest point. Everyone says if you don't speak it like Edith Evans then you can't play it; Johnny Neville said she did a great disservice to the British theatre by playing it so well!'

After its successful opening the production went on tour to major cities in England and Scotland, and in Glasgow it was Nigel Havers who nearly had a heart attack when Martin Jarvis got his own back for a trick played on him. Between the matinée and the evening performance he changed all the clocks, taped the audience arriving and then played the tape of the curtain going up. Nigel was sitting in his dressing-room with curlers in his hair, thinking he still had ten minutes to go, and was galvanised by the noise over the tannoy and the supposition that he had to make an entrance seconds later. Judi and the others were in on the joke, but even with her track record she thought it might have been a little over the top. 'Nigel knew he had to get down the stairs, under the stage and up the other side. He was screaming and throwing the curlers off. He ran onto the stage and we were all there waiting for him, with the safety curtain down. He was completely shattered. I mean, another man *would* have had a heart attack.'

As soon as the Wilde play had opened, the same cast went into rehearsals with Peter Hall for a Pinter triple bill under the generic title of 'Other Places'. Judi was only in the last of the three – *A Kind of Alaska* – in which she played Deborah, struck down at the age of sixteen with the sleeping sickness, encephalitis lethargica. As the play opens she awakens from a twentynine-year coma after treatment with the new wonder drug L-Dopa. The clinical facts were drawn from Oliver Sacks' case notes in his book *Awakenings*, but the factual basis was transmuted into a deeply moving drama by the skill of the writer, director and players.

Paul Rogers was the sympathetic doctor who had to break the news to her that though her consciousness and experience had been frozen at sixteen, her body was that of a woman in her mid-forties. His lines were few, yet he says it 'stands out as one of the highlights of my life I think, because the interplay with Judi made me feel so much part of that extraordinary atmosphere'.

Judi knew that Ralph Richardson's first wife had died of the disease, and she read about its effects and those of the drug that treated it, but one of her most effective pieces of business was based on a shattering experience of her own. 'All I remember on that first night was that moment of getting out of bed and walking towards Paul as the doctor, and I had that absolutely clear flash of thinking, "That's why I snapped my Achilles tendon, so I would know the whole process of learning to walk again. You have to be told, you just put your heel down, you're so frightened when you start to walk again." That stood me in incredibly good stead.' (It was Charlotte Arnold at the Remedial Dance Clinic who had taught her how to walk again after *Cats*.)

The Pinter plays were to be rehearsed while the Wilde company were on tour, but Peter Hall was unable to be with them for the first leg of the tour in Norwich, so the author himself said he would come up and take the rehearsals, which went very well under his eagle eye. In fact the only complaint when 'Other Places' opened, although a loud one, was that there were far too few performances available in what was the National Theatre's smallest house anyway, the Cottesloe. Sheridan Morley went so far as to complain in *Punch* 'that the usual appallingly incompetent NT scheduling means that it is only available for doubtless already sold-out performances in the whole of November'. He enthused about the writing and the playing in the first two parts, 'but both these plays are really only curtain-raisers for the last', which he thought was 'played by Judi Dench in what has to be the performance of even her remarkable career'.

Robert Cushman registered in the *Observer* his response to Judi's own strongest feelings about her performance, 'an adolescent's consciousness in a woman's body is magnificent (and her first efforts to walk a brilliant paring-down of clinical reality); she really is total theatre.'

Michael Billington is the critic who has always been the most responsive to Harold Pinter's fertile genius, and has recently written a most perceptive biography of him; now his reaction in the *Guardian* was that 'never before have I known a Pinter play to leave one so emotionally wrung through; and much of the credit, in Peter Hall's recent production, belongs to the incredible Judi Dench ... Face glistening, she cries, "Of course I laughed, I have a laughing nature", and Ms Dench, an actress to her fingertips, gives one a sense of a deep buried happiness. To convey a feeling of being re-born is a rare achievement; and it is reinforced by the amazed compassionate stillness of Paul Rogers and Anna Massey as the unrecognised relations.'

Irving Wardle was reminded in *The Times* of an earlier definitive Pinter production: 'the portrait has a personal depth that ranks with Peggy Ashcroft's performance in *Landscape*'. It was even deeper for Judi's brother Peter. 'That was just after our Mum died, and Judi was so uncannily like her that it was very, very moving.'

Playing the Wilde and Pinter in the same repertoire for the National Theatre would have been quite enough for most actors, so it was with some astonishment that Nigel Havers burst into Martin Jarvis's dressing room one day when *The Importance* had opened and 'Other

Places' was deep in rehearsal, to say, 'Smarty, have you heard what they're doing?'

'No.'

'They're doing another play!'

'Who are?'

'Judi and Anna.'

'*Another* play? There's hardly time.'

'Yes, there's a notice gone up on the board.'

Apparently the two of them were going to do platform performances of a play by a new writer, Nick Harrad, called *The Crew*, and the two men were anxious to know more. During Gwendolen and Cecily's tea-party scene in Act II of *The Importance*, Martin and Nigel joined Anna in Judi's dressing-room, and demanded, 'What's all this then?'

'Well,' said Anna, 'we were asked to do it, and it's a good script, and we should encourage new young writers.'

'What's the play?' Martin enquired.

'Well, it's about two lesbian truck drivers,' said Judi, 'and it's called *The Crew*. It's very good; it's very funny; and it's very tough.'

The men found the prospect of Judi and Anna playing a couple of butch truck drivers fairly mind-boggling, but the rehearsal notice on the board had Peter Hall down to direct and Diana Boddington as stage manager, so it all seemed quite genuine. (Diana Boddington even used the tannoy to say, 'Would all members of *The Crew* read the noticeboard', which was only supposed to be used for really vital messages, as all three theatres at the National are always vying for the time.) It was not until the tour reached Glasgow that the plot was rumbled. Nigel came into the dressing-room to say, 'Smarty, it's all a wind-up. It's not a play at all. There's no such thing, they've just been winding us up.'

They realised the joke was on them, but in an attempt to turn the tables they launched into a very long story about Judi and Anna rehearsing *The Crew*, during a Radio Scotland interview they did with Ken Bruce. It was broadcast at 7 p.m. the following day, so they strolled into the neighbouring dressing-room carrying a radio at the key moment, but Judi is not so easily thrown, as Martin discovered. 'Judi said with the straight face of the perfect hoaxer (which is also the perfect way to play Wilde), "Yes, well what's so funny? You're talking about *The Crew*, but you obviously don't know very much about the play. You obviously haven't read it, because otherwise you wouldn't have said it's set in a garage. It's not." '

She has never admitted that the whole thing was a fabrication and still regularly talks about Nick Harrad as a real person to Martin. She sent him a postcard two years later, when she was filming *Wetherby* with David Hare in Yorkshire, saying, 'Done six weeks already, so we're halfway, very hard work being only two of us in it, but Nick seems very pleased.' She enclosed a photograph of herself, leaning out of a lorry cab window in a trucker's jacket and cap, fag drooping from the corner of her mouth, with David Hare standing beside her wearing a T-shirt emblazoned on the front with the lettering 'Anna Massey and Judi Dench in *The Crew* by Nick Harrad'.

The mystery is not that she is prepared to go to such lengths in pursuit of a running gag, but how she finds the time in her incredibly full schedule to make these elaborately detailed preparations. Other actors have similar stories to tell, exclusive to their own relationships with her. John Moffatt receives regular calls from an imaginary bag-lady, who hangs around the car park near Oxford bus station. 'She must be about 110 by now. I'll pick up the phone and hear this old crone's voice say, "It's Adelina." She never rings and says, "Hello, it's Judi here." It's always some performance.'

It was during the tour of *The Importance* that Anna Massey and Judi became close friends, spending a lot of time together before and after the show, when Anna recalls, 'I don't think I've ever laughed so much in my life. We laughed so much that sometimes we just had to stop by lamp-posts and cling on.' The only conflict they experienced in sharing a dressing-room was that Anna cannot bear to hear the audience buzz on the tannoy before curtain-up, and Judi positively has to hear it to make her adrenalin flow. Their compromise was to have it switched off until the last five minutes, and then to turn it up full-blast. Anna also registered Judi saying, 'four or five times a week, "I can't wait to go on." She just does adore it, that is her home.'

Judi's double success as Lady Bracknell alternating with Deborah won her another *Evening Standard* Best Actress Award, and her pleasure was multiplied when Paul Rogers and Anna Massey were named Best Supporting Actor and Actress by *Drama* magazine for their roles in *A Kind of Alaska*.

The three of them were, however, then to fall victims to a very public row between the writer and director of that play. The National Theatre production was to be televised, but the publication of Peter Hall's diaries in 1983 and his references to the break-up of Harold Pinter's marriage so incensed the playwright that he refused to collaborate on this or any other work in progress.

The ripples from this situation reached out and touched other actors. When the play was eventually televised some while later, the role of Deborah was offered to Dorothy Tutin. 'When I was offered the part on TV I was unhappy, because I'd seen Judi play the part, but they said she wasn't available. So I wrote her a letter saying how sorry I was, and I didn't get an answer, which rather upset me. A year later I met her at some do and she said, "I owe you a letter." I said, "Yes, you do." '

In fact the 'unavailability' was a euphemism. The TV producer reportedly said, 'I don't want to work with any of the people who've done it before', so it was not offered to any of the original actors. Judi bitterly regrets the lost opportunity, though she does not blame Dorothy Tutin for taking it on, and the brief awkwardness has not impaired their friendship.

Judi lost that TV appearance by one man's decision, and she won her next part because of a sequence of indecisiveness by several other actresses. Hugh Whitemore had written a play about the capture of the Kroger spies, and the effect on their unsuspecting English friends who were forced to help trap them. He and the director, Clifford Williams, wanted Judi from the beginning to play the wife in *Pack of Lies* who is torn apart by conflicting loyalties, but she had just opened as Lady Bracknell and would not be free for a year, and they were reluctant to wait that long. But at least six well-known actresses turned it down and, to compound the frustration, they all took ages to make up their minds – one took three months before she said no. (After it eventually opened one of them wrote the author a very long letter saying, '<u>What</u> a mistake I made.')

After months of this waiting, author and director were feeling very dispirited and sent the script back in one last hope to Judi's agent, where Michael Williams picked it up and took it home. 'I read it under a street-lamp, and you can always tell after the first two or three pages; the standard of writing was so high that I knew straightaway. I said to Jude, "We've got to do this." '

The real-life couple they were to play were called Search, renamed Jackson in the play, and the husband was still alive, so Michael set off to find him in Ruislip with Judi rather reluctantly accompanying him. 'I met this lovely fellow, Bill Search, an electrician, and he called me Sir, which I put in the script. He showed us round the house and we went through to the kitchen where he said, "Dizzy Lizzy came in and sat down on that chair, and died. You always feel the pain will go away and it will become less, but in fact it gets more." I went back to Hugh Whitemore and told him about our conversation.' The daughter, Gay Search, was now grown up and working as a journalist, and she was able to offer more help and advice to the actors.

The play's action was set in 1960, when the Krogers and George Lonsdale, members of what became known as the Portland spy ring, were finally caught. Helen Kroger was played by Barbara Leigh-Hunt, and both she and Judi found it an eerie coincidence that the Krogers had been arrested outside the Old Vic looking at a poster for *A Midsummer Night's Dream*, in which the two of them had played Helena and Hermia.

There were nearly two married couples acting in this play, but Richard Pasco could not be released in time from a previous contract, so Richard Vernon played Stewart, the man from MI5, whose courteous request to use the Jacksons' house for surveillance they feel powerless to refuse. What destroys Barbara Jackson is the necessity to deceive her friend Helen, and the strain eventually kills her with a heart attack soon after the arrests.

The emotional depth of the part is not readily apparent on the page, and was missed by all those other six actresses, but even the author was surprised by Judi's insight. 'She found something in it that was not apparent when we started, and it suddenly came like a racehorse zooming through.' Rehearsals were so easy and jokey that he actually became quite anxious; his anxiety was increased when everything suddenly went wrong on the first night of the opening in Brighton. 'I remember Michael switching on a light, and all the lights went off. One actor went off through a fireplace instead of through a door. It was a disaster.'

His confidence only returned when the production came into the Lyric in Shaftesbury Avenue. At the first preview he was in a side box. 'Sitting across from me in the theatre was a bald man whom I thought I vaguely recognised, and at the end he stood up and cheered. I said, "Who's that man over there?" And someone said "David Jones", and I suddenly thought this might be all right.' (Three years later Hugh Whitemore's screenplay of *84 Charing Cross Road* was directed by David Jones.)

Not all the critics were sure about the play, but there were no doubts about the players. Eric Shorter urged his readers in the *Daily Telegraph*: 'If you have a taste for first rate acting at the level to which Miss Dench aspires in its emotional integrity, the actress will be reason enough to visit the Lyric. But at the same time, in the less showy role, Mr Williams can match her in subtlety as the equally perplexed but less affected husband whose fears for his wife's health are expressed with such delicate restraint.'

For James Fenton in the *Sunday Times*, 'the focus of attention is always on the relationship between Miss Dench and Barbara Leigh-Hunt ... Miss Leigh-Hunt, who is extremely clever at portraying those moments when Helen is making her calculations as a spy, never lets you doubt the warmth of her relationship with the family. For Judi Dench, the tragic dilemma is to understand both that Helen is her friend and that she is a liar and a traitor.'

Michael Coveney claimed in the *Financial Times* that 'Miss Dench has rarely done anything so tight or so moving'; and Robert Cushman in the *Observer* doubted 'if any could match her for anger and anguish. Her emotions seem to be coming from her belly and they hang, immovably and disturbingly, in the air of the theatre.' I found her anguish at the betrayal in this play as moving as her aching sadness in *The Promise* sixteen years before, and somehow this was heightened by the very ordinariness of the English suburban setting.

One production device was to convey a time lapse of several hours by a blackout of just a few seconds; and the playwright Michael Frayn was impressed by her ability to conjure up those emotions at will. 'When the lights came back up she was sitting in the window, and she looked as if she'd been crying for hours. She'd only had two or three seconds to create that impression.'

But for once Judi found it easier to summon up that despair than to shrug it off afterwards. Clifford Williams quite often found her uncharacteristically drooping with depression when he went round afterwards. Michael worried about the strain on her, 'that breaking-down that Jude had to do finally exhausted her. After about three months she wanted to come out, but was persuaded to stay on a bit longer.'

The pressure on her to stay for another two months was because there were now queues around the block for returns, though some fans of *A Fine Romance*, which was being screened during the run, were disappointed to find that *Pack of Lies* did not contain the same dizzy couple they knew from television. The image of the latter did help to ease one moment of strain in the former. Michael and Judi had had a sharp disagreement about something at home, and were sitting in a cab *en route* to the Lyric without speaking, when it stopped at the traffic lights in Shaftesbury Avenue. In Michael's vivid metaphor, 'There were icicles hanging from the roof of the cab, the atmosphere was strained, and there was a woman walking past. She looked in and then she tapped on the window, and danced round the cab singing "A fine romance ...";' it was a bit easier I think by the time we got to the stage door of the theatre.'

But however exhausting the play, it would have been most unlike Judi not to pull at least one practical joke. The intended victim here was Brian Kirk, the company manager, who particularly enjoyed feminine company. When it was his birthday she sent Michael round the corner to the Raymond Revuebar sex-shop to buy some Cleopatra's Black Pearls, a supposed aphrodisiac. In the interval they all presented these to Brian Kirk with a little card.

He said, 'Oh, I don't know about these.'

'Oh go on,' said Judi, 'go on.'

'Well, I'll take one if you'll take one.'

'OK, I will. I'll take one now', and she popped one in her mouth and swallowed it.

They were called for Act II, when Helen entered to say, 'Barbara, you're not looking well.'

'No, I've got a headache.'

'Why don't you take a pill?'

'I already have', by which point the two actresses were almost weeping with suppressed laughter. Judi said, in a mixture of relief and disappointment, 'The pill had absolutely no effect whatsoever.'

For her performance as Barbara Jackson, Judi picked up another pair of Best Actress Awards in 1984 from the Society of West End Theatres and from *Plays and Players* magazine. This made little impression on her young daughter. Finty by now knew enough to make the right approving noises immediately after a performance, but the truth came out when she was staying with a schoolfriend, Kate Congreve. Then she was overheard saying, with all the authority of an eleven-year-old, "It is without doubt the most boring play I've ever seen in the whole of my life." This judgment convulsed Judi when it was reported back to her.

During the run of *Pack of Lies* the Williams family had their own domestic upheaval. With both their mothers now gone, and Michael's father, brother and sister-in-law about to leave it, they decided to sell Charlecote, because they did not want to go on living there without them. Michael saw a picture of a Tudor house in Surrey in *Country Life*, and sent for the details before telling Judi. The price was more than the Charlecote sale had realised, but they thought they might just be able to raise the balance from some savings and the proceeds of a butter advertisement they had just made. Judi went down to view the house with Michael and her friend Susie Bodmer, who only lived about twenty minutes away from it.

As they drove in, Susie said firmly, 'Now, when you get in don't be too enthusiastic about it. Just go round and have a look at it; don't be too over the top or they'll be keeping the price up.' Then she found herself unable to follow her own advice. 'Within two minutes of being in the house, Judi and I were both going, "Oh look at this; look at that; so-and-so would just fit there", so it was hopeless. We came back to my house, and Michael did all the negotiation over the phone from my kitchen.'

The rambling house has equally old barns in the grounds, a swimming pool in the front garden and a large pond behind that is home to a large family of ducks, moorhens and two mute swans that were rescued by Michael and Judi.

When she came out of *Pack of Lies* she spent some considerable time getting the house into shape, helped by Michael when he too relinquished his part in it some while later.

If that play had been emotionally draining, her choice to return to the stage at the end of 1984 was to prove hugely physically demanding.

fifteen

1984–86

From *Mother Courage* to
84 Charing Cross Road

The driving force behind the RSC decision to stage *Mother Courage and her Children* in 1984 was Howard Davies. He had directed other Brecht plays, including *Schweyk in the Second World War* with Michael Williams, which helped him to persuade Judi to take on the title part. He had met her socially through the company, but she took a little while to size up both the director and the play. He had to go and tell her the story, not once but twice, and although on the second occasion she started to question him on the purpose of this scene or that scene, he formed the distinct impression she had still not read it.

His assumption proved all too true when, on the very first day of rehearsal, Judi berated him for failing to point out one vital piece of information, which would have been apparent to her if she had simply read the script earlier. 'I was so cross on that first day. Howard had come to tell me the story, but what he omitted to tell me was that she's never off. I was so angry when I found this out that I said at the first rehearsal, "Well, who translated this? I can't make head or tail of it." Howard relied, "Meet Hanif Kureishi. This is him here." He's never spoken to me since.'

The early rehearsals were quite experimental, while Judi tried out different ways of moving. When the director said he wanted her to march around in a long old army coat, as if scavenged off a dead body of a soldier, Judi found in a skip the one Michael had worn as Schweyk. It reached the floor on her and when she did a stooping Chaplinesque walk, it trailed behind her like a train. It became so much a part of her physical character that when the actual designed coat arrived, its weight and texture were so different that Howard

Davies quickly said, 'Keep the coat you've been wearing for the six weeks of rehearsal, and we'll adjust that one.'

Judi knew how she wanted Mother Courage to look and here there was an immediate rapport. 'I had clearly in my mind that the wig should be red and look as if just anybody had cut it, so it was always standing on end. I was convinced about that and when I told Lindy Hemming on the first day, she produced the design she had already done with red hair exactly like it.'

Howard was keen to break away from what he regarded as the stifling shadow of the famous 1949 Berliner Ensemble production and the alienation effect that everyone talked about. Judi was very quick to go along with that. 'I don't understand about the Brechtian alienation. I know what he means, I've read it and understood it. What I don't understand is how you then involve the audience with the personal predicament. They all spoke about Hélène Weigel and that moment where she heard of the death of her son – well, if what she did was alienation, then I don't understand what the word is.'

Brecht called the play an episodic chronicle of the Thirty Years War, which engulfed much of Europe in the first half of the seventeenth century, but its première in Switzerland in 1941 was naturally informed by sharp parallels with what was happening under the Nazi regime from which he had fled. Mother Courage's travelling canteen is a cart she trundles around the battlefields of the continent with her three children, all by different fathers, and all of whom die in the end. Zoë Wanamaker was once again playing her daughter, the mute Kattrin, and was much happier here than she had been in the Wilde play.

In other plays, Shakespeare in particular, Judi's directors have spoken of how she never merely 'marked' her performance in rehearsal, but went full out from the beginning; but now she did a variant of her earlier diffidence over Lady Bracknell. As he watched her develop the part Howard Davies felt encouraged until nearly the end of the rehearsal process. 'I was surprised by her courage, no pun intended. She was so brave about embracing the ugly aspects of the character; most actors would want to find a point of redemption that would allow the audience to forgive, but she was completely prepared to abandon all those usual actorly habits. But she was quite reluctant to put anything together. I always got the feeling that she didn't want to peak too soon, to arrive at a performance too early. Then there were moments where you'd run a scene and you'd go "Whoa!" and it would be absolutely fantastic.'

But his growing admiration was suddenly clouded at the final run-through, when 'what emerged was a completely different performance that bore no relationship to the brilliant work she'd done before'. He became convinced that someone else in the management had given her a note about her delivery and the RSC style of speaking verse, which was inapplicable here. So they had a private confrontation. 'We spent about an hour together and she got very, very upset, because I was saying, "You've got to restore what you were doing earlier on." I don't think that Judi realised that whatever note had been given to her would have affected her performance that much, but it had. She refused to tell me who it was, she was too loyal, and I think she was shocked by my reaction, because until that time we'd had a complete mutual accord on her work.' She says no one had given her a note, but she was thrown by being told not to make her a heroine.

There was more unhappiness to come, caused by the universal dissatisfaction with the set. John Napier's design was more a piece of machinery than conventional scenery, with Courage's wagon attached by a spindle to a central revolve, and it rumbled around on tracks as she trundled it across war-torn Europe. He had an impressive record of designs for the RSC and Judi had been a fan of his ever since *The Comedy of Errors*, but this time his concept had to be built by engineering workshops rather than by carpenters and painters and it kept seizing up. The director hastens to defend his designer. 'It wasn't John Napier's fault at all, it was just that we had a very bad workshop who made it. They didn't deliver it on time, and they made it terribly; it kept on breaking. I had to stop John doing a Kung-Fu job on the set, because he was so angry. It taught me a terrible lesson, that as a director you have to fight for every inch of what you want, and never accept second best.'

Cast and stage crew grew ever more frustrated trying to make it work in the technical runs and dress rehearsals, and when it broke down at one of the previews, Howard Davies felt he owed it to the audience to go on himself and explain what had happened. 'Just as I was about to walk on Judi appeared behind me and said, "I'll buy you a drink if you get a laugh", which completely threw me, but I got one good laugh so I got a drink. The next time the set went wrong she said, "I'll buy you a drink if you get two laughs." Every time the set broke down she upped the stakes in terms of laughter, and I thought it was typical of her that in the face of adversity she could raise the laughter quotient.'

As everyone now feared, it broke down again on the opening night, when Michael Billington reported with some irritation in the *Guardian*, 'you could feel the tension ebbing away as the actors struggled with a recalcitrant brake mechanism and caravan flaps that remained obstinately stuck. The least one can ask of a theatre design is that it works.'

On the other hand, Michael Coveney was full of praise in the *Financial Times* for the work of both John Napier and lighting designer David Hersey, comparing it to their joint achievement in *Cats*. He also approved of the director's new approach: 'Brecht wanted us to observe detachedly, not become involved. Fat chance of that with any good actress, let alone Miss Dench, an indisputably great one.'

John Peter agreed in the *Sunday Times*: 'Judi Dench's Courage is like a watchful, bustling animal whose prodigious energy is bent only on survival. The face betrays almost no emotion; the eyes glint warily at every opportunity to grasp and gain, and they signal to us that she is a frightened predator to whom missed opportunities mean danger. Her shoulders hunch and move to express both alertness and suspicion; her walk is the loose, cockney shuffle of a professional bouncer which sags gradually into the slouch of a weary dog. This is one of the finest Brecht performances I've seen: dry but gripping, pitiless and unsympathetic but eloquent.'

Philip Brady congratulated Judi in the *Times Literary Supplement* for succeeding in 'banishing those old pictures of Hélène Weigel ... It is a performance full of contrasts – she is witty in a curiously unhumorous way, and she is so coarsened that faced with her daughter's corpse, even her tenderness is ham-fisted.'

Michael Ratcliffe did not surrender so easily in the *Observer*, finding 'a hollowness at the heart of the evening hard to pin down, a lack of intensity and shape', and although he admired aspects of the central performance, he concluded, 'it may be that in the end the rendering of total corruption is beyond her'.

But the most patronising put-down was John Barber's in the *Daily Telegraph*, with a particular sting in its tail. 'Judi Dench is altogether too warm and homely a personality for this holy terror. She works hard to make herself look and talk ugly, and you can see why her vigour attracts weak men. But her quaint scampering around the stage is merely endearing, and she gives no idea of Courage's screaming agony when death strikes down her dearest. It is a role for Glenda Jackson.'

The latter had hoped to play the part herself at the Oxford Playhouse at much the same time for the Triumph Apollo Company, but the RSC had bought the UK rights from the Brecht estate and refused permission for a rival production that was expected to transfer to London. This caused a bitter row at the time and now that the dust has settled one feels more than a twinge of regret that theatregoers were denied the chance of what should have been a fascinating comparison of styles and interpretation.

The production at the Barbican is doomed to be remembered as the one sabotaged by the set. Zoë Wanamaker calculated that out of thirty performances there were only ten where it worked properly. One night, when it jammed totally after just one circuit of the stage, Judi had to go out and make the announcement, but her attempt to raise a laugh fell on stony ground. 'I made this speech, "Look we're the RSC, not the RAC, so I'm afraid we can't fix this wheel, and you'll have to come back another night." I thought it was quite funny, but the audience were furious and they didn't laugh. Zoë and I raced in the car from the Barbican to Joe Allen's for supper. I was meeting Mikey later for another supper, but it didn't matter. Zoë said, "So this is what Joe Allen's looks like on a Tuesday evening at ten past eight." '

The cast tried to cheer each other up with the occasional joke onstage. At one matinée the soldiers who bought drinks from the cart produced an American Express card instead of coins, and Judi pretended not to notice. But for the evening performance she put vinegar in the bottles they had to take a great swig from, which they then spat out all over the stage in a great spray. After Judi cried in the lift about the revolve she found a weeping cherry tree in her dressing-room, as a present from the cast. It now flourishes in her garden.

Judi's second play that ran in tandem in that Barbican season was

Harley Granville-Barker's *Waste*, directed by John Barton. The on-stage requirements for her were a lot less demanding, as her character died before the interval, so she went home without staying for the curtain call, an early departure of which not all her fellow-actors approved.

The play was first prohibited and then neglected. The story of an Edwardian MP who has a brief affair with a married woman and gets her pregnant, and whose career is then ruined when she dies having an abortion, was in itself considered too scandalous by the Lord Chamberlain, who banned it shortly before it was due to open in 1907. Barker substantially rewrote it twenty years later, but it was only staged for the first time in 1936, and never again in the London theatre until 1985, though the BBC did a radio production in the 1950s and one on television in 1977.

John Barton thought it was Barker's best play and was very keen to direct it. He worked on a conflation of the author's two versions and his absorption in both texts provoked Maria Aitken, who was playing the MP's sister. 'He never looked up from these two scripts to watch what we were doing. Judi, with her wicked sense of humour, encouraged me to be naughty. Before the dress rehearsal I said I was going to sew a banana instead of a sampler, just to see if he noticed. When I chickened out at the last minute she thrust a banana at me – and he didn't notice.'

After the suburban dowdiness of Barbara Jackson and the battlefield rags of Mother Courage, Judi told Maria that she loved the idea of wearing nice frocks for a change.

Stephen Moore, who was appearing with Judi as the Chaplain in *Mother Courage*, was not in *Waste*, but by chance was wearing clothes of a matching period in *A Doll's House*, so he nipped down to the Pit from the large theatre upstairs and strolled across the set of Judi's play while she watched him in surprise. She never mentioned it to him, but when Moore opened as Captain Hook in *Peter Pan* that Christmas, he was mid-speech on the ship near the end, and 'when I glanced around at my pirates, there was one very round, very over-dressed pirate sitting on a barrel, smoking a pipe, and it was Judi'.

Judi insists that he failed to recognise her. 'I had a red wig, and a red beard, and a patch over one eye, and still he didn't notice me. He's changed his tune; if he says that now, he's lying.' Then she remembered with horror, 'God, I didn't know how to get off, either.'

Finding her exit then was less of a worry than finding her voice at the opening of *Waste*, until Cicely Berry came to her aid once again and did some special vocal exercises, which made her at least audible as Amy O'Connell. Enough, anyway, for Michael Ratcliffe to note in the *Observer* that 'Dench endows her with irresistible aspirates and the softest of Irish brogues behind which to defend herself in this brutal Anglo-Saxon world.'

Michael Coveney in the *Financial Times* thought that Daniel Massey perfectly captured the MP, Henry Trebell, who ruins Mrs O'Connell and thus himself. 'His scenes with Judi Dench's Amy are superb: his stiff deportment shattered in a moment of cataclysmic lust while she sways, languidly around and through him, bearing the sadness of a woman scorched by an inadequate marriage.'

Irving Wardle waxed enthusiastically in *The Times* about the high 'theatrical music' of the Church and politics debate, but he, too, thought it was overshadowed by the sexual affair. 'Judi Dench's Amy undergoes a staggering transformation from a flirtatious bird of paradise with a soft Irish brogue in the first act to the desperate, businesslike woman who comes seeking a few moments of his valuable time. Daniel Massey, challenged and at bay throughout the evening, turns to pure granite at her demand for an abortion. It is a searingly intimate collision between two people who should never have met in the first place.'

Emrys Jones welcomed in the *Times Literary Supplement* the way in which 'John Barton's firm and sensitive production restores the play to what should long ago have been its place as an Edwardian classic'. However, he dissented over the casting of Trebell, and of the role of Amy O'Connell. 'Judi Dench gives it the right warmth and appealing vulnerability. But neither physically nor temperamentally can she quite suggest the waif-like "little thing" referred to by the others; her maturity slightly unbalances the play.' His greatest praise was reserved for others. He thought the production was lucky to have at least three players superbly equal to its demands – Maria Aitken, Tony Church as the Party Leader, Horsham, and Charles Kay as Lord Charles Cantelupe, who defends the Church against the Disestablishment Bill, with what Jones called 'chilly ecclesiastical ardour.'

According to Judi, it was difficult sustaining that chilliness throughout their scene. 'The two minutes I was on the stage with Charlie were very, very tricky. He's an appalling corpser; we played one bit just not looking at each other at all. The slightest thing sends him right off. I had a fur and as I got up the end of it caught under the chair and came off, so it looked like a kind of hamster. He caught sight of that and we were off.'

The public response to this theatrical rarity was such that the production was transferred from the tiny Pit to the West End and the larger capacity of the Lyric, Shaftesbury Avenue. During the run, while Judi luxuriated, for the only occasion in her career, in playing hookey from the theatre after the interval, she was suddenly offered what is arguably the most demanding and challenging role there is for an actress.

Terry Hands asked her to play Cleopatra in the next RSC season. She immediately said Yes, and it was only afterwards that she suddenly remembered a conversation with Peter Hall at the last night party for *The Importance,* when he had said that 'we should do *Antony and Cleopatra.*' So she rang him up and said, 'Look, Terry Hands has asked me to go and do Cleopatra at Stratford, but we're bound to each other on this. Do you want to do it, because if you do, I will honour our pact?'

He replied, 'Yes, of course, if we can get an Antony.'

There then ensued a tug-of-war between two determined directors, neither of whom wanted to lose her, while Judi was torn between conflicting loyalties.

Terry Hands insisted, 'But she's an RSC actress.'

Peter Hall riposted, 'Don't be so silly. I'm an RSC director, and I asked her first.'

'But I asked her in the office.'

The row became so fierce and protracted that Judi got very upset and told Terry that she would rather not do it at all. He responded with characteristic generosity by writing her a long letter saying she was so right for Cleopatra that she must do it, even if it was not for him. He thought Judi behaved impeccably throughout this painful saga, but he was not prepared to say the same thing about his rival for her services.

Before it was resolved, and before the production could be slotted into the National Theatre's repertoire, Judi had other claims on her attention, most of them for the camera. Between 1984 and 1986 she made six screen appearances, three for the cinema and three for television. There might have been a seventh, but for her congenital reluctance to read scripts.

Whilst they were struggling against the odds to film *Saigon – Year of the Cat*, Judi burst out one day, 'Oh, David, why do you write these bloody difficult things? Why can't you write a play in which I go to Paris and have tea at the Ritz?'

He said, 'Fine, I'll write you a film in which you go to Paris and have tea at the Ritz, it's no problem.'

He wrote it and sent it to her, but she never replied. The next conversation about it between David and Judi came fifteen years later when they were working together at the National Theatre. One day he asked her casually, 'Do you get a lot of mail?'

'Oh, I get all this endless mail.'

'I bet you do. Do you read it all?'

'I read everything, except the scripts you send me. I found that script of yours for *The Butter Mountain*.'

'Oh, you've finally found it, have you?'

'Yes, I found it the other day. Do you still want me to make it?'

'It's too late. I've already made it with Charlotte Rampling.'

Judi enquired, 'How was she?'

David answered with relish, 'Bloody good!'

Judi says if the original title had been *Paris by Night*, as it became, of course she would have read it.

In 1984 David Hare was the director as well as the writer of *Wetherby*, in which a schoolteacher invites a group of friends for dinner at her cottage, and when a stranger arrives at the same time he is invited to join them. At the end of the evening he suddenly blows his brains out, and the rest of the film unravels the impermanence of relationships. Vanessa Redgrave was the teacher, and a strong cast included Ian Holm, Tom Wilkinson, Penny Downie, and Judi for once using her native Yorkshire accent.

Judi asked David just to tell her about her own part, not the whole of the film, which she claims never to have understood. Only very recently she remarked to him, 'Now one day you are going to tell me what *Wetherby* was about, aren't you?'

In retrospect he feels frustrated that the parts were unequal for two actresses of the stature of Redgrave and Dench, especially as it is the only time they have acted together, but he was aware that Judi did it as a favour to him after *Saigon*; a favour he amply returned much later with *Amy's View.*

She only had a small part, too, in *Room with a View,* but enjoyed playing most of her scenes with another contemporary, Maggie Smith, though that was about all she did enjoy. The director, James Ivory, has the reputation of not being particularly helpful to actors, and Judi's only comment on him is terse – 'too uptight for me'. While she received little guidance from the actual director, she was offered some unsolicited advice by one of the youngest members of the cast on how to play a line if she wanted to get a laugh, which unsurprisingly did not go down too well with one of our most brilliant exponents of comedy timing. With or without advice, she turned in a per-formance that won her a BAFTA Award for Best Supporting Actress, in yet another of her screen appearances that she has never seen.

The television parts that followed in 1985 were much happier experiences. For the first she was reunited with Ian Holm; after their brief scene together in *Wetherby,* they now starred opposite each other in *The Browning Version.*

The BBC's studio recording of Ibsen's *Ghosts* also went off happily, until director Elijah Moshinsky rashly asked his cast to improvise a scene at the dinner-table to run under the credits. Michael Gambon was Pastor Manders, Judi was Mrs Alving, Kenneth Branagh her son Oswald, and Natasha Richardson was the maid serving the meal. The intention was to add a music track later over a single camera track round the faces at the table, a moody establishing shot that had only one flaw in it – it began with Gambon. 'I said to Elijah, "Can we speak?" as Ibsen didn't write this scene. So he said, "Well, I could put a slight murmur under the music, maybe." Well that's a red rag to a bull really, isn't it? Kenneth Branagh is the worst corpser in the world and as we all sat down I could feel the table moving; we were already in trouble. Natasha came to me first, and said, "Would you like some potatoes?" They were big potatoes, and I said, "Yes please, I'll have twelve." '

This was too much for the others, who now had to endure a long slow panning shot as the camera moved on from Gambon. It was most difficult for Kenneth Branagh. 'As the camera passed Michael he bent double over his soup and when he looked up at me the tears were rolling down his face. Judi's close-up was next and although the shot revealed only head and shoulders I could see that her hands were white, gripping the tablecloth for dear life. Once the camera had passed her she threw her hands up to her face and stuffed a serviette in her mouth. By the time the camera reached me I was watching two titans of the English theatre in silent convulsions. I was helpless and it was too late. I could no more have produced a straight face than swim the Channel.'

After several abortive attempts at a retake, the director abandoned recording for the day and sent his distinguished cast home in disgrace. The shot was eventually captured the next day, but when the play was transmitted more than one perceptive actor spotted several telltale signs of corpsing from the trio.

Judi exchanged her grey wig in the Ibsen for a brunette pageboy bob in Michael Frayn's *Make and Break*, about a group of salespeople in a Frankfurt hotel over one weekend. Other members of the cast included Robert Hardy, Frank Windsor, Ronald Hines, Jon Finch and Martin Jarvis. The last remembers director Michael Darlow saying right at the beginning, 'I think that's one of the most amazing read-throughs I've ever been at', a refrain that has become so regular it is almost routine when Judi is involved. Her regular fans must have wondered why she had been cast as this nondescript secretarial figure, as she hardly had a line to speak for the first fifty minutes. Then she had a long and moving speech about loneliness at the end, which justified her presence.

Her part was quite small in the last of these screen appearances, *84 Charing Cross Road*, and she really only accepted it because of the other people involved. The screenplay was adapted by Hugh Whitemore from Hélène Hanff's book and the subsequent stage play, and directed by David Jones. The two men wrote down their list of an ideal cast and Hugh says, 'It was one of those rare occasions when we actually got it. Anthony Hopkins rang me up when he'd got to page thirty and said he'd do it, which of course is what every writer dreams about. At the read-through, a rare event itself for a film, he and Judi reduced me to tears. I don't know why Judi did it, because it wasn't much of a part on the page, but she made it seem a terrific part.' Although Judi says she was always very flattered if she was asked to do a film, because of her own lack of confidence in the medium, that and her warm admiration for the author of *Pack of Lies* were not sufficient in themselves to capture her for the part of the bookseller's wife, so David Jones added his persuasive powers. 'She rang me up and said, "Are you serious? She's only got a couple of scenes." But I pointed out that it's a concealed struggle for her husband with Hélène Hanff, and the pivotal role she plays in the final scene.'

But the clincher for Judi was 'because of Tony. It was very good because it broke the ice before we did Antony and Cleopatra.'

There was an instructive interchange between the two actors during the shooting. She said to him in genuine puzzlement, 'You really like filming, don't you?'

'Yeah, I love it. I think it's wonderful.'

'But what is there?' she asked. 'There's no audience.'

'Well, who the hell needs an audience? They're the enemy.'

'What, how can you say that?'

'Well,' he said, 'that's how I think of an audience – the depressing aspect of coming in of an afternoon, for a dreary Wednesday matinée, a half-empty house, people couldn't care less whether you're on-stage or not. I'd rather not do that.'

That conflicting view of the rewards of playing before a live audience would lead to a few major crises when they met again in Judi's preferred arena, and the bond between the two of them forged in the making of *84 Charing Cross Road* was of inestimable help in resolving those crises. For those who appreciate the strength of restrained emotional acting, the film is worth seeing just for itself. In other hands it might not have worked at all, based as it is on letters between two people who never meet – the bookseller Frank Doel who sends books to Hélène Hanff the New York bibliophile, played by Anne Bancroft, who later sends food parcels to help the bookshop staff through the postwar austerity. When she finally comes over to London, Frank has just died. As Nora Doel, Judi's unvoiced jealousy of her rival for her husband's attention speaks volumes.

After the Hopkins/Dench team played man and wife on screen, and before they played on-stage two of the most famous lovers in history, Judi had a prior date with her real husband as a deeply contrasting pair – *Mr and Mrs Nobody.*

diary entry three

---

3 and 8 April 1997

James Bond Film – *Tomorrow Never Dies*
Location – Eon Film Studios, North London

Day 1. 3 April 1997.

9.30 a.m. Arrived at Eon Studios and was met by Gordon Arnel, Head of Publicity, who told me that the Director, Roger Spottiswoode, had met Judi for the first time last night when they had a two-hour rehearsal for today's scene. On a large circular set representing the MI6 Control Room, the principal actors were rehearsing, minus the extras.

10.00. The director broke the actors to light the scene. I was greeted by Judi and Geoffrey Palmer, and we walked back to Judi's dressing-room, which was marked simply M. Geoffrey's said Admiral Roebuck. Judi introduced me to Terence Rigby – playing the Russian General Bukharin – and Colin Salmon – Robinson, M's Chief of Staff. While we waited for coffee to be brought Judi got out her embroidery, saying that she has been working on this piece for ages, but now wants to finish it for Wendy Toye's eightieth birthday on 1 May. 'This is what I love about filming, all this free time to get on with things like my embroidery.'

10.30. Roger Spottiswoode arrived with the other actors to run through the scene in Judi's dressing-room. Judi ribbed Terence Rigby about his chestful of medals, especially what she called 'The Order of Ice-cream', in the shape of a parachute with a white top. A discussion ensued about the script.

Judi: 'After the Cruise missiles are fired, I don't know what I'm supposed to be acting here. I know something they don't know, which is why I'm calm ... Roger, do I really need to say Cruise in this line? We all know what they are by now.'

The wardrobe girl came in and took away Judi's shoes to roughen up the soles; at the first walk-through on the set the soles were so new and smooth that they slipped on the steps as Judi descended, and she went headlong.

Colin: 'I was so impressed by the way you just relaxed into the fall, and didn't break or twist anything.'

Judi: 'Oh, I'm always falling over on-stage', and listed the parts in which she has fallen.

11.40. We returned to the studio for a full rehearsal on the lit set, now with the full complement of extras sitting at computer terminals and walking busily across the room in naval uniform. Together with the full crew, there were about fifty people on the set. Four big video screens stood at the top of the broad flight of seven steps. Large monitor screens standing on the floor of the set replicated the pictures on the top screens; rows of computer terminals all had different images on them – maps, still photos, figures, military information, etc. At the foot of the steps was the main control desk, with six computer monitors operated by Robinson and his assistants. This area was the focus of the action in this scene – the pre-credit action sequence. The main actors were wearing concealed radio mikes, but two boom mikes were also used for general background noise, and to cover the close dialogue between Admiral Roebuck and General Bukharin, while M interrupted in the background. The video camera at the rear recorded the monitors for continuity of the computer signals.

11.50. Second rehearsal.

12.00. Third rehearsal.

12.05 p.m. Call from 1st assistant director: 'Final check.' Make-up and wardrobe attended to Judi and other actors with last-minute adjustments. The naval officers in particular were carefully brushed down. Smoke was blown onto the set by a huge fan. The director checked the shot on the TV monitor slaved to the film camera. Judi stood in her opening position at the end of the control desk.

12.15. Take 1.

12.25. Take 2. At the end the director called: 'Cut. First positions everyone.' After this take Judi and Geoffrey chatted and laughed quietly together.

12.35. Take 3. Roger: 'Cut. Excellent. Print it.' This completed the wide mastershot. The camera was moved to the right to take the close shot of the admiral and the general conferring.

1.00. Take 1.

1.05. Take 2.

1.10. Rehearsal of the later part of scene. Looking in the camera colour monitor I could see how Judi's pale costume glowed in the background, in contrast to the dark naval uniforms, ensuring that she did not lose her dominance of the action, even in long-shot. Some of the younger crew members were audibly wondering when they would break for lunch.

1.15. Take 1.

1.18. Take 2.

1.20. The lunch break was finally called and there was a rapid exodus. I returned with Judi and Geoffrey to her dressing-room. She worried that I had not had a chance to order any lunch and asked the young assistant who brought hers to see if he could get something for me. I chose the salmon salad, and five minutes later he brought one which turned out to be duck, but was delicious. Judi told us about bringing Finty in to watch on the previous Bond film, and giggled as she described her reaction when Pierce Brosnan dropped in to her dressing-room to say hello: 'It was just like that cartoon when the character is splattered across the wall – she kind of reeled back as she saw him come in.' Paul, the assistant, popped his head in to ask if they could go to make-up at 2.05. Later, at 2.15, he returned apologetically to say the camera was now to be rigged on the crane, so there would be a delay before their next call. This proved to be a long one, and at 3.45 Judi exploded: 'This is what I *hate* about filming, all this hanging about!'

'I thought you said earlier that's what you loved about it.'

'No, I've had enough of embroidery for a bit, now. (Pause.) I wonder if the shops are open around here, I haven't got anything in for Mikey's supper.'

4.00. Recalled to studio.

4.15. Rehearsal. Then the principals were replaced by their stand-ins while the lighting was set. Judi, Geoffrey and Colin relaxed on the sofa at the edge of the set and swapped filming experiences.

4.45. The principals were called onto the set. The camera was now very close to the rear of the control desk. Lots more smoke called for.

5.00. Take 1. Aborted in the middle as technicians were suddenly heard clumping around on the roof of the set.

5.02. Take 2. A crew member's mobile phone rang. He hastily switched it off and exited, and the scene continued to the end, but a retake was needed.

5.18. Take 3. Roger: 'Very good.'

5.30. I had to leave. The shooting was scheduled to continue until 7.15 p.m.

Day 2. 8 April.

9.45 a.m. Arrived at the studios and joined Judi, Geoffrey and Colin on the set. Their entry was being filmed in long-shot, with Samantha Bond as Miss Moneypenny in the foreground on the telephone. Eight takes before it is in the can.

10.45. Found Judi teaching Colin the word game I had seen on the set of *Mrs Brown*, while they waited between shots.
   Judi: 'Good job you weren't here yesterday, John, I lost my bottle. I just couldn't say this line, we had to do thirty takes, and never got the close-up. Then Geoffers began to blow it too. I'm sure he only did it to make me feel better. I went home and burst into tears.'

11.30. We went back to her dressing-room and chatted about the filming on Sunday in the City of London, as M and 007 were driven around.

12.00. Called back on to the set.
Judi: 'I hope I'm not on a box again, I'm fed up with playing all these scenes on a box.' But Colin Salmon, who is well over six foot tall, seemed more worried about his height than Judi about her lack of it. Judi: 'Have you

noticed, they keep calling me Judith, and I don't respond, I don't know who they're talking to!' (Mostly this was the American cameraman.)

Different angle close-up for Moneypenny on the phone and the camera pans with her as she turns to see M standing behind her.

Moneypenny: 'James, you always were a cunning linguist.' Turns. 'Don't ask.'

M: 'Don't tell.'

Minister of Defence enters and calls: 'M.'

Long set-up for different angle.

1.10 p.m. Rehearse shot.

1.20. Roger: 'One more for safety.'

1.22. Roger: 'Break for lunch, but I want to rehearse the actors for the next segment.' This was M and Robinson bursting into the control room past the armed guards.

1.40. Lunched with Judi. Spaghetti, Dutch apple pie and ice-cream. We discussed the forthcoming Cannes screening of *Mrs Brown*, and the changed dates for the start of rehearsals of *Amy's View* at the National.

2.50. Called to the set for brief rehearsal with extras and crew. Returned to dressing-room for more chat.

4.20. Recalled to set after relight and track-laying for camera. Judi off-camera as top brass respond to her entrance. Judi to me: 'These are the shots I like, when I don't have to do anything.'

4.55. Take. Roger: 'Good. Print it. One more please.'
Several more takes.

5.05. The camera was turned round to shoot Judi's entrance. Break extras and crew to get cup of tea and cake. By the time I got there, only a few crumbs left.

5.20. Depart.

sixteen

1986–87

Carrie Pooter, Cleopatra
and Sarah Eldridge

George and Weedon Grossmith created Mr and Mrs Pooter in their *Diary of a Nobody* in the 1890s. Ninety years later, Keith Waterhouse wrote an affectionate parody in *Mrs Pooter's Diary*, as a companion piece to her husband's notations. Judi read it on BBC Radio in *Woman's Hour*, and said that she would love to do it as a play in the theatre with Michael. So Waterhouse knitted both the old and the new texts together into a play for Mr and Mrs Williams, entitled *Mr and Mrs Nobody*. Trevor Nunn was slated to direct, but there were so many demands on his time that he kept putting off a production date.

The author became increasingly impatient, so he asked Ned Sherrin to take it over, as he knew he adored the script. The change of director took a little selling to Judi. 'To begin with I couldn't believe he'd want to work with me, because he was such a partner in crime with Caryl Brahms, and she *always* gave me such bad notices. She said, "as Juliet she conveys about as much as an apple in a Warwickshire orchard". Hard!'

Ned was well aware that there was a gulf to be bridged: 'Caryl always referred to her as Dench, J. and she wasn't at all keen on that. I think she thought I was tarred with the same brush. However, once we started working it couldn't have been more enchanting.'

Michael and Judi worried about sustaining a whole evening with just the two of them reading out the letters and diary entries from Charles and Carrie Pooter, but they were very taken with a revolving set designed by Julia Trevelyan Oman. Luckily, Judy was spared a repeat run of her trials with the revolve for *Mother Courage*, as this one was abandoned as totally impractical before they even got onto the stage, but by then the die was cast.

The company was increased to four, with the addition of Penny Ryder as the maid and Gary Fairhall as the general factotum – both mime roles. All the other characters were impersonated by the Pooters. The original script was much too long, at around four hours, so the author and director took their cue from the awful brand of champagne mentioned in it, called Château Jackson Frère and bottled in Highbury. Ned remembers fondly, 'We reckoned that it was a six-bottle job cutting it initially, then still more had to go. I'll never forget Keith's face when we gave some agreed cuts of half a dozen pages to Judi and Michael, and the absolute glee with which she ripped the pages out, making a great ripping noise – you could see the pain in the author's face as it came through.'

Judi's initial apprehensions about their director were soon dispelled, and replaced by worries about the nature of the material. 'Ned was precise, and funny, and very, very astute; then suddenly he'd sit back and say, "They're on automatic pilot." We used to think it was going to be a doddle, a really short evening, get a lot of laughs, and straight home, but it was *desperately* hard work, because you had to create it all yourself. It was good fun doing it, but you had to feel quite well for it, you had to feel really on top of it all.'

One of the illusions they had to create was the presence of all the other people referred to – Mr Cummings and Mr Gowing and the Pooter son Lupin – and they chose an eyeline to a different fixed point in the auditorium to address each of them.

After four weeks' rehearsal there was a pre-London tour to Guildford and Brighton before its opening at the newly refurbished Garrick Theatre on 17 November 1986. Michael envies Judi her ability to pick up her lines without having to sit down and learn them as he does, so he was quite proud of the fact that it was he who helped her out on the first night, when she made a tiny fluff at one point.

Irving Wardle welcomed it in *The Times* as 'the best comedy to reach the West End this year', and Shaun Usher urged his readers in the *Daily Mail* to book tickets, praising the script, designs and direction. As for the actors, 'Judi Dench and Michael Williams are more like the Pooters, one suspects, than even the Pooters were. Their performance is a gentle, subtle, highly-skilful duet hitting notes of harmless snobbery, punctured pretensions and mild bickering.'

Michael Coveney also thought in the *Financial Times* that 'their playing together is a delight and of a high technical order.' But others were disappointed. Although Michael Billington did his best in the *Guardian* to pick out aspects he enjoyed, such as Judi doing 'wonders with a line, coolly dismissing her son's fiancée, like "Her hair is no stranger to the automatic curler",' it still struck him as a thin substitute for a play. 'In my Pooterish way, I want a real night out at the theatre rather than the equivalent of a good read.'

Mark Lawson acknowledged in the *Observer* 'two perfect comic performances', but complained that an icy West End professionalism was present in everything from script to direction and settings, and 'when two Nobodies are played by Somebodies of the stature of Williams and Dench, the pathos is lost.'

Despite all these critical reservations *Mr and Mrs Nobody* ran for nearly five months, and could have run for much longer, if Judi had not been committed to return to the National Theatre to play Cleopatra. Ned Sherrin failed to find anyone willing to take on the role of Mrs Pooter.

While Judi was playing the one and rehearsing the other, she received a message asking if she would meet Kenneth Branagh. She thought he was going to ask her to play in something which she would be unable to accept because of the upcoming Cleopatra. But he totally took the wind out of her sails by asking her to direct a Shakespeare play for his Renaissance Theatre Company. He wanted to recruit experienced classical actors to become first-time directors, beginning with Judi. They had hit it off well in *Ghosts*, but she was very apprehensive of taking on the role of director. It was one of the latter who convinced her. 'I talked about it to Peter Hall, who said, "Absolutely, go on, you've got to do it."' But first she had to get Cleopatra under her belt.

It was a visibly narrower belt than Carrie Pooter's, too. She had padded out under those voluminous Victorian clothes, and now she also slimmed off over a stone in weight for the enchantress of the Nile, to make the most of Alison Chitty's seductive costumes, in the style of Veronese paintings of the classical world.

Judi had seen the 1953 Stratford production with Peggy Ashcroft and Michael Redgrave, but had never read the play, though she did do some background reading on the historical Queen of Egypt, a diversion from the play text which she usually avoids as unhelpful. Anthony Hopkins quietly confessed to her that he had not read Shakespeare's script before the first read-through either. The problem that Peter Hall had hinted at when he said, 'if we can find an Antony', is that leading actors are often wary of the part, conscious of the fact that, after his death, the last act belongs to Cleopatra. But Hopkins had just played two hugely demanding parts in succession at the National – Lambert Le Roux in *Pravda*, and King Lear, eventually clocking up a hundred performances of each, so he rather welcomed the thought of having his death scene first. Quite often as he lay dying in Cleopatra's arms he would look up at her and whisper, 'Just think of it. In a few minutes I'm going to be in the dressing-room, having a nice cup of tea, and you've got all this rubbish to speak for the next hour.'

But he found the early rehearsals a struggle. They began just after he had opened in *Lear*, and he had difficulty in making another great stretch of verse stick in his memory. After a couple of unhappy weeks he confided to Judi that he wanted to give up the part. She immediately told him to ambush Peter Hall on his way back to rehearsal. He offered to relinquish Antony to Brian Cox, but the sympathetic director was very conscious of the strain of mastering two such difficult Shakespearean leads simultaneously and simply told him to take several days off from rehearsals, so he could learn the part.

Peter Hall also had to cope with doubts about the casting of Cleopatra, including those of the actress herself. 'On the first morning of rehearsal she said to me, "Well, I hope you know what you're doing. You are setting out to direct *Cleopatra* with a menopausal dwarf." A number of other people said to me, "You're mad", but one of Judi's qualities is a kind of outrageous sexuality, combined with a decorum, which is why she was so good as Titania and as Cleopatra, and an extraordinary wit – she can make things funny other actors couldn't make remotely funny. What she brought to Cleopatra was a sense of dangerous comedy; she was a dangerous woman. I also think Judi is probably the best verse-speaker in England.'

He believes that this play is the Shakespearean Everest, much harder to bring off than *King Lear*, and also that it is 'probably the best play ever written'. He never doubted for a moment that he had cast it to the hilt; 'from my point of view, I think it's probably the best Shakespearean production I have ever done.'

He was also conscious from the outset of the amount of work needed to reach the summit of this Himalayan challenge and arranged a twelve-week rehearsal period, the first time Judi had had that luxury since *Much Ado* at Stratford. Usually the cast are shown a model of the set on the first day, but Alison Chitty watched them rehearsing for six weeks, sketching her designs all the time, to follow the mood and the movement of the production.

She came up with a blood-red set with sliding walls, and differentiated between the scenes in Rome and Egypt by dressing the former in steel-grey, blue and white, all cold colours, and putting the Egyptians in orange, yellow and pink, earthy colours. She gave the latter decorative tassels and when Antony returned to Rome in formal Roman attire, he wore one of those tassels round his waist as an exotic accessory. The fetching costumes for Cleopatra included two long wigs in the second act made from the hair of fourteen Filipino girls; so when a friend of Judi's, who saw a performance from a seat near the back, came round to say, 'Judi, you have to wear your hair like that!', she could only laugh.

In rehearsal, the actors were encouraged to experiment all the time. For the first entrance Anthony Hopkins asked if he could come on riding on the shoulders of a eunuch. 'I had an image of this couple like Richard Burton and Elizabeth Taylor, just over the hill. All their great beauty has gone, and there's this buffoon standing there on the back of a eunuch.' When he suggested to Judi that they rolled over each other on the ground, she tried it and said, 'Yes, this is going to work, I think.'

The physicality of all this rough-and-tumble, coupled with the uncertainty of exactly what the other was going to do, had one painful side-effect that Judi tried to keep to herself. But Susie Bodmer's keen eye spotted that 'she was black and blue all the way through it, because he threw her all over that stage.'

As they continued to improvise the moves, changing them on impulse from one day to the next, the director suggested another departure from the normal practice, not setting the moves but urging them to keep it fluid in performance, and introducing a couple of follow-spots to make sure the principals were always lit, just as if it were a musical. He told Cleopatra's attendants, 'Just go with her wherever she goes, and stop when she stops; it should be like a shoal of fish.' (There is a similar effect in *Mrs Brown*, when Queen Victoria stops dead, and her ladies-in-waiting swing back into line behind her.)

He gave Judi notes that she found invaluable in approaching the part. 'He said, "Don't think you've got to come in and play all of Cleopatra in the first scene. All you do is play different aspects of her in all the scenes, and by the end hopefully you'll have the whole character." That's a wonderful note to be given.' When she worried about how on earth she could live up to Enobarbus' great speech about her – 'the barge she sat in' – Peter Hall gave her great comfort by saying, 'Don't believe everything everybody says about you in plays is true. Enobarbus has just gone back to Rome, having been in Egypt, and he's in a pub with his friends having a pint, so of course he's going to say, "My God, you could smell the perfume coming across." '

He warned her that the great challenge is that Cleopatra has to have a fifth gear in reserve; 'it's what she goes into after Antony dies, a kind of fifth overdrive, and it wasn't until I did it that I understood it. After we'd played it for about three months Peter came back and said it had got a bit baroque and I thought, "I know exactly what that means, it's when you start to embellish some things." '

Above all, he was concerned with the speaking of the verse and although Judi was no stranger to his rehearsal discipline, even she found this a testing time. 'Peter was like a maestro. He would stand with the text on a lectern, watching that you obeyed the verse, and the half-lines. He took a whole morning over Cleopatra's death scene with Charmian and Iras, until eventually Miranda Foster, said, "our Royal lady's dead", and Peter said, "Thank Christ!" But it was a marvellously intense time.'

One of the trickiest scenes to stage is always the one in the monument. It has to look high enough to make the action plausible, without making it impossible for the actors to negotiate. Tim Pigott-Smith was playing Octavius and he sat in the stalls of the Olivier Theatre with Judi at the first technical rehearsal, as they watched a demonstration of how to lower Cleopatra from the twenty-foot-high platform, which looked very dangerous to all of them. 'The first time somebody did it, she clutched me in horror with one hand and the person on the other side of her with the other, and said, "What shall I do?" We said, "Get them to do it again." But they turned round and said, "Judi, can you come up and have a go now?" And she just went and did it. We had a couple of close shaves with that moment, and every night I thought, "God, I hope Judi comes down from the monument all right." '

Her luck held, but at one preview, as Antony was winched up in his net, he got stuck and audience laughter broke the spell that had been cast by the performance until then. Judi's only accident happened on the first night when she did a running exit and crashed into a wall section, which gave her a swollen lip. She feared that her loud ejaculation, "Oh shit!" might have been heard by the audience, but this mishap went undetected. Apart from that, she thought the first night was the best performance they had yet given, much better than the dress rehearsal.

She always likes to have some last-minute notes on a first night, to concentrate her mind on the performance and distract her attention from the occasion, and she had more than enough to think about on this one. She said afterwards, 'I've never before experienced a first night when my nerves were entirely taken up with problems. Either I was busy preparing to haul Tony up, or leap from the monument, or deal with the snake – it was wonderfully focusing!'

The snake was a real one, and several had been auditioned during rehearsals. Knowing Judi's phobia about worms, Michael suggested giving the snakes names. They chose 'Wilson, Keppel and Betty', after the buskers who did comic Egyptian dances; Betty was always supposed to be hanging round in the wings while Wilson or Keppel went on in the scene. Judi says, with feeling, 'One snake was a keen actor, and one wasn't.'

Her susceptibility to superstition created a new good-luck token for this play. 'Just before the first run-through I found a penny and put it in my bag, and I touched this penny before we did every run-through, and then I had it sewn into my dress.'

The forecasters of doom were proved even more ringingly wrong by this Cleopatra than their predecessors had been by her Sally Bowles, Lady Macbeth and Lady Bracknell. Charles Osborne harked back in the *Daily Telegraph* to the Redgrave/Ashcroft partnership of 1953, which he had thought unsurpassable, 'but I have never seen a more exciting and satisfying production of the play than this new one by Peter Hall. Nor, since Peggy Ashcroft, have I encountered a finer Cleopatra than Judi Dench. In a role which some might have anticipated would be outside the range of this versatile actress, she triumphs completely.'

Michael Billington also ranked this pair in the *Guardian* alongside Redgrave and Ashcroft for their comprehensive humanity, in a production which 'is about two chunkily real people living out some epic fantasy. And no one could be more real than Judi Dench's breathtaking Cleopatra. She is capricious, volatile, the mistress of all moods who in the course of a single scene can switch easily from breathy languor ("O happy horse to bear the weight of Antony") to cutting humour ("How much unlike art thou Mark Antony" to an effeminate messenger) to a pensive melancholy ("My salad days when I was green in judgment") at the frank acknowledgement of the passing years ... she can be highly funny, as when she rushes for the door in affronted dignity at being told Octavia is 30, and highly dangerous as when she fells a messenger with a right hook.'

John Peter hailed Peter Hall's production in the *Sunday Times* as "the British theatre at its spellbinding and magnificent best ... Anthony Hopkins and Judi Dench play the title roles as if they were not star actors ... Both actors speak this soaring, voluptuous, difficult text with that finest of techniques which is based on artistic intelligence and true human feeling: two massive but golden performances from a golden age.'

Irving Wardle speculated in *The Times* that 'perhaps we are seeing this production simply because, for the first time in living memory, the English stage has two actors capable of doing full justice to the roles'. He was impressed by the speed of the playing, with Cleopatra 'as a creature moving too fast ever to be pinned down'.

It was this aspect that also struck Michael Ratcliffe in the *Observer*. 'Judi Dench's glorious Cleopatra is scornful and sassy, blessed with terrific energy, temper and wit. The head swerves with the speed of a snake or a bird at the first hint of a reverse; the round grinning face slumps into a thunderous, sullen and cruelly ageing mask when more seriously put out.'

I found the speed so breathtaking at the time that I had no memory of the performance running for four hours, and it was with real surprise that I registered the duration when I came to talk to all the principal figures involved in it ten years later.

There were occasions when it was still not fast enough for some of them. One night there was so much coughing in the audience that Judi came off and said, 'I can't hear myself.' Anthony Hopkins suggested, 'Why don't we just do the whole thing very fast, just rattle through it? That'll shut them up.' They rattled through it at such a lick that the audience did not dare to cough, in case they missed something. It was even faster than the *Macbeth* speed-runs. Peter Hall came round and remonstrated with them: 'It's far too fast; you've knocked half an hour off the play', but it achieved the desired effect.

Judi only felt the length of the evening when she was marooned up in the monument with Charmian and Iras for twenty minutes, during the scene where Antony's servant Eros ran onto his own sword rather than help his master kill himself. The three of them used to sit there in the dark, speculating about their ideal meal. Judi felt she was very boring about it, because hers was always seafood and a glass of champagne. Miranda Foster and Helen Fitzgerald planned a little treat for her on the last night. 'When I stepped inside the dark gloom they had tiny torches, and they clicked them on and there were three dressed crabs and half a bottle of champagne. We had to wait until Tony shouted out before we could pull the cork.'

Such distractions could throw some players, but in Judi's case they seem to enhance her own performance. In December 1987 the profession celebrated Peggy Ashcroft's eightieth birthday with a packed-out gala performance at the Old Vic, and Judi was billed to come on towards the end of the second half of the programme. Ned Sherrin was surprised to see her standing in the stalls behind a pillar, watching the whole of the first half, and back there again after the interval. 'She was following Eric Porter, and she stayed watching her colleagues from the front until Eric started his long speech, and it was only at that moment I saw her go through the pass-door, with just enough time to get upstage and make her entrance. Most people would be getting into the role and not want to be interrupted, but her technique seems to be to switch it on instantly.'

A week after that tribute to Dame Peggy, her natural heiress-apparent was also created a Dame of the British Empire in the New Year's Honours List. Judi was caught completely unprepared when her usual pile of mail one morning included what struck her as a very official-looking letter. 'I thought, "Oh my God, it's a summons", and stuffed it into the bag with all the other summonses, parking offences, and then I just happened to open it during the matinée. I had a really severe shock; I had to read it several times, and then of course I couldn't tell anybody, though I did tell Michael.' The public announcement on 31 December coincided with the date of Anthony Hopkins' birthday, so before that evening's performance the National Theatre resounded backstage with two musical serenades. The dressing-rooms are grouped around four sides of a central light-well, onto which all the windows look. At a prearranged signal, they were all thrown open on several floors for a lusty singing of 'Happy Birthday dear Tony', followed by a rousing chorus of 'There is nothing like a Dame.'

Other honours for her Cleopatra followed in rapid succession, and she was voted Best Actress by the *Evening Standard*, by *Drama* magazine, and in the Society of West End Theatres' newly renamed Olivier Awards. Peter Hall collected a Best Director Award, but he was just as pleased that his swansong production on the Olivier stage as Director of the National pulled in more than 100,000 people by the end of its run.

The final performance was quite an emotional one, especially for Judi. 'The last night was absolutely wonderful. Peggy came on at the end, and we were all given roses. We weren't sorry to see the end of it, because we had done a hundred performances.' For all the accolades, Judi thought that she only reached the summit of this acting Everest once: 'There was one performance in the hundred that we did, where when I came off I thought that's as much as I can give at this moment, that's really as much as I can give.'

The public sees what she gives on-stage or on screen; only her fellow-players know what she gives them in private, and she never fails to heed a cry for help. Dearbhla Molloy had spent five years away from the theatre when she was asked to play Lady Macbeth, her first Shakespearean part. 'So I rang Judi and asked her if she'd teach me how to speak the verse, which she did. We didn't use *Macbeth* as the text, for obvious reasons, we used *Cleopatra*, which she was playing at the time. I wrote down the rules that she gave me:

1. Remember it's a play, not reality.
2. Obey the metre.
3. Start scenes.
4. Earn a pause.
5. Don't separate.
6. Drive through the speech.
7. Antithesis, pauses, up at the end of lines.
8. Economy, simplicity, and negotiate with humour.
9. You don't have to carry the message, the play does it for you.
10. Trust the play, and your casting.'

These were rules that had been instilled in Judi by Michael Benthall and Peter Hall. Which is the greatest of them for Judi? 'Economy – I think that's the most important thing.'

For Dearbhla this was invaluable, especially when Judi directed her as Ursula in *Much Ado About Nothing* a few months later.

Judi was not, of course, just playing Cleopatra throughout those months. As soon as she had opened in that she began rehearsing her next play in the National's repertoire – *Entertaining Strangers* by David Edgar.

It had started life as a community play commissioned by the town of Dorchester, and performed by a local cast totalling 180. When he adapted it for the Cottesloe Theatre, he reduced the cast to a more manageable 27 with a lot of doubling of parts. Set in Victorian Dorset 1829–73, it hinges on the antagonism between a fundamentalist vicar, the Reverend Henry Moule, inveighing against the evils of drink, and Sarah Eldridge, the local pub-keeper and later founder of the famous Eldridge Pope brewery. A cholera outbreak in the 1850s transforms the way in which they are regarded by the community and by each other.

Tim Pigott-Smith shed the chilly bearing of his Octavius for the passion of the reforming priest, and Judi now became the bustling entrepreneur out to defend her trade from him. Hers was an under-written part, which she found 'strangely unsatisfying', with difficult jumps in the development of her character, though she enjoyed playing it as a regular change from Cleopatra. Peter Hall was again directing and she agreed to play it for him without reading the script. The whole cast piled into a bus and went down to Dorchester for a tour of the Eldridge Pope brewery, and talked to many of the local people. Finty went too, as at the time she had a great crush on Garry Cooper, a young actor in the company.

Tim Pigott-Smith was conscious that his was the pivotal role as written, and was lost in admiration for the way in which Judi's performance made them seem equal opponents. They only had three scenes together, a strong one at the opening, another in the middle, 'and this phenomenal scene at the end when we were both much older. And she practically took the evening in that one scene in the graveyard. I couldn't believe what she did, she just used to turn on the juice – that was a heavenly experience. And that wasn't there in the play, that was her, it was only because she was phenomenally skilled in the way she paced the role.'

She surprised him during rehearsals when she suddenly announced, 'I want to talk to the whole company afterwards.' He thought, 'Judi getting serious? What's going on?' When Peter Hall had left she said, 'Now tomorrow, everybody's got to wear something red, and we'll see how long before he notices.' So Tim put on a pair of red socks, others had a red tie or an Aids ribbon and they were all sitting around the next day like a bunch of self-conscious schoolchildren, when the director walked in and said, 'Oh, you've all got something red on.'

If that gag died immediately, another game between Tim Pigott-Smith and Judi is still running. At Peggy Ashcroft's eightieth-birthday gala he was in a skit on *Jewel in the Crown* and wore one black glove as Merrick, and Judi ribbed him, 'That's strangely attractive, that one-armed acting.' So the next night he wore one glove as Octavius at the end of *Antony and Cleopatra*, to no effect; later he slipped it into the basket with the asp, which did get a reaction. It then became a challenge to return it to the other unexpectedly – handed to him on-stage in *Mary Stuart*, falling out of her parasol in *A Little Night Music*, stencilled inside her dressing-room loo, made up in the form of a chocolate cake for his birthday, embedded in perspex, hidden in a tureen for his wedding anniversary; an intimate game of long range ping-pong that only two dedicated practical jokers could sustain over several years.

Judi's aim was embarrassingly a little less precise at one performance of *Entertaining Strangers*. It was a promenade production at the Cottesloe, with the vicarage at one end and the pub at the other, and the actors moved between the two through the audience, which this night included the director of *Mother Courage*, Howard Davies. 'I saw him sitting cross-legged in the audience, so I wrote a note saying, "I suppose a screw is out of the question?" But then I dropped it accidentally into the lap of the man sitting next to him!'

If he was surprised, so was Judi by some of the audience reactions. There was an effective snowstorm in the graveyard scene, but the flakes also fell on the spectators. 'You would see people tasting it, and you'd think, "Now come on!"'

Michael Billington appreciated the promenade approach because 'it brings you into close contact with the actors and there are two magnificent central performances. Tim Pigott-Smith's Moule is a figure of Brand-like serenity and harshness . . . but the supreme virtue of his performance is that he enlists sympathy for the character by playing him from his own point of view. And the great merit of Judi Dench's Sarah is that she never seeks to soften or sentimentalise the hard-nosed businesswoman more concerned with striking a deal than tending her injured son.'

Roy Porter described the production as a revelation in the *Times Literary Supplement*. 'The cast rises to the occasion. Judi Dench blends Mother Courage and St Joan as the publican while Tim Pigott-Smith's preacher conveys all the callowness of conviction; and they are supported by an ensemble whose dazzling playing is a tour de force.'

Charles Osborne was not keen on the play itself in the *Daily Telegraph*, but keener on the players: 'Judi Dench establishes a firm hold on Sarah, cleverly withdrawing her from the audience's sympathy as the play and the years progress, and passing Tim Pigott-Smith going equally cleverly in the other direction.'

Meanwhile, Judi was beginning to worry seriously about a totally new direction in her career, and whether she would measure up to the challenge Kenneth Branagh had set her.

seventeen

1988–89

Judi the director – *Behaving Badly* – an unhappy Gertrude

The years that end with a 7 always seem to have marked significant milestones in Judi's career. In 1957 she attracted great attention by making her professional debut as Ophelia; her 1967 performance as Lika in the London transfer of *The Promise* established her as one of the most exciting actresses of her generation; her Lady Macbeth took London by storm on its transfer first to the Donmar and then to the Young Vic in 1977; and her Cleopatra in 1987 placed her unquestionably in the forefront of her profession. In each of those years there was always a curious echo of surprise at her achievement – an echo that had completely died away by 1997, and the string of Best Actress awards for her performances in *Amy's View* and *Mrs Brown.*

She was the one who was most surprised by Kenneth Branagh's invitation to direct in 1987. By the time she came to do it the following year, the surprise had grown into something more akin to panic. 'I don't know who was the most frightened, them or me. I didn't ask them to do any audition speeches; I thought, "We'll talk and I'll put them at their ease", so we'd have a cup of tea. I ended up having twenty-five cups of tea or coffee, asking questions and answering them myself, just to put them at their ease.'

The Sunday before she started rehearsals she threw a big party at her Surrey home to help foster the company feeling that both she and Kenneth Branagh were so keen on. The accord between director and leading man was as one from the beginning. When he asked her which play it should be, there was a slight pause, and then the two of them said at the same moment, *Much Ado About Nothing*, in which Judi had had such a success as Beatrice to Donald Sinden's Benedick.

Kenneth Branagh was now to play Benedick and he suggested Samantha Bond for Beatrice, which Judi quickly agreed to after the three of them met in her dressing-room at the National Theatre.

His offer to Judi sprang from a hunch he formed when they acted together in *Ghosts* on television. 'When she's searching for the model for her character, her rehearsal investigation is like a director's. She leaves nothing to chance, and I thought she'd be tenacious as a director.'

That tenacity did not lead her to impose an interpretation on her cast, particularly on Samantha Bond, who often wished Judi would be a lot less oblique in offering her guidance. At an early rehearsal of the scene with the Prince, when Beatrice says to him, 'there was a star danced, and under that was I born', she thought it was going quite well until she looked up from her script. 'Judi was looking at me and I said, "Is that not right?" She just looked back and said, "There is another way." I said, "Is that it?" She said, "Yes." So Richard Clifford and I went out into the corridor and talked it through for about an hour, and the various other ways it might have been between her and the Prince. It was actually a highly successful note to be given, but it wasn't the most helpful thing she could have said. I then re-presented the section and she said, "Yes that's fine." '

For years Samantha believed that she had stumbled into playing the scene as Judi herself had done and it was only much later that she discovered it was quite different, and Judi had coaxed her into playing it in a way that suited her own talents and personality. But despite Judi's determination not to impose a performance, as Michel St-Denis had tried to on her own Anya when she was Samantha's age, what emerged did remind the knowledgeable of that earlier Beatrice. Bob Peck had also been in John Barton's production and when he went to see this one he was 'staggered by how much Samantha Bond resembled Judi vocally and in delivery, her whole interpretation. Maybe it was inevitable, but it was very striking.' Their vocal and physical similarities paid further dividends when they came to play mother and daughter ten years later.

Kenneth Branagh found that he, too, was pushed into finding his own way into the character. 'Judi never gave line-readings, despite my often urgent appeal to tell me how to say a line. She conveys what she wants by force of intuition, though her conversations with Sam were very mystifying to me. It was a joy to play in; one of the most enjoyable things I've ever done in the theatre. Directorially it worked very well, and captured the world of the play – hot, sweaty, and full of midsummer madness. She has a very sharp sense of comedy, and it's easy to be seduced by the play, but she was scrupulous about not milking the laughs.'

Judi was adamant that she did not want to put the men in tights, so she chose the Regency period and Jenny Tiramani designed some fetching costumes for the men and the women. Kenneth Branagh was so taken with the style that he did the same thing in his subsequent film version, which he happily acknowledged was deeply influenced by Judi's stage production, especially in the opening scene.

She only had four weeks' rehearsal, which she was determined to use to the full, so much so that a friend of hers was told by one of the actors 'she goes very, very quickly'. One thing that has always impressed her colleagues is her seemingly limitless energy, but she found she was having to draw on even more of it as a director than she did as an actress. 'After one rehearsal in London I came home and sat down in my coat and the family said, "Do you want a cup of tea?" I said, "No, I don't want a cup of tea." Then a quarter of an hour later when they were watching the news I walked out and went straight to bed, and slept from a quarter to eight until quarter to eight the next morning.'

Even more draining was the first time her work was unveiled to an audience. The production opened in the Birmingham Rep Studio, which only holds 150 people, and Kenneth Branagh could see her sitting there looking white-faced with nerves at the first preview, and scribbling in her notebook.

The actors' nerves made them mistime some of their lines and the laughs failed to come as expected. It was by no means a total disaster, but sufficiently off-key for Judi to shake her cast afterwards by saying, 'What are you all doing? It's like watching a multi-car pile-up on the M1!' That was meant less as a criticism of their acting, than as an expression of frustration at her own inability to affect the direction in which they were travelling at the time.

When the others all went off to an Indian restaurant for their own post-mortem, Judi stayed behind and unburdened herself to Branagh. 'Oh Kenny, it was like giving birth to a baby that isn't breathing properly. You watch it trying to walk and then it falls over and can't get up, and you can't do anything. It's agony.' Judi's assistant director Rachel Kavanaugh was the daughter of her old friend Pinkie Johnstone, and the two of them talked late into the night about the production.

Judi was full of self-doubt about her judgement of the play, even mistrusting her own sense of humour. But after a short night's sleep she rang Michael to say, 'Don't come up, I'm all right', went in with an armful of notes, got her actors to relax much more, and at the second preview that Friday night the laughs began to come. Judi was very glad that this was the performance Frank Hauser attended.

The following Tuesday was the press night, and Judi had an earlier engagement that day at Buckingham Palace, to be presented with the insignia of a Dame of the British Empire. Her hat was being made for her by Janice Pullen from the Wardrobe Department at Covent Garden, and it was awaiting her when she got back from Birmingham at one in the morning from the final dress rehearsal. 'I went upstairs and put it on, and it wasn't quite big enough. The crown kept shooting up, so I had that extra worry.'

Michael and Finty accompanied her to the Palace, and she was thrilled that it was the same day as the honours conferred on the heroes who had saved lives at the Zeebrugge ferry disaster. She was amused that, when she walked up to the Queen, the band played 'Half a Sixpence'. Then the family went on for lunch at the Savoy Hotel, where Daphne and Peter Dench were awaiting them.

In the afternoon Michael and Judi caught the train to Birmingham for the first night of *Much Ado*. The cast had made her promise to come in her outfit for the investiture and show them her Royal Award. Richard Clifford had only what Judi thought 'a paltry badge' to wear as Don Pedro, 'so I gave him my DBE to wear, and it sparkled like anything. I said, "It's the only time you ever get to wear it." They didn't want any notes, all they wanted to know was what I had to do, so I did it all again for them.'

The performance went well and the local press approved, apart from one critic who enraged the star by describing Benedick as 'rotund'. He thought they found their feet on the tour, but when Judi caught up with them in Brighton, 'she gave us a severe dressing-down. "You've all gone very West End; everyone is talking out front, not to each other." She came back at regular intervals, and had a long memory for what had changed, for the better or for the worse. She was a very good editor, and kept it fresh.'

By the time it came in to London for a short run at the Phoenix, in repertoire with Geraldine McEwan's production of *As You Like It* and Derek Jacobi's of *Hamlet*, it was very polished, and received a rapturous critical reception.

Jack Tinker's headline ran 'Much ado about everything in Dame Judi's subtle debut', in the *Daily Mail*. 'This is as triumphant a celebration of the Bard's most complex piece of courting as ever roused an audience to roar its approval at its conclusion ... Credit for its unexpected insights, its astute shadings of sublime lightness and shadowed tragedies, must lie at the feet of Dame Judi Dench, making her directorial debut thanks to the policies of the Renaissance Company.' Samantha Bond's struggle over that early scene was now rewarded. 'Her gently-turned refusal of the Prince's half-proposal has never, for me, been so delicately underscored.' Judi's rigour over the speaking of the text, passed on from Peter Hall and Trevor Nunn, reaped other dividends in this review: 'Of Mr Branagh's Benedick it is impossible to speak too highly. He offers the words as if they had just tumbled in his consciousness; lifts phrases with the bafflement of a nimble wit suddenly out of its own depth.'

Nicholas de Jongh compared it favourably in the *Guardian* with the current offering from the RSC in Stratford, praising Judi's 'fresh and refreshing version' and the performances she had drawn from her young cast. 'I have rarely seen the turbulent relationships between Beatrice and Benedick and Claudio and Hero interpreted with such inventive and convincing psychological insight.'

Judi was both happy and relieved that the Branagh gamble had brought such praise for his Renaissance Company, but she was just as pleased by all the letters she received from schoolchildren and their teachers, saying that they thought the story so clear that it helped them enormously, and they found it both funny and very, very sad. 'That's the greatest compliment, and that's why I think the theatre is important, to make that audience of tomorrow want to go and see Shakespeare played, and the stories properly told.'

In between playing Benedick, Touchstone and Hamlet, Kenneth Branagh was desperately trying to set up his planned film of *Henry V.*

Now the roles were reversed between he and Judi – he was to direct her as Mistress Quickly, and their mutual trust carried them through some deeply frustrating technical problems. What he had thought of as her glorious performance in the death of Falstaff speech proved in the next day's rushes to be technically unusable, so they had to shoot it again. The director recorded in his diary: 'But against all the odds, an even better performance from the ever patient Dame. It was 7.30 in the evening before we had cracked it. I'd insisted on the whole thing being done in one shot, a five-minute take where many things could go wrong. The tension on set as we attempted the umpteenth take was almost unbearable. Only Judi's example prevented me from flying into an impotent rage against someone or something. Not worth it, love.'

Her patience and his persistence paid off. The rushes this time were perfect and her playing with Richard Briers, Geoffrey Hutchings and Robert Stephens – as Bardolph, Nym and Pistol – conveys a feeling of relationships that reaches back for years, and a shared pain at the loss of Falstaff, which was enhanced by seeing the fat knight in flashback, personified by Robbie Coltrane.

The young first-time film director was also playing the title role, and he had to suffer a certain amount of press sniping at his presumption in repeating Laurence Olivier's famous double-task in his wartime *Henry V.* Judi thinks these personal attacks deeply unfair, but that did not stop her from chaffing him about his directorial flourishes. She said, 'I've never seen anyone give themselves such an outrageous entrance', as two great doors clanged open and he marched forward with cloak flying.

From Shakespeare Judi switched back into a modern role that she had been waiting to play for nearly five years. When *A Fine Romance* ended, Humphrey Barclay was casting around for another project for her when a friend of his, Moira Williams, brought him a novel by Catherine Heath, *Behaving Badly*, and said, 'Read a bit of this. Who does this remind you off?' As soon as he looked at it he thought, 'It was Judi, all over the page.'

When he sent it to her she was captivated by the opening scene when the wife is asked, 'What did you think when your husband told you he was having an affair with a younger woman?' She replies, 'I thought about turbot', because she was cooking it at the time. When

Judi met Humphrey for lunch at the English Garden in Chelsea she told him, 'Whenever you do this, I will make it. I want to do it that much.'

He had now left LWT and was working as an independent producer. He was glad that Judi had made him that promise, since they had such a long wait before all the elements slotted into place – her availability and the final go-ahead from Channel 4 for the four-part, one-hour drama series.

Moira Williams did the adaptation, and was quite unaware of Judi's system of judging scripts. At the first read-through of all four episodes, she and Humphrey assembled everyone involved, including all the heads of departments as well as the cast and production team. Moira was thrilled with Judi's reading of the first two scripts, and how she immediately captured the spirit of the wronged wife who suddenly decides to stop being long-suffering, and moves back into her ex-husband's home. At this point in the story, Judi leant across to the designer, Eileen Diss, and said, 'I'm absolutely dying to know what happens next.' Moira Williams' insides knotted up as she realised that Judi did not know that her character ended up going off with the juvenile lead half her age sitting at the other end of the table, Douglas Hodge.

At the end of the four hours there was an absolute silence as everyone knew they were on to a winner, a silence which Judi broke by turning to Ronald Pickup, playing her husband, and said with great feeling, 'Our job is to keep it as that – we have to hold it like that.'

Which they did, but not without a few tricky moments along the way. Moira Williams was entranced with the way in which Judi instantly inhabited the part, with nothing ever having to be explained, so she was caught by surprise when the director, David Tucker, came to her with a complaint.

'Moira, I just don't know what to do about Judi. I need your advice. It's her behaviour in rehearsals.'

She said, 'What do you mean, her behaviour in rehearsals?'

'She hums when I'm talking.'

When she was not in a scene, Judi would flop down on a bed or a sofa and hum, which Moira guessed was her little gesture to a director who was working on his first show outside the BBC, and was committing the cardinal sin in his leading lady's eyes of taking himself much too seriously. He was not sure how to cope with her behaviour and Moira sensibly advised him, 'I should let it go, David', as Judi was giving such a faultless performance.

It took a little longer to calm down Judi's co-star on the first day they moved into the studios at Elstree. Judi's bright wheeze was to arrive early and change the dressing-room labels. There were a lot of extras coming in that day, with purple hair and bones through their noses, so she got their clothes rails and moved them into Ronald Pickup's dressing-room, and changed the label on the door to read 'Male extras and Mr Pickup'. Moira was apprehensive about this joke, with good reason, when she was grabbed outside the door by the outraged leading man.

'Moira, there's been a terrible misunderstanding.'

'Oh dear, it's been such a dilemma. We knew you wouldn't mind.'

He exploded, 'But I *do* mind,' and stormed in to Humphrey Barclay to complain about his treatment.

Judi was protesting her innocence with a straight face, but it was not long before it was clear who was the culprit, and the Pickup wrath subsided.

The strong cast also included Gwen Watford, Frances Barber, Maurice Denham, Hugh Quarshie, and Joely Richardson; Channel 4 trailed the series hard, and scheduled two transmissions a week per episode. After the first one, the *Daily Mail* thought it 'will surely become the year's best TV production', and its stablemate the *Mail on Sunday* said, 'How cheering to know there are three more Monday slots to come. Judi Dench served up yet another stunningly strong performance.' For the *Financial Times* it was 'like watching a Munch painting come to life, or Cleopatra take leave of Antony', while the *Birmingham Evening Mail*'s imagery was less high-flown: 'Judi Dench has the skill to put the bristle in a doormat. Roll on next Monday.' But the *Daily Mirror* found it 'disappointing', and the biggest cavil came in the *Independent*: 'this is what people with no discrimination call "quality television".'

'Quality TV' or not, the series drew high viewing figures for Channel 4 and, flushed with its success, the Humphrey Barclay/Moira Williams team were soon collaborating with Judi again on a TV recording of her second venture into direction, again for the Renaissance Company. This was John Osborne's *Look Back in Anger*, with Kenneth Branagh as Jimmy Porter and Emma Thompson as his wife Alison. The original plan was for just one week's run in Belfast, to raise money for Northern Ireland charities, where it brought in £50,000. An additional Sunday night performance at the London Coliseum, in the presence of the Renaissance Patron, the Prince of Wales, raised even more for Friends of the Earth. 'And that,' complained Michael Coveney in the *Financial Times*, 'after a grand total of eight performances is that', which he found regrettable, and expressed the hope that 'maybe Judi Dench's fine production will receive a reprieve from whoever controls the London stage rights'.

In place of that, the television recording was seen by far more people than could have attended even a long run in the West End. Both stage and TV versions were put together in a remarkably short time. The first had only two weeks' rehearsal, and even they were not consecutive. Judi took an anti-sentimental view of the play and was very concerned that the final scene of the 'squirrels and bears' reunion should be played against that sentimentality.

David Jones was brought in to work with Judi on the studio recording, which only had one week of rehearsal. They sat together in the control-room and, whilst she usually deferred to his expertise in camera direction, he always gave her the last word on which take best captured her actors' performances. Because the actors knew it so well, it was recorded in quite long takes of fifteen minutes or so. David Jones heard later that the author was quite pleased with the final transmission. It received further accolades in the United States, winning a Golden Globe, a Cable Ace, and an Emmy nomination.

Judi retained her director's hat briefly, for a production of *Macbeth* by students at the Central School, and by coincidence her next play at the National Theatre was the same one she was in when she first left that training ground – *Hamlet*. The role was different, but her unhappiness in it was not much less.

She was playing Gertrude, in which she had watched Coral Browne make a great impression at the Old Vic, and she was very keen to try to emulate her. But there were a number of factors that conspired against, not just her success, but that of the production as a whole. It was Richard Eyre's first since taking over as Director of the National from Peter Hall, and he says he was distracted by simultaneously trying to get to grips with running that complex structure. He also found it difficult to get on with his Claudius, John Castle, though it was the problems facing his Hamlet, Daniel Day-Lewis, that eventually captured the headlines.

Judi's problem was convincing herself that she might have given birth to this Hamlet, so she tried thinking herself into the persona of his actual mother. 'I thought I'll try and play it like Jill Balcon, but I tried playing it very tall and dark, and I couldn't do it.'

Her stage son was all too successful in merging his acting bereavement with his grief over the recent death of his real father, and some way into the run his confrontation with the Ghost reduced him to such a state of collapse that he could not carry on.

Michael Bryant was coming up the stairs to make his next entrance as Polonius, 'and I found him in the corridor on the floor, crying his heart out. I took him to his dressing-room and held him like a baby while he sobbed and sobbed.'

Judi went to find Jeremy Northam, who was playing Laertes but understudying Hamlet, to tell him he would have to switch parts for the remainder of this performance. He went white, but was changed and on as Hamlet within a few minutes, and reached his death at the hands of his understudy as Laertes with great relief.

Grappling with all those problems of temperament, Richard Eyre found it a great comfort to have Judi's steadying presence; and he believes her unhappiness as Gertrude was more rooted in the shortcomings of the part. Jill Bennett had also found it frustrating in his previous production at the Royal Court, and so have several other strong actresses.

The production got mixed reviews, but Irving Wardle for one had no reservations in *The Times* about Judi's performance. 'Whatever the deficiencies in verse-speaking elsewhere, her delivery of everything from the Ophelia elegy to her dying emphasis on "my *dear* Hamlet", gives you a memory to cherish.'

Judi cherished another when the production travelled to the Dubrovnik Theatre Festival in July 1989, which had previously seen her Ophelia with John Neville. She was not the only one for whom her visit rolled back thirty years – she was followed around at the first night party by an admiring and sentimental Yugoslav television crew with long memories.

Daniel Day-Lewis's insistence on playing every scene flat out, which was a contributory factor to his collapse at the Olivier Theatre, also nearly laid him out when he forgetfully banged his head emotionally against the solid stone walls of Fort Lovrjenac, with a crack that made the audience gasp in horror.

During the run at the National, she received a visit from a young man of twenty-three who had just had a great success at Chichester with a production of Gorky's *Summerfolk*, and who wanted her to play Ranevskaya in *The Cherry Orchard*. They sat in the canteen and chatted about the Trevor Nunn era of the mid-1970s – *Macbeth* and *The Comedy of Errors*.

Judi asked, 'Did you see any of them?'

He said, 'Well no. I was ten years old.'

Judi went, 'Aaaarghh', and put her hands round his throat as if to throttle him.

His name was Sam Mendes and, despite his youth, she decided to put herself in his hands for what turned out to be a sequence of three plays in rapid succession.

eighteen

1989–91

The Sam Mendes trio – Madame Ranevskaya, Bessie Burgess and Mrs Rafi

It was the producer Michael Codron who brought Sam Mendes and Judi together, and after that canteen lunch Judi agreed to appear for him in *The Cherry Orchard*. Several people had used the term 'Chekhovian' to describe his recent Gorky production and he quickly showed he had an affinity with both Russians. He had the advantage of a brilliant new translation by the playwright and Russian linguist, Michael Frayn.

Sam Mendes admits now that he was a bit scared of directing Judi, an understandable apprehension in a twenty-three-year-old, but one that came as news to his star. 'Oh, was he? He never, ever let on. I remember saying once, "I'm not going to do that; I'm going to try something else." He said, "Well, you can if you want, but it won't work", and he turned away and wouldn't watch! He seemed very sure of himself, and he was terrific to work with.'

The admiration was mutual, and he observed, like others before him, that emotional change of gear which makes the watcher catch their breath. 'That's her speciality. She did it in *The Cherry Orchard* to an incredible degree. She'd be roaring with laughter and then she'd be close to tears. I remember her raging against her lover in Paris, ripping up his letter, with Michael Gough as Firs trying to take the remains of the letter away, her just talking about something else and covering it up and putting it in her bag later. It seemed almost imperceptible. She hated him but loved him, and she can do that in a line, in a second; she has enormous speed of thought and speed of emotion.'

He discovered that her emotional control was strong enough to contain her own corpsing within it, and to fool the audience. 'Nicholas Farrell said one of Trofimov's lines the wrong way round, and she was weeping and laughing, corpsing but continuing to cry simultaneously for about two minutes through an entire speech, and she pulled it off, it just seemed natural. Nick didn't know what to do. Try acting opposite that!'

Verbal slips are meat and drink to Judi. When Michael Gough could not remember Gaev's full name one night he clutched at the only Russian name he could think of, so Firs said, 'Vladimir Ashkenazy is out without his coat again.' Judi's response was to offer a prize to everyone who could work other Russian names into their performance, so there were several new touches, like exclaiming 'Shos TA Kovich' as if it were a sneeze.

Ronald Pickup, as her brother Gaev, was by now used to these games and well aware they did not betoken any lack of respect for the intentions of either the playwright or the director. 'Sam is a brilliant director, and he didn't treat Chekhov with the wrong kind of reverence, but it needed somebody to pull it into its sombre centre nevertheless, and Judi always did that. I used to listen to her do Act III every night, as I only came on at the end with a packet of herrings, and hearing her swirl around the emotional rollercoaster of that act was an example to any actor inhabiting a stage.'

Judi did her utmost to help particularly the younger members of the cast. Every night, just before they all burst onto the stage for the dance scene, Judi told the others a risqué joke so they were already laughing in a party mood as they came on.

The rehearsal period was quite a short one, but Judi's natural leadership of a company, which Joseph O'Conor had perceived in another Chekhov play twenty-five years earlier, quickly knitted this cast into a family. Even an unwitting challenge to that solidarity made her fiercely protective. Soon after the opening, Michael Gough was interviewed one morning on the radio and said, 'I am working with three of the most attractive women in the West End'; so that evening Judi got together Miranda Foster, Lesley Manville, Abigail McKern and Kate Duchene, and the five of them lined up in front of him, while Judi said, 'OK, Michael, which is the three?' Talking his way out of that slip of the tongue was quite a task.

She overreached herself, however, when she extended her confidence in her fellow-players to Carlotta's little dog, Pepper. 'I said to Kate Duchene after we'd been doing it for a bit, "Please, in the last scene don't take that dog on on a lead. It knows what to do; it's wonderful; just let it walk across on its own." He walked straight across and tried to squeeze in between the scenery. We were all falling about. I fell down and then it bounded on again. It had to be put back on the lead after that. That taught me a lesson.'

The theatre housing the play was the Aldwych, the original London home of the RSC where Judi had first appeared in it, so she was thrilled to get a good luck note from John Gielgud – 'To my favourite actress in my favourite play.'

One interruption at that performance could well have thrown less experienced players. A car alarm went off outside the theatre and no one could stop it. Since the police are only empowered to act if it is causing an obstruction, some infuriated members of the audience went out and lifted it into the middle of the road in desperation. Whether or not this distracted the critics, there was certainly an undertone of disappointment in their response – a feeling that the production could have done with that bit of extra rehearsal time that the RSC or the National would have lavished on it. But, despite that, Michael Billington recognised in the *Guardian* a 'Ranevskaya which, even by this actress's standards, is a remarkable performance'.

Jack Tinker, too, regretted in the *Daily Mail* that with 'such an impressive and awesomely experienced cast the whole never quite adds up to the sum of their various parts', but enthused, 'there is real passion, real joy, real sorrow, and real breeding in abundance whenever Dame Judi is on the stage'. She showed her power in the scene with Bernard Hill's Lopakhin – 'when she hears that the Cherry Orchard has been sold to the good and faithful former peasant she turns a look on Mr Hill that would have turned lesser men into a nasty mess on the carpet'.

Irving Wardle expressed no such reservations in *The Times*, praising the inventive production, and the acting, above all 'Judi Dench's Ranevskaya, whose wonderful performance is built on sequences of lightning emotional reversals. At one end of the spectrum she is the indolent Parisian prodigal, at the other the harsh-tongued Russian landowner. It is the speed and decisiveness that count: going down on her knees to beseech Trofimov for sympathy, then repulsing him and denouncing him as an ignorant prig, then flying after him with appeals for forgiveness. Every transition is articulated to the limit, most of all after her briskness in the last act, when she falls sobbing into the arms of Ronald Pickup's Gaev.'

Judi herself retains a grain of disappointment in her own performance and feels she got nearer to the character in Richard Eyre's television production nine years earlier. But her stage director was thrilled by this first collaboration.

Sam Mendes came to the conclusion that Judi's ability to plumb great emotional depths was more than just a supreme technical skill: 'I think there's a great, great sadness somewhere in her life, a great well of sadness she digs into. She doesn't hide behind a character, she doesn't hide behind an accent, she's an inside-out actor.'

She was required to use an accent in their next play together, her second by Sean O'Casey, *The Plough and the Stars*. This reunited her with Dearbhla Molloy, who was with her in *Juno and the Paycock*, and she rang her up to ask about the story and her part of Bessie Burgess – the drunken, slatternly Protestant in a tenement full of Catholics during the 1916 Easter Rising in Dublin. Dearbhla said, 'Judi, it's not a very big part', thinking that perhaps she would only play leading roles. So she hastily added, 'Look, all the really great female Irish actors have played it, and she has a wonderful death.' Judi's response was, 'Terrific! That's terrific. I'll do it.'

When it came to rehearsals, however, she shied away from her death scene until quite late. She revelled in Bessie's monstrous behaviour in the first three acts, and showed convincingly in the fourth how that rough, tough exterior concealed a heart of gold, as she nurses Nora Clitheroe in her nervous breakdown. When Nora runs to the window at the sound of shooting outside, Bessie drags her away and is fatally wounded herself.

Sam Mendes began to grow a little nervous as Judi kept putting off rehearsing that scene. 'She said, "Don't make me do this scene; I'm not ready; please don't make me do this scene." Then four days from the end of rehearsals I said, "Look, Judi", and she said, "Fine, I'm ready to do it now." '

The only technical direction he gave her was what he had gleaned from a man who had been shot, who told him it was like being run through with a red-hot poker, at the same time as being kicked by a horse with a force that knocked him off his feet. He turned out all the lights in the rehearsal room and did it by candlelight, with the rest of the cast who had just left the stage sitting around.

Then he saw that Judi was indeed ready. 'It was such a humiliating death – she begs and pleads, curses herself for getting in the way, then she falls and talks about how much blood is coming, and almost monologues her own death. Judi followed her own instinct and knew just what to do; she just went to the end and I said, "That's it." I didn't really direct that scene at all, and it was one of the best moments of the play. You almost couldn't watch, it was so degrading, and she was so bitter about it. When you see the craft of acting done to such a degree, at such close quarters, it becomes the mark against which you hold truthful acting.'

Judi's instinctive insight into whatever character she is playing is accompanied by very sensitive antennae for the troubles of her fellow-actors. Dearbhla Molloy experienced this in both the O'Casey plays she did with her.

During *Juno and the Paycock* her younger sister, who was nineteen, was knocked down by a motor bike and severely injured. She was put on life-support machines and had a weekly series of operations for months, so every Wednesday Dearbhla and her brother, who was a priest, fasted as a way of focusing their minds on their sister. Judi noticed, and when she found out why, she announced that she would fast as well on that day. When she told Michael, he joined them, in a fast that continued for about eighteen months. At one point Dearbhla was told that her sister might have to lose her leg, but two nights before the planned operation the surgeon said to her, 'The most extraordinary thing has happened. There is no need to do this operation. I cannot explain to you why.' But Judi is convinced she knows why: 'It was not the fasting that did it, but the concentration of a lot of minds on one day on one subject that did it – it was a victory of mind over matter.' She has adopted the same tactic several times since in an attempt to help those close to her who have been seriously ill.

As rehearsals began for *The Plough and the Stars* Dearbhla was enduring another emotional trauma – the break-up of her marriage. 'I don't reveal myself that easily, and yet on day two of rehearsal Jude came over and said, "There's something terribly wrong, what is it?" She took me under her wing, took me home with her and made me tell her the story on the way down. So she's nursed me through two of the most terrible things that have happened to me in my life.'

Their stage relationship was very different from the mother and daughter in *Juno*, but just as strong for Paul Taylor in the *Independent*, who admired the richness of detail in the production and especially Judi's 'magnificent portrayal' of Bessie, 'a tatty bundle of bellicosity with a wretched-urchin, booze-florid face, she is always twitching to launch herself like a furious distempered terrier at her Catholic neighbours. Her disputes with Dearbhla Molloy's wonderfully lugubrious Mrs Gogan are miniature masterpieces of raffish, unsentimental comedy.'

Michael Billington thought them well-matched, too, in the *Guardian*, and he warmed to the way in which 'Judi Dench offers us not a star turn but a crafted piece of ensemble acting: she makes Bessie both a Thersites-like commentator on the futility of conflict and a blotchy-featured boozer with a fundamentally good heart.'

Jack Tinker paid glowing tribute in the *Daily Mail* to her 'tottering, brawling rag bag of twitching rage at her lot' as 'a towering performance in a production crowded with marvellous moments'.

With these descriptions of her convincingly blowsy look, it is perhaps not surprising that when Judi was waiting behind a flat one night to make her entrance onto the Young Vic stage, she overheard one woman in the audience say to another, 'She played Juliet once', which elicited the response, 'You are joking!'

During the run Judi suffered another great personal loss, when Peggy Ashcroft died. 'I went up to the hospital to see her that day, and the registrar of the hospital came and said, "Would you like to come this way?" He took me into a room and said, "She died about twenty minutes ago", and I was so glad I heard that way. I had to make an announcement at the end that night and I thought, "I don't want to call for silence, because Peggy wouldn't have wanted that", so I called for applause. We could have stood there for half an hour while they clapped."

Peggy Ashcroft had been one of her models from the earliest days, had supported her through the difficult times with Michel St-Denis, offered her enormously helpful advice over the years since, and become a dearly loved friend. At the memorial service in Westminster Abbey, there was a particularly moving moment when Judi and

Dorothy Tutin together read the dirge from *Cymbeline* – 'Fear no more the heat o' the sun' – which they rehearsed with Trevor Nunn the night before, when they both decided to wear contact lenses. They seemed to support each other in their grief and the emotion of the occasion was highlighted when John Gielgud, who had partnered Peggy on so many memorable occasions, invoked Shakespeare's epitaph for Cleopatra as 'a lass unparallel'd'.

She mourned Peggy deeply and was grateful for the distraction of a new directing challenge – the Rodgers and Hart musical *The Boys from Syracuse*. Judi fell in love with the show at its Drury Lane première in 1963 and her affection for it was, if anything, enhanced by her success in *The Comedy of Errors*, on which it is based. Ian Talbot invited her to choose something to direct at the Open-Air Theatre in Regent's Park and jumped at her suggestion, as it had never been revived in London since that original production.

One of the Antipholus twins was played by Bill Homewood and the other by Peter Woodward, the son of her old stage partner Edward. Peter had known Judi from when he was a little boy and his affection for her did not diminish his awe of her talents. 'She was very good at not doing too much showing. I mean we knew that she could play all the parts, male and female, better than we could, but she never made us aware of it.'

He was also playing Macbeth in that season and had given himself some exhausting fights in that play, so he felt guilty at sometimes feeling tired in Judi's rehearsals. 'She expects everyone else to have her enthusiasm and energy, quite rightly, and I think she's always surprised when people don't, especially young actors. If they get bolshie she's surprised and disappointed, and I don't think she can understand why anyone would want to be in the theatre if they're not as happy in it as she is. And she's absolutely right: it's a job where you have to be one hundred per cent enthusiastic, or you really shouldn't do it.'

Judi infused so much of her enthusiasm and energy into this young cast that the opening night triumphed through showers of rain that suspended the action three times, but the audience sat tight to the end under steaming umbrellas.

Jack Tinker urged his *Daily Mail* readers to go to this 'fresh-as-a-daisy revival'. Claire Armitstead delighted in the *Financial Times* in 'a

With Finty.

"What does King Lear say?"
"Never, never – FIVE times!"

With Finty – two generations of graduates from the Central School of Speech and Drama.

With Michael and Finty at Buckingham Palace in 1988 after becoming Dame Judi Dench.

With Richard Warwick, Susan Penhaligon and Michael in *A Fine Romance*, directed by James Cellan-Jones, LWT 1980.

'People shouldn't demean situation comedy, because it's so difficult.'

With Maurice Denham and Michael at the première of *84, Charing Cross Road*, directed by David Jones, 1986.

'It wasn't much of a part on the page, but she made it seem a terrific part.'

With David Hare on location for *The Crew*. Postcard to Martin Jarvis: 'Very hard work, being only two of us in it, but Nick seems very pleased.'

With Edward Jewesbury, Emma Thompson, Kenneth Branagh and Gerard Horan – the cast she directed in *Look Back in Anger*, 1989, at Birmingham Repertory Theatre, and on TV.

'Judi took an anti-sentimental view of the play.'

The spy-chief 'M' in *Goldeneye*, her first James Bond movie.

'I think she was genuinely terrified of playing 'M', which she does like falling off a log really.'

Christine Foskett with Corey Johnson as Butch in *Absolute Hell*, directed by Anthony Page, National Theatre 1995. 'Judi Dench makes the club's proprietress a sexily rump-twitching figure, constantly caught between laughter and tears.'

Desirée Armfeldt with Laurence Guittard as her lover Frederik in *A Little Night Music*, directed by Sean Mathias, National Theatre 1995.

'Her voice cracks unforget-tably in *Send in the Clowns*, as she confronts with genuine despair life's missed chances.'

Esmé with Samantha Bond as Amy in *Amy's View*, directed by Richard Eyre, National Theatre 1997.

'A major dramatist has written a strong, rich play, and a major actress has done him proud.'

Queen Victoria with Billy
Connolly as John Brown
in *Mrs Brown*, directed by John
Madden, Ecosse Films, 1997.
'The film makes such effective
drama from tiny convulsions
of feeling that a look can
seem an embrace, the touch
of a hand can seem like
ravishment.'

Nominated for Best Actress
at the Academy Awards
ceremony in Hollywood,
March 23rd 1998.

'The whole thing is amazingly
tatty, and absurd, and we had
a wonderful time. I wouldn't
have missed it for anything.'

deliciously actor-centred confection, as pleasing to the eye as to the ear'. Paul Taylor responded to 'the joyful freshness of Judi Dench's production' in the *Independent*; and Michael Billington claimed in the *Guardian* that it 'actually seems closer to Shakespeare than Ian Judge's campily heartless version of the original play at the Barbican'.

After that diversion, Judi returned to the National Theatre to complete her hat-trick of performances for Sam Mendes with Mrs Rafi in a revival of Edward Bond's *The Sea*. Described variously as 'a small coast-town Clytemnestra' or 'an East Anglian Lady Bracknell', this part was a true monster of a woman, who rules the eccentric members of her small community with a rod of iron. When a young man is drowned in a storm, his death sets off a crisis in the local relationships, which soon descends into black comedy. It is set in 1907, and Mrs Rafi's grand costume made her look indeed not unlike a demonic Lady Bracknell.

By now the director had twigged that Judi was not going to read the whole play in advance, so he persuaded her to do it by telling her the story, and showing her Mrs Rafi's big speech at the end alone on a cliff. He understood the reasons for her refusal to sit down alone with the script: 'it robs her of her instinct to read the play without anyone else there. You know why when you work with her: she can't act without people in front of her. I'm always asking her to do Beckett's *Happy Days*, and it clearly fills her with absolute horror.'

She is psychologically incapable of doing a one-woman show, though she is often asked. When her husband opened his solo act as John Aubrey in *Brief Lives* in 1997, she said her admiration was unbounded. 'I *could not do that*, I couldn't do it if I was paid a million for each performance. There's no one to bounce off, no one to share it with. It all comes down to the fact I don't like being on my own, and the thought of going to that dressing-room on my own – I just couldn't do it. I suppose it's a huge flaw in my character, in that I'm so reliant on other people, but I am, and I recognise it now even more.'

That reliance is far from one-sided, which Sam Mendes had fully grasped by the time of this third production. 'The wonderful thing she does in rehearsal is that she acts *with* people. She says, "Come on, do this with me", and she raises everyone else's game, because she's so fantastically alive and alert from moment to moment. She never tramlines; she never does the same thing twice; it's always fractionally different, always shifting, catching the light. You can feel people wanting to act with her, to respond to her, being drawn towards playing an emotional scene with her. They'll never ever shy away from her. With a lot of big actors, their energy is so overpowering on the stage that people want to run away from them and play their scene over there somewhere, but you find many people give their best performances with Judi.'

In *The Sea* she worked for the first time with Celia Imrie, who shared her highly developed sense of the ridiculous. She was playing Mrs Rafi's downtrodden companion, who rebels at the funeral by outsinging her employer, and she had not met Judi until the read-through. 'Sam made the fatal error when we got to the hymn of saying, "OK, go on then, sing." My character had to outdo her in the descant, and Judi had to try to outdo me. Well, it's one thing if you're talking and trying not to laugh, but it's quite another if you're singing and trying not to laugh. We were sitting opposite each other, and when we looked up we both had mascara down our cheeks like pandas.'

When they got down to work after the hysteria of the read-through, the director met with some resistance from Judi once again, in the scene where Mrs Rafi rehearses some amateur theatricals. 'She just refused to show off, because as an actress she's absolutely *not* a show-off, and eventually I stood up and said, "You've *got* to show off, Judi." She said, "I don't want to, I can't." I said, "Look, this woman has just got to be monstrous; she's got to tell everyone else how to act the whole time, which is what you never do." She got a bit tearful, but said, "I'll get it up at home", (that phrase so familiar to her other directors) "and came in the following day and did it straight off, just like that.'

Edward Bond came to one rehearsal, and his reputation had pre-ceded him. The violence in his other plays like *Saved*, or his version of *Lear*, though transmuted into savage humour in this one, led them to expect a very fierce author to arrive. Their reaction conjured up a vivid image for Judi: 'All the cast were terrified. I looked at the rest of them huddled in one corner looking down, and thought, "I know exactly what this looks like, it's like the sheep in the shedding-ring." But Edward Bond was lovely, in fact.'

However, it is hard to believe that the author would have been as forgiving of the leading lady as the director found he had to be once it opened. 'There was a scene where they had to study costume drawings for the play that she was directing on-stage, and every night she replaced the drawings by something else – nude pictures, people in suspenders, she defaced the costume designs, wrote graffiti about Celia Imrie, and they would stand with their backs to the audience and roar. People might think, "Oh, so it's all right to mess around", and then she'd go straight in to the scene absolutely bang-on, while everyone else would be spiralling out of control.'

Celia Imrie always had a slight shiver of apprehension as this scene approached, and one night she had a particular surprise. Judi asked her, when she first read the credits in the programme, 'Excuse me, what's this I see? *The House of Whipcord*. What's that?'

'Oh Judi, it was a porn film I made when I was about twenty-one.'

'Oh, I don't believe it. You're making it up.'

'I'm not. It was soft-porn, and I only threw a Bible out of the window, I didn't take my clothes off, OK?'

'You're joking, I don't believe you.'

A couple of months later, as the two of them launched into what everyone had come to regard as the booby-trapped scene with the costume designs, Judi kept pointing to a box on the table. Celia thought, 'Oh Lord, had I better open it, then?' Inside was a video of *The House of Whipcord*, which she had never seen, and nor had anyone else as far as she knew, since it was made back in 1974; but that was hardly a challenge to such a knowledgeable and determined shopper as Judi has always been.

Both the play and the production seemed to catch the critics on the hop. 'I never expected to enjoy a play by Edward Bond', wrote Charles Spencer in the *Daily Telegraph*, but 'this production of *The Sea* is one of the year's most welcome dramatic surprises, leaving the audience stirred rather than shaken.'

John Peter was overwhelmed in the *Sunday Times* by this author's heroine. 'Only an Englishman could have dreamt up this frightful, mesmerising woman, shrill and indomitable, both nemesis and nanny. Judi Dench plays her like a demented empress who has graduated from some ghastly academy of deportment, forever outfacing the menace of imaginary disorder, cutting very small people down to size, and despising the world which doesn't have enough sense to be saved by her. It is a consummately stylish performance, fiercely and coolly funny, genteel, evil and preposterous in equal proportions.'

Michael Billington wished in the *Guardian* that the author would more often exercise this 'gift for rueful, regenerative comedy', so well brought out by Judi with 'the great actress's eye for detail. When, in the draper's, she remarks, "People are judged by what they have on their hands" she casts a faint withering glance at her companion's gloves; and, assuming the role of Orpheus in amateur theatricals, she tosses her shawl over her shoulder with the imperiousness of a country-house Bernhardt.'

For Nicholas de Jongh in the *Evening Standard*, in that scene 'she attacks her role [as] if she had a grudge against it', vindicating the director's early pressure on her to make the most of Mrs Rafi's showing off.

She was pleased that Celia Imrie won the Clarence Derwent Award for Best Supporting Actress in *The Sea*, but made sure she heard her say, 'Oh, now I suppose we'll have to go to Oxfam to buy her another cardigan.' This began another of her long-running gags, pretending that Celia should always stick to cardigan parts and never, ever attempt to be glamorous, saying it doesn't suit her at all.

Judi's own audiences had got used to seeing her in a succession of wigs – glamorous, imposing, drab, or grotesque – that it came almost as a shock suddenly to see her on television without one, in a new situation comedy, *As Time Goes By*. This had a couple of similarities to *A Fine Romance*: it employed the same writer, Bob Larbey, and it too was commissioned for just one series, with no longer life antici-pated for it. That was in 1991, and in 1998 it is still going strong.

nineteen

1991—93

As Time Goes By — Coriolanus —
The Gift of the Gorgon

The Theatre of Comedy was founded in 1983 by Ray Cooney and thirty of the best-known stars of British comedy, to produce both new plays and classic revivals. Its success soon led it to branch out into television as well, in association with the American producer Don Taffner, who set up a UK arm of his business to handle it.

An early script to be considered was entitled *Winter with Flowers* by Colin Bostock-Smith. (Much later, it was changed to the more explicable title of *As Time Goes By*, underlined by the signature tune so familiar from the Bogart/Bergman relationship in *Casablanca*.) Geoffrey Palmer read it and liked the basic idea of a romance between a nurse and a subaltern who lose touch when he goes off to the Korean War; they marry other people and only meet again thirty-five years later when she is widowed and he is divorced. The original writer seemed unable to develop the idea, so the writer of *A Fine Romance*, Bob Larbey, was invited to take it over. At this stage the proposal was for Jean Simmons to play opposite Geoffrey Palmer. He suggested the highly experienced Sydney Lotterby as the director, and the three men went to discuss the project with the prospective leading lady over lunch at the Pomme d'Amour restaurant in Holland Park.

Negotiations then drifted for some months, until eventually Jean Simmons chose to do a mini-series for American television instead. None of the principals concerned can remember who suggested Judi to play Jean Pargeter, though they all agree it is impossible now to think of anyone else in the role. She says she accepted it because she wanted to work with Geoffrey Palmer, despite their two previous encounters having been slightly awkward ones. 'I was in the General Trading Company with Finty one Christmas, and he tried to pick me up. He said, "I'd rather be anywhere in the world than here."'

He says he hesitated over whether to say hello or not at that chance meeting, in case she did think he was trying to pick her up. Later on she heard that Tenniel Evans, her actor-friend from the York Mystery Plays, wanted to become a lay priest and that Geoffrey had said to him, 'Rubbish, you mustn't do that.' When she went with Michael to see *An Evening with Peter Ustinov*, she found herself sitting right in front of the Palmers and she turned round and said, 'I hear what you've done to Tenniel Evans. How dare you!'

But despite these two hiccups, Geoffrey was so delighted at the prospect of working with her that he was downcast when the director told him that Judi was not available for the April dates allocated by the BBC for recording, and they had been asked to recast. After about ten days' gloom he rang up and said, 'Look Syd, this is bollocks. I don't want to do it without Judi. We've been hanging around for eighteen months already, so what's another little delay?' Sydney Lotterby said he did not want to do it without Judi either and, rather to their astonishment, the BBC agreed to reschedule the recordings for October.

The younger members of the cast only met Judi when rehearsals began and were unsure at first whether to address her by her title or not, an uncertainty that was resolved within the first five minutes. Moira Brooker, who plays her daughter in the series, was more surprised by the realisation that, 'considering she's been at it so long, she's totally uncynical, and I find that incredible. She's determined to enjoy it every day.'

When she was a drama student, Jenny Funnell used to write to lots of actors she saw in shows, 'and Judi was the only one who ever replied. I saw *A Kind of Alaska* at the National four times because I loved it so much, and when I wrote to her I got the most amazing letter back, saying, "Good luck, and I hope everything goes well at drama school." I've still got it in my scrapbook.' She has now played the secretary, Sandy, in seven series of *As Times Goes By*, and has still not told Judi about the impact of receiving that first letter.

Judi created her new company family in no time. When Jenny broke up with her boyfriend she was heartbroken, and Judi just swept her up and took her home for Christmas. Jenny's eyes glistened as she remembered walking back across the fields after Midnight Mass and seeing candles lit in all the windows, creating a magical effect. 'Then we had a champagne breakfast with the most amazing Christmas stockings.'

Judi has always put a huge amount of thought and care into those Christmas stockings, and Geoffrey Palmer was made to wish he had not let slip that his wife Sally still did one for him and their children (now middle-aged), but he never made one up for her. 'What?! You mean *she* does a stocking every year for *you*, and the children, and *you* don't do one for her?'

Two days later she arrived at the BBC rehearsal rooms in Acton with a stocking and a small present. 'Do you think you could manage the other things yourself? I'll give you lots of ideas.'

The two co-stars' approach to their work is totally different in the way they prepare. Geoffrey likes to read all the scripts in the series before work begins on episode one; Judi arrives for the read-through as usual, not even having read that one. 'There is something about the whole business of reading it, and knowing that's the particular jump you've got to do. It's a bit like going to look at Becher's Brook in the Grand National. I wouldn't be one of those people; I'd think, "Well, I'll know how high it is when I come to it." I wouldn't be a careful jockey.'

His analogy is drawn from a different sport. He says he has to try and get ahead of the game, because 'acting with Judi is like playing football with Pele; it's a whole different league.'

Philip Bretherton, who plays the street-wise Alistair, has the same reaction. 'She can look at you, and it's almost as if she has a switch somewhere and this light goes on. You think, "Where the hell does that come from?" This light just zings across and takes your breath away.'

Sydney Lotterby's pedigree in television comedy embraces the creation of *Porridge*, *Open All Hours*, *Yes, Minister*, and *Last of the Summer Wine*, so he was not unused to comic invention from stars like Ronnie Barker and David Jason, but Judi still managed to catch him out.

One day she brought her little dog, a Shih-Tzu named Henry, who sat quietly on a chair watching the rehearsal. When the director went out of the room briefly, Judi suddenly commanded them all to hide. Unfamiliar as yet with this side of her, the others looked at her in puzzlement. 'Just hide', she said urgently, so they hid in various pieces of property furniture placed around – wardrobes and cabinets, leaving Henry on his chair. Philip Bretherton says, 'It worked exactly as she planned it, because Syd came back and obviously thought, "Oh I must have told them all they could go for a break." So he shrugged his shoulders and started talking to the dog, just as you would if you thought no one could hear you, and you were in a room on your own. Judi's always the first one to break her practical jokes, because she always laughs before everyone else does. The metal cabinet she was in started to shake, and that's what gave it away.'

At one script discussion of what turned different people on, Sydney remarked, 'The thing I find really sexy is long black dresses, short sleeves, bare elbows and long black gloves – that little bit of bare flesh is just wonderful.' Two weeks later, on the Tuesday when everyone usually comes in early, he found he was waiting to start the read-through, and asked impatiently, 'Where the hell are all those women? Where've they all gone?' Then they all trooped in wearing long black dresses, short sleeves and long gloves. This developed into one of the standing jokes of this series, and a large group photograph of the whole team was painted over to put everyone in black dresses, including all the men in the cast and crew.

The constant joking makes the rehearsals very relaxed, a necessary ingredient in a series recorded weekly, when Judi is often also playing in the theatre every evening and one or maybe two matinées as well. The cast assemble on Tuesdays, and by Friday morning must be word-perfect for the run-through in front of all the studio technicians. Saturday morning is two fast run-throughs, and camera rehearsal starts on Sunday at 10.30 a.m.; the recording before an invited studio audience begins at 8 p.m. By then the pressure on the actors has really built, on even the most experienced like Geoffrey Palmer, who says, 'I have spent forty-eight years pretending I'm relaxed, and I get tense, but Judi gets an absolute knot across her shoulders. Squeeze her there and you can feel it, it's like a lot of ball-bearings.'

Much of that is the tension building up in her about going out and talking to the audience beforehand, none of whom would sense the slightest nervousness either then or during the recording. One of her compensating gifts is the ability to catnap at will for several minutes when she is not needed, and not just in the rehearsal room. According to Geoffrey, 'in the studio, if she's not wanted in the scene after we've been in bed, she'll be asleep in seconds, always.'

After a Monday off, the whole process begins again on the Tuesday. Adrenalin does much to carry Judi through this performing treadmill to the last episode, but combining that during the seventh series in 1998 with playing *Amy's View* nightly at the Aldwych was such a heavy load that the day she finished the last television recording, she went down with a viral throat infection and nearly lost her voice. Only her determination kept her going without missing a performance in the theatre.

As Times Goes By was an instant hit in 1991, drawing an audience of over twelve million, and a second series was immediately commissioned by the BBC. Sydney Lotterby received an unexpected deputation from the studio crew at the end of the first, to ask if they could all please work on any future series, a request he has managed to bring off so far in six subsequent series – quite a logistical and managerial feat in an operation the size of the BBC. So Judi's ideal of a company family is quite a big one for this show, and the resultant rapport between cast and crew in the studio is palpable.

One thing was not repeated in any series after the first. At the press call to introduce the opening episode a woman journalist outraged Judi by asking her, 'Who was the first person you slept with, and where was that?' She vowed she would never appear at another press call, and she has kept to her word.

At the end of each series since the second one, everyone has thought that it would be the last, but Bob Larbey has sustained the narrative development beyond Lionel and Jean getting married, and feels that their relationship has more potential left in it. The audience clearly agrees with him, since though it has fluctuated a bit in numbers depending on its time slot, for the recent series it was back up to the size of the first. It has also sold well abroad and has been a particular success on the Public Broadcasting network in the USA, where it is running a couple of series behind the UK transmissions.

With her new sitcom series well launched, Judi's next date on-stage was as Kenneth Branagh's mother again, in *Coriolanus*. She agreed to play Volumnia the moment he asked her and quickly communicated to him her vision of the part. 'She doesn't want to fall into the traps of other actresses; she has a very strong sense of what will work for her. She wanted a very sexy relationship with Coriolanus, more as a rival to his wife.'

To mark the thirtieth anniversary of the Chichester Festival Theatre, its Director, Patrick Garland, invited the Renaissance Company to open the season with this play that had never previously been seen there, in the hope that it would be the first of many such visits, a hope as yet unfulfilled.

He attended the first rehearsal in London and the director, Tim Supple, gave a very serious talk about the play before it began. The seriousness of the read-through, however, failed to last beyond Act IV, when a Roman greets a Volscian with the line, 'I know you well, sir; and you know me; your name, I think, is Adrian.' This struck Judi as deeply incongruous, and she echoed, 'Oh, Adrian!' and shrieked with laughter.

The battle scenes are difficult to stage convincingly, and the numbers for the warring armies were made up by recruiting fifty-three local amateurs. Iain Glen was playing Coriolanus' adversary, Tullus Aufidius, and their sword fights produced some deep cuts; Coriolanus had to don protective gloves after he fractured his finger. But the accident which drew most attention was Judi's, partly because it happened at the Gala Performance in June attended by the Renaissance Patron, the Prince of Wales. She sprained her ankle in one scene and the stabbing pain brought the action to a halt. Off-stage, the tannoy went dead; Branagh came rushing up to help carry her off, and the appeal that everyone dreads had to be made – 'Is there a doctor in the house?' Luckily there were two, who both hurried round to the stage door. Patrick Garland was rung in his office and ran over to find Judi white and shaken.

She said, 'I feel I've let them down, Patrick.'

He asked her, 'What would you like me to do? Shall I stop the performance, or cut your last scene?'

'You can't possibly cut the scene; you'll have no play. No, no, I'll go on and finish the play.'

After an anxious fifteen-minute hiatus, a bandaged Volumnia hobbled back on-stage with a stick and completed the performance. When Kenneth Branagh led her on by the hand for the curtain call, she was met by thunderous applause for her courage in carrying on to the end. She was so embarrassed by this ovation that he joked to defuse it: 'As we turned round to go off Kenny said, "Get off-stage, you limping bitch!",' which provoked the intended giggle.

She played the next few nights supported by a stick, but jettisoned it as soon as possible, hating to look as if she was appealing for sympathy, and never missed a performance. The box office appeal of the two stars, plus Richard Briers as Menenius, and Susannah Harker as Virgilia, packed the theatre for its limited run, despite some decidedly lukewarm notices.

Michael Billington sighed in the *Guardian* that the production lacked a point of view, and that the occupant of the title role lacked vulnerability, though 'he has, I believe, a still-better Coriolanus lurking within him that a great director might discover'. The other characterisations were damned with faint praise, but 'a shining exception, however, is Judi Dench as Volumnia. She may lack the character's tactile sensuality but at least she suggests a specific human being: one first seen enthusiastically sword-fighting with her grandson and last glimpsed assuming a masked impassivity at the realisation that she has, in effect, signed her son's death warrant.'

Paul Taylor in the *Independent* also found it unilluminating, with no real sense of danger. 'If the production is worth seeing, it's for Dench, whose climactic entreaty to the hero is a thrilling mixture of desperation and calculation.'

Benedict Nightingale was one of the few to respond warmly, in *The Times*, particularly to the aggression of Coriolanus: 'I haven't heard anybody, either actor or aspiring politician, sneer so stylishly in ages ... There are no tendentious interpretations, no fancy "directorial concepts" here; just Branagh's electricity, Dench's truculent punch, Richard Briers's Menenius, a complacent housemaster out of his depth with a prefect as headstrong as Coriolanus; and some capable supporting performances.'

When the run ended Judi returned to the Royal Shakespeare Company in a new play by Peter Shaffer, *The Gift of the Gorgon*, directed by Peter Hall, in which she gave a performance that was hugely admired by everyone except her. She ended up hating the part and the play even more than Portia and *The Merchant of Venice*.

She played Helen, the widow of playwright Edward Damson,

living on a Greek island. She is visited by Edward's illegitimate son Philip, who wants her permission to write the biography of the father he never met. Over the next two days she tells Philip the story of her eighteen-year marriage, moving in and out of flashback and the present day. There is much reference to Greek myth, and Helen is compared to Athena who helped Perseus slay the snake-headed Gorgon, and then watched him become what he had killed.

Jeremy Northam played the young stepson, and his father was Michael Pennington, who had played Mirabell to her Millamant. Now his character was named Damson, the joke between them was that he got all the plum parts. 'So we're Mr and Mrs Plum to each other, and I suppose we always will be.' He loved the play and was very keen to do it and to this day he is mystified by Judi's antipathy to it. This showed itself early on and there came a morning when she ground to a halt, threw the script up in the air and locked herself in the ladies' loo. When Ella Kenyon, an actress in the company, asked her, 'Is there anything you want?' Judi wailed, 'Yes, I want to go home to Michael.' While Peter Shaffer and Michael Pennington sat and waited in the Clapham rehearsal room, Peter Hall then had a long private talk with Judi, trying to calm her fears. Her long-standing trust in him had led her to accept the part without reading much of it, for which she reproaches herself. 'If I'd read it to the end I'd never have agreed to do it. My admiration for Peter Shaffer was unbounded. *Five-Finger Exercise* and *Royal Hunt of the Sun* had made a huge impression on me, and at the same time as this I was doing a radio play of his – *Whom Do I Have The Pleasure Of Addressing?* It was just this play I found so difficult.'

However, Peter Hall's persuasive powers kept her on board, as they had similarly conquered Anthony Hopkins' deep reservations about his ability to play Antony to her Cleopatra.

Judi cannot articulate what it was in her that so resisted it, but her close friend Pinkie Kavanaugh is absolutely convinced that it was the theme of revenge in the play that Judi found so repugnant, as the very idea is so alien to her nature. Her unhappiness by no means inhibited her performance, and her co-star soon realised that he was going to have to be as much on his mettle as he had in *The Way of the World*. He puts the challenge in the highest league: 'She's very fast, like John Gielgud is very fast. Their speed is something to do with real quality, you don't miss a word, the mind is moving at the same speed as the tongue. Anyone can go fast, but it's the speed of both those two actors, mentally and emotionally, that's so impressive to watch.'

When it opened in the Pit at the Barbican it was a knockout with the public and the press. For Michael Billington in the *Guardian* it was 'bracingly theatrical, endlessly alive and fiercely ambitious, the best thing Shaffer had done since *Amadeus*', and he much admired Peter Hall's production. 'Judi Dench as Helen also reminds us why she is one of our greatest actresses. Michael Pennington as Edward shrewdly suggests the vanity and cruelty lurking inside the daemonic dramatist, and Jeremy Northam brings to the academic son a nice touch of filial puzzlement.'

He thought it almost burst out of the confines of the tiny Pit and so did Jack Tinker in the *Daily Mail*, who found it a 'profound and disturbing play ... Dame Judi, the ringing voice of civilised reason, reconstructs her late husband's history in dramatised and anguished flashbacks, giving it the sort of intensely moving compassion of which she is the past mistress.'

Judi took some of her personal anguish out on the new Director of the RSC, Adrian Noble, when he came round with his executive producer, Michael Attenborough, to wish her good luck before the last performance at the Barbican; because she hates the building even more than she hated that play. She says the dressing-rooms are like cells, with dirty windows looking out into the underground car park. 'I loathe it. I think it's a monstrous building, and I told Adrian and Michael that I would never go back there to do a play, whatever the circumstances, I'm afraid. I simply cannot believe you can have a company feeling when you're going up and down in lifts all the time, and you never meet the other actors.'

Not that she was all that keen to transfer to the West End with *The Gift of the Gorgon*. She resisted for a long time and tried to enlist Michael Pennington on her side. 'She kept urging me to price myself out and ask for too much money, so that the whole project would collapse. This was jocular stuff, but the day I said, "No, I've made terms", she nearly killed me, mockingly.'

She eventually succumbed, reluctantly, when Peter Hall rang her up and said, 'Look, Judi, are you really prepared to put all these other people out of work?' When it moved to the much bigger space of

Wyndham's Theatre, it was sold out as quickly as it had been at the Pit. The cast were nervous about adjusting it to this new arena and Michael Pennington found he was not alone in a certain actor's ritual. 'We both have a tendency, like Joe Louis, to have a look at the ring before the other fighter appears; I remember prowling around the stage at about half-past six, only to find her prowling around the stage as well, just trying to get our feet attached to the ground.'

It was another part of her anatomy that transfixed Samantha Bond when she went to Wyndham's. 'The curtain went up and Judi was by a table, leaning on one arm, and this arm was so full of pain and awfulness that my whole heart came into my mouth, and I thought, "What has happened to that poor woman?" I knew three of the other actors in the play as well as Judi, and I didn't go backstage afterwards because I didn't want to break the spell, so I wrote them all cards. I won't ever forget that arm. I have a moment in *Amy's View* when Dominic's been horrible and I come on and lean on the table, and I always think, "I'm going to do my best arm now for her"; but I've never told her, because if I said, "From the moment I looked at your forearm . . ." she'd think I was really barking.'

Judi played out her contract for the West End run but flatly refused to extend it, even though it was still playing to packed houses after six months.

When she is playing every night rather than in repertoire, Judi likes to work on something else during the day, and she slipped her director's hat back on in the early summer of 1993 for *Romeo and Juliet* at the Open-Air Theatre in Regent's Park. It was more than three decades since she starred in Zeffirelli's production, but she had just renewed her acquaintance with the play as the Nurse, in a radio production with Kenneth Branagh.

She cast two young unknowns as the lovers, Zubin Varla and Rebecca Callard, but felt that she let them down because she could not devote enough time to the production. She had to stop rehearsals by 4 p.m. each day to go and lie down before her evening performance and found that she just 'ran out of steam'. Any regrets she had were unallayed by the generally sharp response from the press, led by Nicholas de Jongh's description of it in the *Evening Standard* as 'a lame-duck production, which lacks a clearly defined concept of or response to the play'. Judi distrusts terms like 'concept', which for her can mean directors or designers imposing an interpretation which may be far from the author's intention. But she has not directed again since that frustrating experience.

A much happier occasion, at least until its last day, was the radio production of *King Lear*, with a stellar cast supporting John Gielgud in the title role, to celebrate his ninetieth birthday – 14 April 1994. It was recorded the previous September over several days, with Judi as Goneril and Kenneth Branagh, who had proposed this Renaissance co-production with the BBC, as Edmund. It was cast right down to the tiniest roles with star actors, all of whom wanted to be part of this special tribute to Gielgud.

On the night before the last day's recording, Judi returned to her home in Surrey. Finty was now living in the Hampstead house with two friends and she awoke around 1 a.m. to discover that a burning candle had set fire to the curtains. She called the fire brigade and it was nearly 4 a.m. before it appeared to be put out. By great good fortune no one was sleeping upstairs when a second fire blazed up at 7 a.m. This time the house was virtually gutted, but luckily no one was hurt. Judi rushed up from Surrey to check that everyone was safe and her relief outweighed the loss of so many of her possessions and career mementoes. But the shock of seeing the burnt-out shell of the first home she owned was enough to make her burst into tears.

Professional as ever, even in such a crisis she sent a message to the producer, Glyn Dearman, to say she would be a little late in the studio, but could carry on with the recording so long as nobody mentioned the fire. He managed to warn all the cast, with one notable exception. When she arrived, nothing was said to her about the night's events until John Gielgud came in and rushed over to say, 'Judi, my poor darling, are you insured?' At which point she collapsed sobbing into his arms. Later he sent her a little box that had belonged to Peggy Ashcroft, as a memento to help replace personal treasures lost in the fire. When the programme was broadcast, there was no audible trace of the emotional pressure she was under at that time. (Goneril and Regan are both associated with unhappy experiences for Judi, and it seems a shame that she never played the youngest sister; she would have been much better suited to Cordelia, but that role is one of the very few glaring omissions in her Shakespearean gallery.) The Hampstead house took months to restore, and when it was habitable again Finty moved back in. It is her house now, and Judi only stays overnight on rare occasions, preferring to drive home to Surrey even when she is playing in London six nights a week with a couple of matinées as well. She says she could not bear 'to live in the smoke again', now that she is so settled in her ideal home in the country, even if it does often mean long drives early in the morning or late at night.

1993 was a year she was glad to put behind her, with such unhappy memories in both her private and her professional life. Now she looked forward eagerly to rejoining the National Theatre for a run of plays, in an ambience that she really loves. 'It's wonderful. All the dressing-rooms look out on each other; you can see everybody getting ready, and we can all talk to each other – the National's heaven.'

The first play was to be *The Seagull*, directed by John Caird, with several of her old friends in the cast.

twenty

1994–96

The Seagull – Absolute Hell – A Little Night Music

John Caird had known Judi since she played Imogen at Stratford in the 1979 *Cymbeline*, when he was directing other plays for the RSC, but they never actually worked together until *The Seagull*. So when Richard Eyre invited him to direct it at the National, with Judi as Arkadina, he leapt at it. The only other decision taken for him was that it had to be in the large Olivier Theatre, when he would have preferred the studio ambience of the Cottesloe.

He was given a free hand with the rest of the casting but, as soon as word got out, he was inundated by requests to be in it. One was from Norman Rodway. 'I did something I've never done before. I wrote to John Caird and said, "I hear that Judi's doing *The Seagull*. Can I be in it please, because it's the only Chekhov I've never been in, and I'd really like to play the Doctor." Then I got a phone call asking me to play Sorin, so having played her husband twice, I now got to play her brother.'

The director was used to actors canvassing for parts, but says he was subjected to a lot more of it than usual for this play, 'no doubt because of her association with it. If you have Judi Dench then you have top-quality actors queueing up, because they know it's going to attract attention. It's not just self-serving. Everybody wants to work with Judi because it's such a blast.'

Bill Nighy played her lover, Trigorin, and he noted her impact on rehearsals. 'There was a sublime moment when she was telling Masha "You're young", and she suddenly did a little tripping walk just like a fifteen-year-old, entirely light on her feet, and it was quite heart-stopping. You just thought this was inspired acting, and there was no warning of it.'

There was a bit more warning of what became one of the most remarked upon inventions in this production, as Arkadina tries to reassert her sensual hold over Trigorin when she fears losing him to the much younger Nina. John Caird told them it was a sex scene that in a film would be set in the bedroom, and it lacked all conviction if the actors played it in upright positions. 'I said you can't sexually dominate someone by sitting in an armchair. I talked about the bedroom feeling and I remember Judi's eyes lighting up. So she got him as horizontal as she could, as quickly as she could, on the floor, because in that position her sexual power over him is manifest. The objection to it I think was ignorant, and tradition-bound. The laughter at that scene was absolutely Chekhovian laughter.'

Bill Nighy found it a bit difficult to get right first time, but came to look forward to that scene in performance. 'Frankly speaking, on nights when I was able to be less than fully engaged in the moment, I used to lie on my back in the centre of the Olivier stage, with the foremost Dame of the British theatre crawling all over me begging me not to go, and think, "What did I do to deserve this?"'

Nina and Masha were played by Helen McCrory and Rachel Powell and, after watching that scene, they went and locked themselves in the ladies. When they emerged, Bill Nighy asked them why, and they said, 'Because how on earth are we going to go on the same stage as her?'

But they found it was difficult to remain in awe of an actress so prone to play jokes at every opportunity. Edward Petherbridge, playing the doctor, phoned in one morning to say he would be about a quarter of an hour late. This delayed the start of rehearsals just enough to irritate the director, who said, 'What shall we do to him when he comes into the room? We should do something to make him feel rotten for just a few seconds.' Judi immediately suggested one of her favourite games: 'Let's hide.' So everyone hid behind the big black drapes in the rehearsal room, which then appeared totally empty when the actor arrived. Momentarily flummoxed, he said out loud, 'Good Lord', and Judi erupted out of her hiding-place in triumphant laughter. John Caird says with a grin, 'You do something like that at 10.15, and the whole of the rest of the day is that little bit more cheerful. It's a wonderfully childlike sense of fun, and things like that happened all the time.'

He admired her lack of any sense of hierarchy and her insistence on being treated with equality, but he also noticed that if anyone tried to take advantage of that equality, or her own care was reciprocated with carelessness, a very beady look came into her eye. 'If anybody has the right to feel proud of their achievements it's Judi, but she never does, she just lives in the moment. So for her of all people to meet others who are bombastic, or pretentious, or vain about their achievements, is preposterous, and she is always very amusing then in her analysis of those pretensions.'

This was an attitude that Judi unquestionably inherited from her mother. Olave used to have a saying that punctured any smugness instantly. One day in York when a group of actors were present and one was rash enough to remark, 'Oh, I think I did that rather well. I don't know that I've ever done anything quite as well as that', Olave said quietly, 'Pity he's dead.' Barbara Leigh-Hunt enquired, 'Pity who's dead?' 'His trumpeter.'

Judi heard that a foreign actress making a guest appearance at the National had said imperiously to her dresser, 'I am a *star*. You are nothing. Fetch me fizzy water *now*!' That became Judi's catch-phrase for weeks and she convulsed her hearers with a wicked take-off of the diva concerned, barking out those commands in her best fractured French accent.

Judi's delight in sending up others is perhaps only exceeded by her pleasure in being on the receiving end. She particularly treasured a poem from John Moffatt that came through the post one day during these rehearsals:

> Dame Judi Dench ... known as Jude
> Was excessively vulgar and lewd.
> If she got no applause
> She would shout 'Up Yours!'
> To the audience. Dreadfully rude!
>
> From the first act right through to the last
> She'd insult the rest of the cast.
> She would sometimes yell 'Balls!'

To the orchestra stalls
And leave *ev'ryone* simply aghast.

The director said sadly 'Oh, dear,
Dame Judi's too vulgar I fear.
For the lead in The Seagull
I'd have liked Anna Neagle.
What a pity she's no longer here.'

Judi enjoyed the rehearsals of *The Seagull* enormously and this enjoyment was shared by her colleagues, especially Bill Nighy. He says he has an anxious disposition and normally comes off on a first night thinking, 'Oh God, I didn't do that as well as I did in the run-through.' But when he came off as Trigorin he thought for the first time in his life, 'What we've just done is good. If anyone else has a problem with it, it will remain their problem. I can't collaborate with them.'

He was not even thrown by the ten-minute delay caused when one of the false proscenium arches got stuck as it was being dropped in for the second scene. The critics savaged this design concept of an extra arch flown in for each of the four scenes, though the director believed the intensity of their hostile reaction was only because of the unfortunate hiatus on the press night.

Few of them were very keen on Pam Gems' new translation, either, comparing it unfavourably with Michael Frayn's, but there was a greater welcome for the acting. Alastair Macaulay was particularly taken in the *Financial Times* with Bill Nighy's interpretation of Trigorin, and 'Judi Dench plays Arkadina to brilliantly funny, absurd effect; I love her daring in showing the character's most odious, selfish side from the very first. Her hilarious masterstroke comes in pulling Trigorin to the floor in Act Three and making love to him while praising his literary skills.'

It was Judi's 'toweringly comic performance' that appealed to Paul Taylor in the *Independent*. 'Dench turns the scene where she re-bandages her son's head after his suicide attempt into a hilarious slapstick routine.'

Michael Billington in the *Guardian* had several reservations about the production, but none about the central performance. 'Dench illuminates every movement large or small: when her son refers to two pious ballet dancers who lived in the same block, she emits a dirty chuckle that evokes a wealth of life experience yet, as she hears the final revolver shot, the blood seems to drain from her face as she stands stock still in ashen foreknowledge. This is real acting.'

He admired several other players, including Norman Rodway as her brother Sorin, 'raging furiously against the extinction of his wasted life'. Norman used to ad lib in character, trying to make Judi corpse in the last act when they were both upstage, saying *sotto voce* to her, 'You're still fucking that writer aren't you?'

When Geoffrey Palmer came to see it, she alerted him to a little surprise she was planning of her own. 'She told me beforehand that she'd tell Norman on-stage that I was out-front, and said, "Watch his lips for his reaction." She did, and he said, "Is that boring fucker out there?" *On-stage!*'

There was very little risk of performances getting stale or repetitive with actors playing tricks like this, without ever detracting from the power and truth of their acting.

Judi now regarded the National Theatre as home, but her loyalties have always been to people rather than the theatres they ran. It was John Neville who lured her to Nottingham, Frank Hauser to Oxford, Peter Hall and then Trevor Nunn to the RSC, Peter Hall again to the National, and Richard Eyre who kept her there. Throughout those peripatetic years one figure had been constantly at her side or on the end of a telephone – Julian Belfrage, who had represented her from her Old Vic debut onwards.

He was much more than an agent; he was one of her closest friends, whom she had leant on for the thirty-seven years she had been on-stage. Now he was dying of cancer and very weak, but by a huge effort of will he managed to attend the surprise sixtieth birthday party Michael arranged for Judi. Many of her friends came, including the cast of *As Time Goes By*, which was recording its fourth series at the time. Jenny Funnell says, 'Judi sat with Julian and her whole attention was on him; he died soon after that and she was in pieces; it took the bottom out of her world, I think.'

To those who knew her well, it was clear that Judi was still feeling bereft by the time of his memorial service on 7 March 1995. Julian's clients and friends turned out in force; the other readers included Ian

Holm, Alan Howard, Penelope Wilton and Daniel Day-Lewis. Ned Sherrin was in the congregation and wrote in his diary, 'Judi read Canon Henry Holland's "Death is Nothing At All". I've never seen her so moved or stronger in exerting iron control between each sentence to get through.'

Even two years later her voice shook a little when she first talked to me about how much she owed him, and what a wonderful friend and adviser he had been. In the last couple of years of his life his wife Victoria, known to everyone as Tor, moved into the business to help him and has kept it running since his death. She quickly learnt how to juggle Judi's punishing schedule of plays, films, recitals, radio and television broadcasts, and all the attendant promotional appearances and awards ceremonies.

Combining her several careers has meant that Judi has three times enjoyed the challenge of playing the same part both on stage and on television – Princess Katharine, Major Barbara and Madame Ranevskaya – but they were for different directors in each medium. Now she arranged for an interesting double – Christine Foskett in *Absolute Hell*, this time for the same director in both versions, Anthony Page.

Rodney Ackland's play was originally entitled *The Pink Room*. It is set in a West End drinking-club, La Vie en Rose, which combined different elements of the French Club, the Colony Rooms and the Gargoyle Club. The time is 1945, as the results of the General Election are awaited, and the large cast is made up of a group of misfits, Bohemians, and lost souls of various sexual persuasions. When the play was first staged in 1952 it was savaged by the critics, especially Harold Hobson, for its unsavoury characters and moral bankruptcy, and it failed disastrously. The embittered author rewrote it under a new title, *Absolute Hell*, for performance at the little Orange Tree Theatre in Richmond in 1988; in the more open moral climate of the day, Ackland was able to be more explicit about the homosexuality of some of the characters.

Three years later it was televised by the BBC in a production by Anthony Page, who had rediscovered Ackland's work in the 1970s, and at last managed to get this play seen again. He wanted Judi to play the raddled club-owner Christine because of the demands of the scene where she gets drunk, and he was convinced she could best plumb those emotional depths from watching her as Lady Macbeth on television. Judi read the script on a train journey and immediately said she would do it.

The BBC were concerned about the cost of the large cast and wanted the duration cut to ninety minutes, but Anthony Page succeeded in beating them up to two hours. He went to see Rodney Ackland in hospital, who later came to rehearsals and helped with the cuts from the full-length stage version. The director recalls the rehearsals as being exceptionally easy, not least because of Judi's positive influence and her watchful attentiveness when she was not in a scene.

Bill Nighy was playing the failed writer Hugh Marriner and he shares Anthony Page's view. This was his first experience of working with Judi and he prizes it as much as he does their later stage-partnership in *The Seagull*. His nervousness was completely dissipated in rehearsal. 'There is a line in *Absolute Hell* where a chap comes in with a gun and says, "Who wants a bullet up the botty?" Judi just looked at me in the most unprofessional look that I think anyone has ever given me, the first time that came up, and I just turned upstage and wobbled. The old-fashioned looks she can give you are just irresistible and we never got through that scene without corpsing.' But somehow they managed to get through it for the recording.

Anthony Page invited the author along to the recording at Television Centre, and he watched it from his wheelchair in tears. He died shortly afterwards, so he never saw the National's subsequent stage production. Judi was saddened by that, but touched by his response to the TV recording, when he said to her, 'I didn't realise I had written such a good play.'

She so enjoyed letting her hair down in this part that she said to Anthony Page, 'Wouldn't it be lovely to do this in the theatre?' He agreed, but it was another four years before they came together again to do it in the Lyttelton. Richard Eyre decided to put it on to mark the fiftieth anniversary of the end of the war, encouraged by Judi's enthusiasm for the play. The director and star were the same, but many others of the cast were new, with Greg Hicks succeeding Bill Nighy as Hugh Marriner.

Judi felt she had made Christine too genteel on TV, so she made her coarser and more drunk. 'In fact, although we were of course only drinking coloured water, I used to feel absolutely stotious after-wards.' Less enjoyable was the fact that she had to smoke, a habit that makes her feel physically sick; but she is prepared to endure even that if the character requires it, as Esme did too in *Amy's View* later.

Peter Woodthorpe played the monstrous film director Maurice Hussey, and he now remembered his schoolboy doubts about her voice. 'I watched her weep, weep, weep at the dress rehearsals of *Absolute Hell*, and was moved by her vocal ability to pull off that long string of "Hells" at the end of the play. She's like Len Hutton, she always seems to have that much more time to play a stroke.'

The 1995 production was well received, even if the critics felt the play fell short of greatness. Charles Spencer said, 'Let's drink to a flawed masterpiece' in the *Daily Telegraph*, but he thought it came satisfyingly close, and was whole-hearted about the playing of the central character. 'In a marvellous performance in which she totters unsteadily on her high heels from sluttish imperiousness to maudlin sentimentality, you are made increasingly aware of a woman at her wit's end, desperate for company to keep the horrors of life at bay. Dench's spine-tingling howls at the end do indeed seem to be issuing from a soul in torment.'

For Michael Billington in the *Guardian*, 'Anthony Page's archaeo-logically exact production contains two perfect performances. Judi Dench makes the club's proprietress a sexily rump-twitching figure, constantly caught between laughter and tears, whose boozy con-viviality conceals a desperate terror of solitude. And Greg Hicks is her equal as the creatively blocked novelist whose dithering charm disguises a genuine fury at his critical rejection.'

Gay Times headlined its review 'Hell of a dame', and Tilly McAuley urged readers, 'If you only go to one show in the coming months, make sure it's this one – it's worth the ticket price just to catch Dame Judi . . . It is a performance of such poignancy that it takes your breath away. Dench doesn't just play Christine, she *is* Christine.'

Anthony Page's desire to restore Rodney Ackland's reputation was fulfilled, even if the author had not lived to see his work reach the National Theatre. The production was a hit and could have run for much longer, but the Lyttelton was required for the next shows, and Judi was needed on the bigger stage of the Olivier Theatre.

However reluctant she was to leave Christine behind, she looked forward eagerly to assuming the fading glamour of Desirée Armfeldt. The decision-making sequence was the same as for *The Seagull*. Richard Eyre decided to put *A Little Night Music* into the Olivier Theatre, offered the leading role to Judi, and invited Sean Mathias to direct it and complete the casting.

His first thought was for Ian McKellen to play her lover. There was a question mark over whether he was up to singing what was a very difficult part musically, but he was keen to play opposite Judi in something so totally different from their previous partnership. The same thought occurred to at least one newspaper, which ran a headline: 'The Macbeths sing!' But it was not to be. When the finance at last came through for his film of *Richard III*, he relinquished the role to the American actor Laurence Guittard.

Siân Phillips joined the cast after a chance remark of hers to Sean Mathias, when they were working together on a studio workshop of what later became her show about Marlene Dietrich. She had recently sung the role of Desirée on a recording, but said that if ever *A Little Night Music* came up again she would love to play her mother on the stage.

He said, 'Are you serious?'

'Yes.'

'Well, I'm going to do it. Would you really like to play Madame Armfeldt?'

'I'd love to.'

'OK. There's only one thing. You'd have to play Judi's mother.'

The two actresses are much the same age, but with the right wigs they thought they could carry it off, and they loved playing together again, after the fun they had had in *The Gay Lord Quex*.

It was as well that Sean Mathias had one person in the cast with whom he had worked before, as it took Judi a long while to get used to his rehearsal process. He refused to do a read-through, and began with lots of exercises, including a very complicated one with bamboo sticks, which she positively hated doing and made no attempt to conceal it. She asked Siân Phillips several times, 'Is this going to work? Does he really know what he's doing?' Because she had worked with him twice before, Siân assured her, 'Yes it will work, it will be absolutely wonderful, don't worry about it.'

For once Judi was unable to act on that advice until after the show had actually opened. The set was a complicated one, combining the use of the revolve with big hydraulic lifts on which scenes rose and sank, so it required a whole week of technical rehearsals to coordinate the movements of the set and the cast. The director sensed that Judi was terrified of the hazards of the revolve at first, but saw her start to relax as the week wore on and, unlike the *Mother Courage* revolve, this one actually began to work. She sent him a bottle of champagne with a little note, the first real sign of confidence in him that she had yet displayed.

Stephen Sondheim happened to be in London, and was asking to come to rehearsals, but Sean Mathias kept putting him off, because they were still ironing out the problems in the production. He was right to be nervous, although in a recent newspaper interview Sondheim had said he was really happy that his show was being directed by Mathias, because of the sexuality of the piece and the darkness that he would bring to it. When he finally got to see this production at the first dress rehearsal, his reaction devastated the director. 'Sondheim came up to me and said, "What have you done? You've made it all so *dark!*" I didn't know if he meant the lighting, the morals, or the ambience; I didn't know what he meant. But he was in a kind of frenzy, and he went back to the Savoy and said he was going to stop his partner from coming to see it, so I was terribly depressed.'

He kept the composer's reaction from his cast and although the first preview had some rough edges technically, the audience loved it. At each preview it got better, but Sean Mathias was dreading the one which was a huge gala benefit to raise money for the front-of-house rebuilding fund. 'It took £350,000, but I was in a complete state, because it was a preview and we were still working on it.' He screamed at Richard Eyre, 'How could you put me through this?' The Director of the National Theatre calmly replied, 'You've got no understanding of what it is to run a theatre, and how important fund-raising is.'

Sondheim relented and came and worked with the actors, and became happier with the production as he saw the audience appreciating it, but it never displaced his affection for Hal Prince's original creation twenty years before. However, he helped Judi a lot with her part, and when he said he would not offer her a single note for the

'Send in the Clowns' number, saying, 'No, that's yours now,' that was a tremendous boost to her confidence.

The show is based on Ingmar Bergman's film *Smiles of a Summer Night*, in which a group of the Swedish bourgeoisie at the turn of the century succumb to sexual infidelity and relationships dissolve or are resolved over one weekend in the country. Desirée was the second actress in a year that Judi had represented on the Olivier stage, but this one was a much more appealing character than Arkadina.

The music critic of the *Independent on Sunday*, Michael White, was not enamoured of the production, particularly the choreography, but was convinced by the performances of Patricia Hodge and Siân Phillips, 'and Judi Dench plays Desirée like it is one of the great character roles of modern theatre – as maybe it is – with an endearing shabby grandeur and incredible finesse.'

Sean Mathias said he hated the fact that it was a musical, and directed it just as if it were a play, moaning in rehearsal every time his cast had to go off for a music-call, 'Oh God, this music.' This may be why he got better notices from the drama critics, who responded most warmly to the acting.

Michael Billington asserted in the *Guardian*, 'the great thing about Judi Dench's Desirée is not that she is some ethereal goddess but a warm, funny, beer-swilling touring pro whom you can genuinely believe has given her Hedda in Halsingborg ... But Dench also has the quality of heartbreak and her voice cracks unforgettably in "Send in the Clowns" as she confronts with genuine despair life's missed chances.'

That was also the high point for Sarah Hemming in the *Financial Times*, epitomising the perfect mood captured by the production. 'Her husky-voiced rendition of "Send in the Clowns" may not be the most beautifully sung version ever, but it is immensely moving, full of vulnerability and pain, and it gathers together beautifully all the longing and despair in the show.'

This view was reinforced by the response of one of her old RSC colleagues, Ian Richardson: 'The night I went her voice was completely off; she went flat a couple of times in "Send in the Clowns", and the tears were pouring down my face, because she just instinctively knows where to pitch the performance.'

The production ran for a year in the repertoire, and was so popular that it had to return for an unbroken eight-week run in the Olivier, playing eight performances a week. As soon as the posters went up showing Judi in her seductive red evening-gown, it sold out for that too. She extracted every ounce of humour there was in the part, and now and again some that should not have been there at all. On New Year's Eve, when she turned upstage and opened her dressing-gown to her ex-lover who now wanted to return, she had written Happy New Year over her corset, which was tricky for Laurence Guittard, and trickier still for the band at the back who could also see it. On the last night the message read, 'Go home, Yank.'

Despite its great success, the director of *A Little Night Music* says he never wants to do another musical, though he would love to direct Judi in a great play. He found he was completely frustrated when he came back to check on the production after he had been away for some months making a film. 'I went to Judi's dressing-room and gave notes, and she said, "Oh I don't think we can do that Sean, honestly. We've worked so hard on that, and there've been so many problems. Now we've got it working this way, I just don't think we can do what you're asking." I said, "Oh all right", and went to Siân's dressing-room, and gave her a note for a completely different scene. She looked at me and said, "If it were a play, I could do that, but it's a musical, so I can't."'

Their judgement was almost certainly right, because by the time it closed it had become the National's biggest hit, taking £3 million, compared with £2 million for *Carousel*. Judi reaped a unique double, winning a pair of Olivier Awards in 1995 – for Best Actress in a play with *Absolute Hell*, and Best Actress in a musical for *A Little Night Music*.

Anna Massey was playing Queen Elizabeth I in *Mary Stuart* at the Lyttelton during the 1996 season, and she got a card or a little present from Judi on the days when they were both performing, not, she says, that she needed any reminder, 'as I could always tell when she was in the building anyway, because you could feel her aura of concentrated calm – it somehow permeated the whole of the National Theatre backstage'.

The normally calm and unflappable Peter Hall did, however, have a jolt to his equilibrium when he was rehearsing *Oedipus* one day. 'I had the chorus for the first time in costumes and full masks, and one of them came out of the chorus and started walking towards me. I had no idea who it was, but this small malevolent creature came right up to me, and I said in some alarm, "Who are you? What's the matter?" She took her mask off and it was Judi. She'd got the wardrobe to kit her out in full costume.'

Her invention seems as boundless as her energy. She is Patron of the Yvonne Arnaud Theatre at Guildford and when it was under threat of going dark she gathered a group of theatrical luminaries for a fund-raising gala on Sunday, 25 February 1996. Peter Barkworth was one of them, and he remembers how they all felt a bit frayed after the long rehearsal which only ended at 6.30 p.m. 'Judi then went round all the dressing-rooms, collecting guesses from everyone, at fifty pence a go, on what time "this unending gala performance would finish". Her entire time between 6.30 and curtain-up at 7.30 was spent collecting and writing out the list of all the guesses, thus ensuring that backstage was a very happy place that evening.'

On the penultimate night of the run of *A Little Night Music*, the cast put on a late night cabaret after the performance, for friends in the other National Theatre companies and from outside. Judi wore flaxen plaits and a dirndl, to sing a wicked parody of 'I am 16, going on 17' from *The Sound of Music*, with Brendan O'Hea. She was used to him constantly making ageist jokes against her and Siân, saying, 'It's amazing you both get on-stage at your age, it's wonderful. Here you are, at the end of your careers, and I'm just at the beginning of mine.' He even risked Judi's wrath by singing 'You are 60, going on 70.'

But far from being at the end of her career, she was just about to conquer one medium that she had mistrusted for so long, and that had too often failed to do her justice – film.

twenty-one

1997

Judi the movie-star – M
and Queen Victoria

By the 1980s Judi had scaled the highest pinnacles in the theatre – she was the leading lady at the National and had won a clutch of the most prestigious stage awards. But her handful of appearances in the cinema was limited to often quite small supporting roles, in art-house movies that were never contenders for huge box office success. She had virtually written off any thought of a significant film career, when she was suddenly offered the part of the spy chief 'M' in the first Bond movie to star Pierce Brosnan as 007 – *Goldeneye*. The real chief of MI6 was actually code-named 'C'; more importantly for changing the gender of this role was the fact that it coincided with the appointment of Stella Rimington as the first woman Director General of the domestic counter-espionage agency, MI5.

Judi leapt at the chance of giving Bond his orders, and of playing in her first blockbuster film. She particularly relished the opportunity of accusing one of the most famous heart-throb heroes of the big screen of being a 'sexist, misogynist dinosaur'.

She has said since that she was more scared of her first Bond movie than anything she had yet done, but concealed that at the time from virtually everybody except the star, which Pierce found very comforting. 'It was trepidation for me, stepping into the shoes of Bond, and it was also trepidation for me, sitting across the desk from an actress of Judi's talent. But what took the sting out of it for me was when I said to her, "Do you like filming?"

'She said, "Oh, it terrifies me, I'm absolutely terrified."

'I said, "Well, you obviously prefer the stage."

' "No, no," she said, "only if I can be downstage, in the dark, with my back to the audience."

'You laugh at that, and then you sit opposite her, and once she catches you in her eyes you get your own performance for nothing really, because she's so there. It was wonderful from my point of view that she had the grace to be nervous, and to be open and free, it makes the work a lot more exciting; as opposed to someone who's trying to mask their nerves, or trying to rise above it all and be distant from you.'

He smiled reminiscently as he said, 'I think she was genuinely terrified of playing M, which she does like falling off a log really.'

She only had three days' shooting on the film, but although the role is small, M is crucial to the setting-up of the plot, and the producers of *Goldeneye* made the most of her presence in the publicity campaign for the film. On the evening of the glittering West End première Judi had an earlier engagement on-stage in a sketch with Alan Bennett. She begged him not to mention it, but as she left he announced to the audience, 'She's off to the première of *Goldeneye*.'

Eon Productions sent a huge limousine to drive her the short distance from the National Theatre to Leicester Square and she took an innocent glee in being observed by other actors as she clambered in at the stage door. It was a little more daunting walking the gauntlet of the flashing cameras and the clamorous crowds calling out, 'Hi Judi, hi Mike', outside the cinema. Judi said, 'It was so kitsch' – it was her first experience of the movie-world hype, but not, as it turned out, her last.

There had been a six-year hiatus between the last Bond film, with Timothy Dalton as 007, and Pierce Brosnan's debut in the role, but this one was such a commercial success that the next was much more quickly set up, and the cameras rolled again only two years later, in April 1997. The director of the first was Martin Campbell, with whom Judi had enjoyed working; Roger Spottiswoode was hired for the second, *Tomorrow Never Dies*.

He inherited the new regulars, Pierce Brosnan, Judi Dench and Samantha Bond as Miss Moneypenny – and a more long-standing one, Desmond Llewellyn, who had played Q, Bond's tetchy gadget instructor, from the very first film in the series, *Dr No*. Many of the scenes between M and 007 in the original script by Bruce Feirstein were now cut, not for the better in Judi's view; and the director gave the impression that he would have cut out both M and Q altogether if he could.

He tried very hard to recruit Anthony Hopkins to play the villain, a power-mad media magnate who schemes to provoke a war between China and the USA to boost his worldwide TV and newspaper sales. Hopkins was keener to accept the title role in *The Mask of Zorro*, which he was offered at the same time. 'So Roger Spottiswoode phoned me and said, "I know you've got that other part, but please give consideration to the Bond." I said, "It's a very good script." He said, "No, don't worry about it, we're going to rewrite it." Then the alarm-bells went off. I thought, "Rewrite what's already good?" That's always the interference of the megalomaniac. So I phoned my agent and said, "OK, I've made up my mind, I want to do *The Mask of Zorro*." Thank God I didn't do the other one.'

His judgement was a wise one. Jonathan Pryce, who eventually played the villain, was hampered by a rewritten script that never allowed him to be as worthy an opponent for 007 as Donald Pleasance, Charles Gray or Christopher Lee had appeared to be in earlier Bond films.

Colin Salmon, who played M's assistant, is over six feet tall and the director was so concerned about getting the two of them in the camera frame together, that he had Judi walking up ramps and standing on boxes, while Colin was standing with his legs uncomfortably splayed to reduce his height. A lot of filming is based on deception of the audience, but this seemed a clumsy way of achieving it.

A more enjoyable one was the drive in the Rolls-Royce, simulated on the trailer of a low-loader, screaming through the streets of London and swaying round corners. At the end of this hectic ride, Pierce could not resist ad libbing a line on-camera, 'Nice smooth ride, M.' So 'smooth ride' became the catch-phrase of the day, to the amusement of Agent 007: 'She's got a raunchy sense of humour, and I don't know how this is going to look in print, but the raunchier the better for Dame Judi Dench.'

Judi was required for six days this time, but had to endure being given new pages of script on each of them. The schedule was a punishing one. The car was calling for her in the morning at around 5 a.m., driving her to Eon's Frogmore studios near St Albans, long days filming, and she had barely got home one night at a quarter to ten, when a motor bike courier delivered to her home ten new pages for shooting the following day. Samantha Bond fumed when she heard this, 'You want to say, "Well when? When do I do this? When am I supposed to learn this stuff?" It was very uncomfortable for her, and made her very unhappy.'

When the film was edited, Judi was called in to re-record some of her dialogue, what is called 'looping' in the business, lip-synching her lines to her own picture on the screen – quite a skilled and demanding technique. On the appointed day her car got stuck behind a broken-down container lorry in central London, so she called in on the car-phone to explain that she would be a little late. She arrived on foot and when Roger Spottiswoode said 'Come on, come on, come on!' and denied that he had got her telephone message she refused to shake hands with him. After the looping, he said in a surprised tone of voice, 'You're very good at this', and her long-simmering frustration burst. 'You know, it was very off-putting indeed to have learnt the script, and at a quarter to ten the night before to get a new script. That's not fair.'

'Well,' he said, 'we didn't start with the right script in the first place.'

'That's hardly my fault'.

'Well, I apologise. By the way, would you like to be in my new film with Jonathan Pryce. My car's at your disposal to take you wherever you're going'.

'No, I'd rather walk.'

She laughs wryly at the memory now, saying, 'God, I can be difficult when I want to be', but it might have confirmed her in her dislike and distrust of the medium, had she not just completed a much more demanding role in a five-week shoot under appalling weather conditions, but which became the happiest and most rewarding experience of her whole film career to date.

Tomorrow Never Dies was a big money-spinner, but it was *Mrs Brown* that won all the critical plaudits. The original title was *Her Majesty Mrs Brown* and it tells the story of the relationship between Queen Victoria and her Scottish ghillie, John Brown. Summoned from Scotland by the Queen's Private Secretary, Sir Henry Ponsonby, to try to draw her out of her inconsolable grief at the death of Prince

Albert, Brown succeeds all too well for the Court, when she becomes so emotionally dependent on her servant that tongues begin to wag about the depth of her attachment to him, and *Punch* nicknames her Mrs Brown.

The independent TV company, Ecosse Films, pitched the project to BBC Scotland, with Billy Connolly's name attached to play the focus of the Queen's affections. The Ecosse Managing Director, Douglas Rae, sent an early draft of the script via Tor Belfrage for Judi's perusal, and then took the scriptwriter Jeremy Brock to meet her for lunch at the National Theatre during the run of *A Little Night Music*. Before they could open their mouths, she opened her Filofax and said, 'When do we start?' Then Douglas Rae told her, 'But I want you to know that Billy Connolly's first choice for Queen Victoria is Bob Hoskins.' Judi said, 'That's all right, it quite suits me to be Bob Hoskins' understudy.'

Once she had agreed to do it a lunch meeting was set up at the Caprice for her to meet Billy Connolly. Both the executive producer, Douglas Rae, and the director, John Madden, elected not to attend that lunch, as they thought it was important for the two co-stars to establish their own working relationship. They were nervous of each other beforehand, but Judi was as big a fan of his as he was of hers and they immediately clicked; when Douglas Rae arrived at the coffee stage he found the two of them roaring with laughter. They shared a sense of humour and an appreciation of the absurd, which kept them, and everyone else, in a state of permanent hilarity off-set, and quite often on it, too.

Before they started shooting the director had a long discussion with Judi about the script, and about the character of Queen Victoria. She read one biography of her, and her Highland Journals, and quite often before the camera turned over Judi would go to John Madden and say, 'Just talk to me about this scene.' The script went through several drafts, but the final version was completed well before filming began. By then the director said he had 'a very strong sense of where the scene was going to be emotionally, with the music of the lines in my head, but Judi always transcended that, particularly in the quiet moments, the moments between the lines where she is so astonishing. If you notice how her eyes move on screen, they register a fluidity of emotion, and the energy within her in every frame was so dynamic that I was never forced to cut where I didn't want to.'

He meant cutting in the editing room, because he was all too frequently forced to call 'Cut' on an individual take and go again, most often because of the horses. The Queen's pony, Bluey, had a tendency to flatulence, particularly on-camera, and it broke wind through several takes of the scene where John Brown led it through the grounds of Osborne House with the Queen in the saddle.

Even worse was the scene when they were both on horseback, and he had to dismount and lift her down from her side-saddle. Brown tries to resign in her best interests, and she refuses to let him, saying: 'I cannot allow it because I cannot live without you. Without you, I cannot find the strength to be who I must be.'

In the only moment of explicit affection seen in the film she takes his hand and kisses it. Capturing this very important scene proved a nightmare for the director. 'The process of getting Judi off the horse, with the voluminous skirts and underskirts, took care of about ten takes, horse-farts took care of another five, one horse bit another, and then it pushed Judi out of shot. At last we thought it had all really happened perfectly, until she walked away and her costume caught on his radio mike, so they were attached to each other. We went to twenty-one takes before we finally got it.'

Needless to say, all these glitches made the actors corpse helplessly, but on the final take there is not a hint of these previous frustrations and the scene is one of the most moving in the whole film. I knew about all the problems when I watched it, and was still totally held by it.

Billy Connolly had never been to drama school, and had done far more stand-up comedy than straight acting; so he read everything he could lay his hands on about acting and the pursuit of reality. 'When I read "be real, don't get caught acting", I thought, "How the hell do you do that?" It wasn't until I worked with Judi that I realised what that meant. In the first scene when we met at Osborne she was remarkably real. We'd been laughing in the morning, and then she showed this grief for Albert which was so unbelievably real. She just carried me along in her slipstream; you could only react in kind.'

The reality was nearly too much for a group of unsuspecting visitors to Osborne. At one break Judi, in full fig as the Queen, went to use the ladies' loo in the House. As she emerged and swept down the corridor, a party of tourists being shown round stopped dead at the sight of this royal apparition. Judi just inclined her head regally, and swept on.

The Scottish locations were so far from the hotels, and so difficult to reach, that Judi was often called before 5 a.m. to allow for the long drives, and the ninety minutes or more in make-up, in order to begin shooting by 10 a.m. It was November, so it began to get dark by 3.30 p.m. When it rained, as it often did, with gale-force winds, things were then delayed further.

Douglas Rae worried that the tight schedule was too exhausting for her, although she never complained. 'One night when we were all having dinner together Judi was talking to me, and she actually fell asleep in mid-sentence. We gently picked her up and took her up to bed.'

Geoffrey Palmer played Ponsonby, and by now he was so associated by the public with Judi's husband in *As Time Goes By*, that there were a few worries about his plausibility in this role, but within moments his stiff-necked bearing and full set of Victorian whiskers erased that other character from the mind. Richard Pasco agreed to play the small part of the Queen's physician, Dr Jenner, when Judi pleaded with him that they would all have such fun in Scotland. His lines may be few, but the lifted eyebrows between these two men over the Queen's behaviour with Brown raise many laughs. Judi put on her Queen Victoria face as she berated them both after the first screening, 'I think it's outrageous that you two get so many laughs without saying anything!'

This was partly to get back at Geoffrey, who observed she was word-perfect from day one, and commented reprovingly, 'Why can you do that for them, and not for Syd and me in *As Time Goes By*?'

John Madden had a little initial difficulty in casting Queen Victoria's daughters, who were present in several scenes, but had no lines; until he had a sudden brainwave and asked to meet Finty. When she agreed to play one of them, he cast the other with an actress friend of hers with a strong resemblance to Finty, so the family scenes have a very authentic look.

The only real casting problem was for the ghillies' ball when the Queen dances happily with John Brown, as her family and Court watch disapprovingly. The Scottish location manager telephoned all his friends in the local nobility, who turned up with their own costumes and knew all the steps of the eightsome reel, but did not look totally convincing as the servant class. This matters less than it might, as the eye is taken more with the foreground players, who did actually have to learn the dance.

Real life imitated art a little too closely in Scotland. In the Balmoral picnic scene John Brown chases off some scandal-seeking journalists he catches spying on them through telescopes. One evening in the hotel, as about nine of the company were dining together, another guest, seemingly the worse for wear, kept pestering them to let him take a photograph, supposedly for his son. To get rid of him Billy said, 'You can take *one* photograph', and the man asked if he could take it of just him and Judi. Three days later the picture appeared in one of the Sunday tabloids over a caption reading, 'Billy takes Judi to a secret hideaway.' The actor's language was vividly unprintable.

That incident upset the production team far more than the appallingly difficult weather conditions which beset so much of the five-week shoot. When it ended, Billy Connolly presented Judi with a brooch, a wonderfully garish crown in coloured glass, 'and she gave me a wee embroidered velvet cushion, which I'll treasure all my life, with To J. B. from V. R. stitched onto it'.

Mrs Brown had been commissioned for BBC Television, but when the edited film revealed the quality of the acting and direction, it was quickly snapped up by Miramax, one of the big American film distributors, for a prior release in the cinema. Their instincts were sound, as most of the newspapers showered praise on it.

Nigel Andrews wrote in the *Financial Times*, 'The film makes such effective drama from tiny convulsions of feeling that a look can seem an embrace, the touch of a hand can seem like ravishment.' Cosmo Landesman asserted in the *Sunday Times* that 'Judi Dench has surely given the definitive performance as Queen Victoria.'

The film critics eagerly tried to claim her talents now for their medium, such as Adam Mars-Jones in the *Independent*: 'Judi Dench's face is a crossroads of imperiousness and vulnerability; it's shocking that she has never before played the lead role in a film, but here she has her revenge.'

Matthew Sweet supported his colleague in the *Independent on Sunday*: 'Judi Dench's Victoria is the jewel in *Mrs Brown*'s crown: a creation of breathtaking sensitivity, exquisitely modulated between icy indifference, warm fragility and imperial rage. She never sentimentalises her character – even at her most unguarded, Victoria retains a capacity for defensive cruelty. The theatre has hogged her for too long.'

She was similarly welcomed to the celluloid world across the Atlantic, where Rex Reed regretted in the New York *Observer* that her genius had been 'cruelly denied to American audiences. She has never invaded Broadway, and her screen appearances have been ruefully rare. But if fame on American shores has eluded her, the situation is about to change. In *Mrs Brown* ... this great actress turns her first leading screen role into a blazing triumph of power and artistry.'

The film was seen as a refreshing import to challenge the native product. In *USA Today* Mike Clark thought 'this intimate import is seemingly designed to prove how tasty a British telepic can be. And oh, do we need one in a summer of homogeneous Hollywood blockbusters.' Thelma Adams greeted this 'bracing historical romance' in the *New York Post*, '*Mrs Brown* highlights the love that dare not speak its name in contemporary Hollywood: a powerful bond between two articulate, intelligent, middle-aged, white heterosexuals.'

When the film crossed the Atlantic Judi was prevailed upon to accompany it for a brief promotional tour. She had not set foot there again since the Old Vic tour of 1958/9, four decades earlier, partly, she says, because she had such a marvellous time then that she was afraid she could not repeat it. But far from being disappointed, she had a wonderful week, being fêted in New York and Los Angeles. Larry Guittard, her co-star in *A Little Night Music*, accompanied her to the premières in both cities.

It got off to a good start on the flight from Heathrow to JFK airport, when she picked up a copy of the *Sunday Telegraph* to see a story about the Chancellor of the Exchequer under the headline 'Brown says the Queen must pay for her own helicopter.' She cut it out and had it made up into cards in New York, to send to all her friends.

She became a little worn down by the endless stream of interviews, where the major light relief was hearing Billy Connolly in the next room screaming, 'She was a *nightmare* to work with', to make sure she could hear.

After the New York première on the Wednesday, the team flew on to Los Angeles for the Hollywood screening and an even more intensive conveyor-belt of interviews, where Judi wearied of telling the same stories about the film over and over again, until her voice started to give out. She wrote in her diary, 'A script arrived for me today. They have to be joking.' Less of a joke for her were the questions asking what she had done before appearing as M and Queen Victoria. But she was amused to hear that when Finty rang her hotel and asked, 'Can I speak to Dame Judi Dench?' the operator asked, 'Is that all one word?'

She loved her brief visit, though she was far from convinced that she wanted to go and work in Hollywood. But the launch of *Mrs Brown* in the United States had been so successful that it gave her for the first time an international profile, and a subsequent presence at by far the biggest event in the world of show-business – the Academy Awards ceremony. That was nine months away; for the moment she was committed to return to the National Theatre to appear in the latest play by David Hare.

diary entry four

---

1 May and 9 June 1997

Amy's View – National Theatre

Day 1. 1 May 1997.

Arranged to meet Judi at the stage door of the National at 11.30, in advance of the first read-through scheduled for 12 noon. It was a gloriously hot sunny day and also Election Day. Joyce Redman arrived first and we chatted about my biography of Ralph Richardson, for which I had interviewed her.

'What are you doing here?' she asked me. I said I was coming to the read-through.

'Oh, what are you playing?'

'That's a lovely thought, but I'm only here because I'm now writing Judi's biography.'

Judi arrived, full of apologies for being ten minutes late, but she had had trouble getting into the theatre car park. Ronald Pickup came in at that moment and they hugged and exchanged greetings, before we all went up to the canteen for coffee.

'I'm so glad you're here', Judi said, 'I'm so nervous, and I haven't read the end of the play yet!'

She guided us to Rehearsal Room 1, where everyone else was already assembled. Judi introduced me to David Hare and we arranged to meet in three weeks' time to talk about his work with her. Richard Eyre repeated to me his innate reluctance to allow observers into his rehearsals, because he saw them as essentially a private process only accessible to those taking part; but he did now agree to my attending a later run-through.

12 noon. After the director had introduced everyone present by name and function, the press, costume, management and the other personnel all left. He then gave the briefest of introductions, and made a jokey reference to an actor, now deceased, who had worked with David and himself, who

used to tear out all the pages of his script where he didn't appear. 'If any of you make a habit of working like that, perhaps you could wait until you get home! David, do you want to say anything?'

'Only that if anyone is unhappy with anything in the text, do please say so sooner rather than later, as I'm quite happy to rewrite where necessary, but it's much easier to do that when I'm around in the first couple of weeks, than later on.'

Richard: 'Right, shall we begin at the beginning.'

The first two acts were read straight through – the actors all speaking very softly, with no attempt at projection. The scripts that I could see had been already marked up by the actors on their own lines, but Judi's was not marked at all.

1.15. Break for coffee. As we all moved back to our seats Judi whispered to me, 'This is going to be the tricky bit, I haven't read the end!'

David laughed a lot at the actors' delivery of his funny lines, especially Judi's. At the end of Act IV, Richard said, 'Great', and announced a sandwich break of fifteen minutes.

Judi said, 'Come along, John', and as we exited into the labyrinthine corridors leading to the canteen, she asked, 'Did it show I hadn't read it?'

'No, you didn't fluff any more than any of the others.'

I mentioned the climax of the play, when Judi and Christopher Staines enter from a howling storm at sea.

'Yes, that's going to make a *great* curtain call, isn't it, dripping wet?'

Day 2. 9 June 1997.

1.45 p.m. Arrived at the National stage door and was directed down to Rehearsal Room 1, where the cast and crew were assembling. Judi was eager to know what David Hare had said when I interviewed him the previous week. I hedged and said, 'You'll read it all in due course, Judi.'

'No, I want to know now. What did he say about me?'

'Well, he thinks you're such a great dramatic actress, you shouldn't waste your time appearing in television sitcoms.'

I realised in a split-second that this was a mistake, as Judi exclaimed, 'Oh, does he?!' and swooped across the floor to punch David Hare on the shoulder, saying, 'How dare you say I shouldn't do sitcoms, how dare you!'

The author gave me a very dirty look, even though he had said to me,

'You can quote me on that, Judi knows that's what I think.'

But this had not been the best moment to quote him to the subject herself.

2.00. I took a seat at the back and observed press-cuttings from 1979 and 1985 pasted up on the walls, as background information for the cast. When the run began, few prompts were necessary, and there was only the briefest gaps between the acts. At the end of Act III the author and the director leapt up and moved the heavy sofa, in such a synchronised movement that they have clearly got used to doing this at every rehearsal.

In Act III Esme wept as she embraced Amy – everyone watched motionless at the power of the emotion. Judi exited at the end of the act and wiped away real tears.

Toby's line at the end of Act IV about the director not coming to the performance – 'He's off angling for a new musical' – which got such a knowing laugh at the first read-through, has now been cut.

At the end of the run-through, Penny Ryder, Judi's understudy, was in tears and there was a generally muted atmosphere, as if everyone had been wrung through the emotional wringer. Richard gently asked me if I minded leaving now, before he gave them all notes.

twenty-two

1997–98

Amy's View and Oscar Night
in Hollywood

One of the hallmarks of Richard Eyre's tenure of the National Theatre was the series of plays by David Hare that he commissioned and directed there. They ranged from the epic sweep of his State of the Nation trilogy about the Church, the Law, and the State, all in the Olivier, to the more intimate *Skylight*, staged in the Cottesloe. The second of these intense personal stories, and his eleventh play to be staged at the National, was destined for the Lyttelton Theatre, and was entitled *Amy's View*.

The play stretches over sixteen years, from 1979 to 1995, and sets a generational conflict against the changing fortunes of an actress, from the West End to a TV hospital soap, to the lead in an unnamed avant-garde play. David Hare did not set out to write the part of Esmé for Judi, but by the time he was halfway through writing it, he did tell her he thought he had a play for her. Once that idea was planted, he found it affected his writing of the last act in particular, where a young actor talks about how Esmé's technique draws the audience in. Hare says he wrote that act, and that speech, knowing Judi would play it. 'It is a mystery why one actor can pull the audience in without seeming to do anything, whereas when another actor tries that technique it doesn't work at all.'

Two weeks before rehearsals began he wrote her a fan-letter, with a mock-challenge at the end.

Dear Judi,
Somebody sent me a tape of *Mrs Brown*. I think it's one of your greatest performances. It's certainly your greatest film performance. I loathe

the bloody monarchy, as you know, but even I found your grief for Albert & your relationship with the ghillie unbearably moving. It is <u>great</u> acting.

I'm thrilled we start soon. No need to reply to this. Oh, one thing: why not be as good in my play as you are in the film?

Many congratulations –

Love

David.

Getting to be as good in his play proved to be much harder than she anticipated. One of her gifts that fellow-actors so envied was that she always seemed to learn her lines by osmosis. After a few rehearsals they were imprinted on her memory and she cast the script aside; she never had to sit down and study them, like nearly every other actor in the business. This time that failed to happen, which was a real shock to her system. When her husband came home one night, 'she was in floods of tears. She said, "I just can't learn the script." I said, "Yes, of course you can", and we got stuck into it, and we got over that, but I'd never seen her like that before.'

Desperation drove her to sitting down with the script every evening, or rather lying down with it. 'I used to come home, say hello to Mike, go up and run a bath, and get into the bath with the script. I would do an hour in the bath, just going at it every day. I don't like working like that, but it was a necessity.'

It was only of limited comfort when she discovered that the rest of the cast had the same problem, including Ronald Pickup and Joyce Redman, and even Samantha Bond, as Amy, who normally shared Judi's facility for just absorbing the lines in rehearsal. Richard Eyre was understanding about their problem, having met it before in previous Hare plays he had directed. 'David's dialogue is illusory, because it gives the impression of being naturalistic, it's all fitting together, it seems to be an effortless musicality, but actually almost every sentence is inverted. It's very stylised, like David Mamet or Harold Pinter, very rhythmic, and if you get words wrong it doesn't go, so you've got to get it right.'

Midway through the six-week rehearsal period she was still struggling with the lines and the playwright was growing frustrated, waiting to be shown his play come alive. Then, as Judi grew more confident over the words, she unleashed that phenomenal actor's energy that had left earlier observers breathless. For David Hare, 'It was the most ruthless two weeks I've ever watched of an actor just simply annexing parts, becoming confident in them and then never going backwards. I've seen actors always take two steps forwards and then one step back, she doesn't take the step back, she just goes on; the bit that she knows she can't do she'll say, "Today I will work on this", and then she'll do it, it's formidable.'

He admired her professionalism even more on one particular day near the end of rehearsals, when she suddenly discovered that a situation in the play came close to one in her own life. Act I pivots around Esmé guessing what her daughter has failed to tell her – that she is pregnant. When Finty gave premature birth to a baby boy in June 1997, her parents were both shaken that they had not guessed she was pregnant, and that Finty had not told them earlier. She says, 'I was planning on telling them that weekend, and then Sam just went, "Oh to hell with this, I'm going to come out now, and you're just going to have to tell everybody." Because I actually had two more months to go.'

This unanticipated news that she was now a grandmother made it particularly difficult to go into the National and rehearse that opening scene with Amy; so Judi went in early and confided the news to the author and the director, both of whom were impressed and moved by her courage and determination in working on a scene that now had so many deep personal overtones for her.

She was distressed by the way in which some of the newspapers chose to handle the story, but not by the event itself, 'because Sam is such a star, he's so joyous a person, we're so thrilled with him, and she's such a good mother'. Seeing them together, it is obvious that no child could have a more doting grandmother, or grandfather.

The press reaction brought to a head her growing reluctance to grant interviews, purportedly to discuss her latest film or play, which then turned into an inquisition into her private life. As I observed over the months I spent researching this book, she is outraged by intrusions into that privacy. After one particularly crass article she told me with some asperity, 'I've made up my mind I'm not going to give any more interviews, I feel like Paul Scofield, they've got enough now, let them make do with that.' She gets upset when suddenly ambushed by photographers staked out at a restaurant, or stalking her with a telephoto lens when she is out shopping.

Knowing that she was adjusting to this unexpected increase in her family, David Hare watched her at work with a sympathetic appreciation, work that continued right through the week of previews. She had one line about her late husband, Bernard, 'But always with him I felt whole.' Judi had not asked for any rewrites, despite the author's expressed willingness at the read-through, but she said to him during that last week, 'This is a very short line for the meaning it has to convey. I shall try and make it last twice as long.' His eager anticipation was fulfilled as 'this she then achieved without seeming either to pause inside it, or to stretch it out unduly. The line expands miraculously to take the weight she wants it to.'

He watched her technique admiringly as she reduced the weight in other passages. 'Once she knows a joke is working she'll take her foot completely off the pedal, because she knows it will work without her being seen to make any effort at all. She's just got the most complete acting brain I've ever seen, in terms of almost working on it as if it's a painting, or something outside herself.'

There are good jokes in the play, but essentially it is a drama of emotion. Esmé's daughter Amy loves a man who is opposed to everything that Esmé believes in. Dominic is a critic who becomes a TV pundit, and eventually a successful director of explicitly violent films, and he hates the theatre. He brings little but unhappiness to Amy, their marriage breaks up, and Act III is a huge emotional confrontation between mother and daughter. By Act IV Amy has died, Esmé has been financially ruined in the Lloyds' Names crash, and Dominic visits her in her dressing-room as she prepares for the evening performance.

On the page, the last act reads like a dying fall after the heart-wrenching tears of the previous one, but when the author ventured the view that 'it must be floating downhill, that last act', Judi's quick response was, 'Don't be ridiculous, I'm working harder in the fourth act than I am anywhere else.'

The director understood why Judi said that, and for him it was the most powerful part of her performance, built on what had preceded it. 'It's like the charcoal in the barbecue, that flares up in Act III, but Act IV is like when it's gone ash-coloured, with that white heat in it. So it's the fuel for Act IV, and without that emotional vortex of Act III, I think it would be astonishingly difficult to play Act IV. I would say that Judi's acting in that last act is among the best I've ever seen in the theatre. Everything gets cut away to the bone, so it's the most exquisitely minimalist performance in the fourth act, everything is done with the least possible gesture and movement, everything is distilled and that's a lifetime's experience. When the young actor is telling her how his mum is his mate, and she's putting make-up on her face, she just stops for almost a micro-second, it's barely visible, and your heart leaps, because it's so exquisitely observed.'

The young actor Toby was played by Christopher Staines, who began to worry that when Esmé kissed him on the cheek he was starting to look away, so it began to feel unnatural. He plucked up the courage to ask if it bothered her if he looked at her before she came to kiss him or not. He half-expected her answer: 'Well, I don't know about you Chris, but for me it's just whatever happens; one night you'll find you're looking at me, and one night you'll find you're not.' He felt rather like Toby feels about Esmé: 'What's so good about working with Judi is that it just feels so free and natural, I think I've learnt that from her more than anything else – just to relax and go with it.'

It was not relaxation that was called for on the night of the gala preview, another great fund-raising event for the National. Richard Eyre bore the strain of this with more aplomb than Sean Mathias had managed on the similar occasion for *A Little Night Music*, but it certainly tested the star and the author. He told her afterwards that he could see that she had come on and thought, 'I refuse to be intimidated by this.' She said that was exactly what she had thought: 'I haven't worked forty years in the theatre to let this lot of dinner-jacketed stiffs oppress me.'

Much of the stiffness came from the presence in the audience of so many people who had been Lloyds' Names themselves and lost a lot of money, and the actors could sense a real tension in the auditorium during the Act III argument about the financial disaster that befalls Esmé. At the supper afterwards one woman was in tears, saying, 'That's my story too.'

When some of the sponsors started criticising the play, and Eoin

McCarthy's Irish accent as Dominic, David Hare lost his temper. 'I started shouting, and I told them to fuck off, it was the strain of the whole situation. Richard told me it was a disgrace that I'd lost my temper, but when I told Judi she said, "Ah, thank God somebody told them, how wonderful", and she cheered up like a child. She loves trouble, loves it.'

The gala preview on the Tuesday had been so traumatic for all concerned that the press night on the Friday seemed just like any other regular performance, and the cast just sailed through it, with none of the usual nerves.

Michael Billington expressed a couple of lingering doubts about the play in the *Guardian*, but thought it contained a gift of a part for Judi: 'Dench is excellent at giving portraits of actresses: here, even though the play is emotionally on her side, she makes Esmé tough, caustic and durable, not least in the final bare-walled dressing-room scene when she confirms Hare's old observation that "acting is a judgment of character".'

Benedict Nightingale shared that view in *The Times*: 'To see her at the end, staring dark-eyed into her dressing-room mirror as she remembers the greatest blow she has suffered, is to feel twice blessed. A major dramatist has written a strong, rich play, and a major actress has done him proud.' In a longer notice he wrote for the *New York Times* he praised the way she developed Esme's character, 'the mix of brisk mulishness and good-natured scattiness that Dame Judi plays so well has become bleak self-knowledge combined with gritty resilience, qualities she plays even better.' He seemed to be more familiar with her work than Susannah Clapp, whose surprising comment in the *Observer* was that 'physical wit is her most undervalued talent as an actor'. She must have missed rather a lot of Judi's previous performances.

John Lahr welcomed 'David Hare's new smash' in the *New Yorker*: 'For me, *Amy's View* ranks with *Racing Demon* as his best work. Broadway doesn't beckon – it positively waves and shouts.'

Hal Prince added his voice to that plea. He went round after seeing it and said, 'You've got to come to New York with this.' Judi replied, 'I want to go to New York with this, but I saw Meryl Streep and Glenn Close in here last week, and I thought, I see what's going to happen.' The next morning the American director sent her a note: 'Meryl Streep and Glenn Close are too goddamn smart to try to muscle in on your role, come to New York.'

Once the play had opened, Judi fell into her regular routine during a run. She rises at 8.15 on the dot, and is physically incapable of lying in. 'When I was a little girl I remember going to bed and hearing the boys playing cricket in the garden, hearing the life going on outside. I simply couldn't bear it, and it's still like that. I don't like missing things, I would hate to be in bed and hear people talking downstairs, because I'm far too nosy, I *have* to know what they're on about.'

Then she will do the shopping, make lunch and do the washing, (though she no longer does the ironing, ever since Moyra Fraser told her she was absolutely mad to do that chore herself). She might lie down for half an hour after lunch, but more often drives in to the theatre and has a rest there. She is usually one of the first of the actors to check into the building, at about 5.30 p.m. She says she always has to do the same things. Her dresser makes her a cup of tea with no milk but with honey in it and she also steams her voice, a singer's habit she picked up in *A Little Night Music*. A steamer is shaped like a teapot with no handle, but a cork and a long tube. This is half-filled with boiling water, then she puts her mouth to the spout and breathes in and out without taking her mouth away.

Ever since the RSC she has done vocal warm-up exercises in her dressing-room, after undressing and getting into a dressing-gown. Then she takes what she calls 'guano' because of its colour – a little phial of ginseng and royal jelly. 'It's just like drinking pure honey, and I always have one of those before each performance, matinée and evening. I wouldn't feel right if I didn't have that.' She always has the tannoy on in her room (apart from that one compromise with Anna Massey on tour).

Once she used to go out to tea after a matinée, but now she will not even go to the canteen between shows. *Amy's View* was so exhausting that she always had a sleep after a matinée, and put a sign on her door, 'Do not disturb – sleeping'. *Under Milk Wood* was playing in the Olivier and the cast tended to be very vocal backstage. Ian Holm was playing *King Lear* in the Cottesloe and had the dressing-room next to Judi's; he heard her open her window and roar 'Shud-dup!!' at the noisy Welsh cast when they disturbed her rest. He says admiringly, 'She can be quite fierce when she wants to.'

She listens to music cassettes while getting ready, and also when she is going to sleep between two shows, always classical music of some kind – Beethoven, Mozart, or the Brandenburg Concertos. At home she listens all the time to the BBC – usually Radio 4, sometimes Radio 3. She is a devotee of *The Archers*, and once when Eileen Atkins, another fan, was away in America, Judi sent her a fax of the entire plot she had missed.

Judi's preference is for the repertoire system, which means she is not playing every night, but when ticket demand exceeds supply she often has to. This happened again with *Amy's View*, which transferred to the Aldwych in January 1998 for a continuous run, where it played to packed houses into April. To her great delight, her husband's solo performance as John Aubrey, *Brief Lives*, came in to the Duchess Theatre in the next street, so Judi just strolled round the corner and they were able to travel home together.

But his opening night in the West End was fixed for 23 March which happened to be the date of the Oscar Awards in Hollywood, so Michael was unable to accompany Judi to Los Angeles. His loss was his daughter's gain, as Finty went with her mother instead.

Miramax, the American distributors of *Mrs Brown*, bought out the Monday and Tuesday performances of *Amy's View* to allow Judi to attend, and the National Theatre had to extend the Aldwych run by another week, so they could offer alternative performances to the people who had booked for those two nights. Judi's biggest regret was that her understudy, Penny Ryder, was thus denied the chance to play Esmé while she was away.

From 27 February, when she heard she was being released from the play for two nights to go, Judi kept a fitful diary, writing at the top of the first page:

<u>Countdown to the Oscars!</u>
or Will I be the only unlifted face in Hollywood?

Zandra Rhodes and Donatella Versace both offered dresses – but I shall go to Nicole Farhi and keep it in the family.
(Mrs David Hare!!)
  On Friday at the half a huge bouquet of blossom and yellow roses arrives at the theatre + a bottle of KRISTAL champagne from DUSTIN HOFFMAN, who has seen *Mrs Brown* and is v. com-

plimentary. I shall be able to write a book entitled *My life with the stars*!!

3 March.
Interview with Marylu Dent down the phone to L.A. 'This may be indelicate but you seem to have a lot of energy for someone of your age . . .' Veteran – old – Old Guard etc.

Tuesday 10 March.
8.00. Had to talk to James Nochty [Judi's phonetic spelling of Naughtie] for the *Today* programme. Live!!
 I mumbled a lot and didn't really come up with the goods.

4.30 To Fouberts Place to meet Nicole. Fints would <u>love</u> the Autumn collection. She'd done several designs and we chose one of them. We decided on the grey organza not the frost.

Monday 16 March.
Fitting at 117B Fulham Rd with Nicole and Barry & the design team. Saw a wonderful trouser suit. They are altering it for me. Got a 4 leaf clover from Van Cleef & Arpels for luck.
 Turned down Asprey!!!

19 March.
Critics Circle Lunch.
 They all wished me well.
 Fitting with Nicole 4.30. Got Fints a bracelet to match the choker. Trouser suit fitted on me. Looked at jumpers. Tor faxed me through diamond earrings from VC & A's. Chose figure of eights – they are <u>only</u> 50 thousand dollars a pair!

Friday 20 March.
Richard from Nicole F came with dress and trouser suit and sweaters. I sent them a case of champagne.

Saturday 21 March.
Long talk to P. Hall who rang to wish me luck. Note from Liam Neeson. Cards. Flowers from Pauline & John Alderton. GPS [Geoffrey Palmer] & Sal rang.
 After the show when I'd taken my wet dress off all the crew and company were waiting with champagne & a lovely card & Ronnie made a speech.

Sunday 22 March.

Geoff came at 9.45 & we went off, waved goodbye by Mikey and Sammie. Got to Terminal 4 and were met as we checked in. The staff at <u>Gatwick</u> had sent good wishes. Changed £200 into dollars. Our dresses were <u>hand carried</u> to the plane – WE HOPE!! Fints had pink champagne & I had a coffee & danish pastries. Phoned Mike. Called at last to the plane – <u>photographed</u>. Sat right at the very front of the plane L & R.

Champagne, lunch and crashed out for a while. Watched Morgan Freeman (what a <u>good</u> actor) on the TV. Invited on the flight deck for landing – Fints not keen though. At 10.30ish I went up on the flight deck and watched us coming into LA. Incredible. Temp 70°. Met by v. nice man who escorted us through customs etc. Dress bag had been put with luggage. Tor met us & we all went to 4 Seasons. Great welcome from the hall porter and the staff. Suite 712 the same as I had before. Then we bathed and changed and by 5.20 Tor, Gene Parseghian (William Morris Agency), Fints & I all went off in a S.T.R.E.T.C.H. limo along Rodeo Drive to the Beverley Wilshire Hotel. Finty got frightfully excited when she recognised it as the hotel in *Pretty Woman*. Up to a room to be interviewed by 4 or 5 reporters (All British). Then downstairs and into Harvey Weinstein's Party (Miramax). Saw Beverley, Veronica, Sinclair & Lisa (up for the Make-up Award for *Mrs Brown*). Saw Dougal (Rae) & Jane, & Harvey who said H. B. Carter & I had to do a skit on *Good Will Hunting* [another of the Oscar-nominated films]. I nearly freaked out. Madonna & Demi Moore were sitting at the next table. Anyway – we did it and had to be 2 construction workers wearing hard hats. I was someone called CHUCKIE & had to say fuck a lot. It brought the house down.

Robin Williams was Mrs Brown but kept lapsing into Billy Connolly! We were given a box of chocs with a little Oscar attached. When I opened it, it wasn't chocs, but a framed photo of John Madden talking to me as Queen Victoria.

Then we left – by now it was 10 to 8 our time (4 a.m. English time). We were driven to a lovely house in Beverley Heights where we had more champagne & delicious things to eat. At 9.30 I knew I'd had it so F & I were driven back to the Four Seasons.

Judi's diary entries run out at this point, as she was overwhelmed by the events of the Oscar Awards day itself. The morning was taken up with having her hair done by John Barrett, an Irish hairdresser who now owns the most fashionable salon in New York, above Bergdorf Goodman's, and being made up by a top make-up artist, Trish McAvoy. After lunch Judi called Michael at the Duchess Theatre. 'He said they cheered a lot, so then a great big weight fell off us, and we were in a great mood to go to the Oscars. We got dressed, and at 3.15 we got into this *vast*, vast, limo, and went out to the Shrine. When we got there they said, "Are you ready for the red carpet?" Nobody prepares you for that! It's about 100 yards, and it took me an hour to get along it, with all the photographers and microphones. They said, "Will you wave to the helicopter?" I said, "You're joking." Then as we were going in, Fint said, "Mama, look", and up in the sky at that minute a plane had done a huge white heart, with a vapour trail, that was lovely. Then we went in, by which time my feet were killing me. As soon as I sat down I saw Vanessa [Redgrave] and Franco Nero, so we had a bit of a chat.'

Her many fans were acutely disappointed when the Best Actress Award went not to her but to Helen Hunt for *As Good As It Gets*, only slightly assuaged by the American's gracious acceptance speech, when she said she was sure that Judi had won when she saw *Mrs Brown*, and then paid tribute to the three other British nominees – Helena Bonham-Carter, Julie Christie, and Kate Winslet.

But Judi herself was not disappointed at all. 'I didn't expect for a minute to win, and I didn't feel one single twinge of anything. The whole thing is amazingly tatty, and absurd, and we had a *wonderful* time, I wouldn't have missed it for anything, I can't believe I've been.'

Her sense of the absurd public response was sharpened on yet another red carpet, going into the Miramax party afterwards, when a microphone was thrust at her and a man said, 'A nation weeps.'

Judi said, 'Oh, *come on!*'

'You must be very disappointed.'

'No, I'm not disappointed at all. I didn't expect to win.'

She had invitations to several other big parties, but she let the others go on and took her limo back to the hotel. 'God I was glad to get my shoes off. I have no recollection at all of going to sleep, or of getting into bed. I've never had that before.'

The following day, after a relaxing swim and a busy shopping trip, she took off from Los Angeles in a storm at 5.45 p.m., landed at Heathrow on

Wednesday at 11.30 a.m., and was at the Aldwych by 2. 'I had a couple of hours' sleep then, and then I went on. It was fine, just as if I'd never left, all dreamlike.'

It was not quite as if she had never been away. The company greeted her with a lot of 'You were robbed' commiserations, but it was the audience response that took her aback. The moment she entered they rose to her in a standing ovation. As she hugged Amy she hissed, 'What do I do now?' Samantha Bond hissed back, 'Go on hugging me.' It was some while before they could carry on with the play. This happened not just on that Wednesday, but every night of that week.

It was a telling indication, if any such evidence were still needed, of the great affection in which she is held by the public.

Not long afterwards the profession seized its first opportunity since the Oscars to demonstrate its similar feelings. At the British equivalent – the BAFTA Film Awards – when Judi was named Best Actress for her performance in *Mrs Brown*, the Great Room in Grosvenor House erupted in delight. As she walked up to accept her award the ovation was such that her husband Michael, no stranger to such events, was visibly overcome with emotion; the TV director cut back to him twice as he mopped his eyes. This time, ironically, Judi could say quite literally, 'I was robbed', as the trophy was stolen even before she left the hotel; BAFTA was so quick in replacing it that Judi said in astonishment, 'It must happen all the time!'

Happily for us, she betrays not the slightest interest in resting on her laurels, or of slowing down. 'Mike's given me a little talk a couple of times about taking it more easily. I don't know why I would want to do that. There aren't enough hours in the day for me, there really aren't. Unless you're there and people see you, they won't remember. I'm too frightened of that. You do see people who work towards an age, and then at sixty or sixty-five you see them go into a deep decline. Why? Why? You don't need to retire as an actor, there are all those parts you can play lying in bed, and in wheelchairs; like Newton Blick, he came off-stage and died in his dressing-room. Lucky Newty, I say.'

She is a long way yet from any wheelchair parts. At the age Judi is now, Peggy Ashcroft entered on a new screen career; John Gielgud is as eager to work in his nineties as ever he was; Gwen Ffrangçon-Davies was enchanting audiences on her hundredth birthday and beyond; so this should be regarded as only an interim record of Judi's career to date, with even greater challenges yet to come. One thing seems certain – we shall continue to be as surprised as we are thrilled by the vehicles she chooses, in any of the performing media.

We can also be sure that she will, by turns, move us to tears and laughter, and give us that insight into the human condition that only truly great acting can offer. It is only a handful who qualify for that accolade in any acting generation, but unquestionably amongst them will be found the name of Judi Dench.

After Queen Victoria her next screen monarch was Elizabeth I, in *Shakespeare in Love* and she jokes, 'I can only play Queens now.' Long may she continue to reign over us.

Acknowledgements

My first and greatest debt is to Dame Judi Dench, who has trusted me to write her life and given unstintingly of her time, allowing me access to her diaries, correspondence and photographic albums; and from the moment she agreed to collaborate has offered me a constant stream of suggestions of who else I should talk to, and which rehearsals and locations I should attend. I am grateful too to her family – her husband Michael Williams and daughter Finty, Jeffery Dench, Peter and Daphne Dench.

I would not have started this book without Judi's consent, and if I had I certainly could not have finished it, as all her friends and colleagues understandably wanted to know whether she knew about it before they would talk to me. For their time and patience I would like to thank: Joss Ackland; Maria Aitken; Humphrey Barclay; Peter Barkworth; John Barton; Tor Belfrage; Cicely Berry; Susie Bodmer; Samantha Bond; Kenneth Branagh; Philip Bretherton; Moira Brooker; Paul Brooke; Pierce Brosnan; Michael Bryant; John Caird; James Cairncross; James Cellan-Jones; Billy Connolly; Chris Cooper; Howard Davies; Maurice Denham; Margaret Drabble; Tenniel Evans; Sir Richard Eyre; Moyra Fraser; Michael Frayn; Stephen Frears; Jenny Funnell; Sir Michael Gambon; Patrick Garland; Sir John Gielgud; James Grout; Sir Peter Hall; Terry Hands; Sir David Hare; Frank Hauser; Janet Henfrey; Sir Ian Holm; Sir Anthony Hopkins; John Hurt; Celia Imrie; Martin Jarvis; David Jones; Pinkie Kavanaugh; Bob Larbey; Barbara Leigh-Hunt; Charles Lewsen; Sydney Lotterby; Gillian Lynne; Anna Massey; Alec McCowen; Sir Ian McKellen; John Madden; Sean Mathias; Sam Mendes; Sir John Mills; John Moffatt;

Dearbhla Molloy; Christopher Morahan; Paul Moriarty; Stephen Moore; John Neville; Bill Nighy; Trevor Nunn; Joseph O'Conor; Anthony Page; Geoffrey Palmer; Richard Pasco; Bob Peck; Michael Pennington; Siân Phillips; Ronald Pickup; Tim Pigott-Smith; Hal Prince; Douglas Rae; Joyce Redman; Roger Rees; John Reynolds; Ian Richardson; Norman Rodway; Paul Rogers; Peter Sallis; Vera Sargent; Ned Sherrin; Sir Donald Sinden; Christopher Staines; John Standing; Wendy Toye; Dorothy Tutin; Zoë Wanamaker; Stanley Wells; Hugh Whitemore; Clifford Williams; Moira Williams; Peter Woodthorpe; John Woodvine; Edward Woodward and Peter Woodward.

For assistance with my research I am indebted to the staff of Julian Belfrage Associates; Emrys Bryson, former drama critic of the Nottingham *Guardian-Journal* and *Evening Post*; Barry Norman and his colleagues at the Theatre Museum; Marion Pringle at the Shakespeare Centre, Stratford-upon-Avon; Michelle Roberts at the Theatre Royal, York; Nicola Scadding at the Royal National Theatre; and Gordon Stratford, formerly of the Oxford Playhouse.

I owe particular thanks to Ion Trewin for commissioning the book, for his encouragement, advice and support throughout the writing of it, and for all the care he and his staff at Weidenfeld & Nicolson have devoted to its production.

Finally, I would like to record my thanks to my wife Aileen for translating what I fear was occasionally my near-indecipherable scrawl into a typescript fit to present to my publishers, and for her unfailing interest in this book from start to finish.

John Miller
1998

Bibliography

Ackland, Joss, *I Must be in There Somewhere*, Hodder & Stoughton 1989

Bailey, John, *The Nottingham Playhouse, 1948–78*, Sutton 1994

Barkworth, Peter, *More about Acting*, Secker & Warburg 1984

Bate, Jonathan & Jackson, Russell (eds), *Shakespeare, An Illustrated History*, OUP 1996

Billington, Michael, *Peggy Ashcroft*, Mandarin 1993

Branagh, Kenneth, *Beginning*, Chatto & Windus 1989

Elsom, John, *Post-War British Theatre*, Routledge & Kegan Paul 1979

Eyre, Richard, *Utopia & Other Places*, Vintage 1994

Hall, Peter, *Making an Exhibition of Myself*, Sinclair-Stevenson 1993

Jacobs, Gerald, *Judi Dench*, Weidenfeld & Nicolson 1985

Lewis, Roger, *Stage People*, Weidenfeld & Nicolson 1989

Lowe, Tirzah, *Peter Hall Directs Antony & Cleopatra*, Methuen 1990

Redgrave, Vanessa, *An Autobiography*, Hutchinson 1991

Sherrin, Ned, *Sherrin's Year*, Virgin 1996

Sinden, Donald, *Laughter in the Second Act*, Hodder & Stoughton 1985

Sprague, Arthur Colby & Trewin, J. C., *Shakespeare's Plays Today*, Sidgwick & Jackson 1970

Trewin, J. C., *Shakespeare on the English Stage 1900–64*, Barrie & Rockliff 1964

Wells, Stanley, *Royal Shakespeare: Four Major Productions at Stratford-upon-Avon*, Manchester University Press 1977

Zeffirelli, Franco, *Autobiography*, Weidenfeld & Nicolson 1986

Chronology of Parts

Theatre

Date	Play	Role	Theatre
1957	York Mystery Plays	Virgin Mary	St Mary's Abbey

The Old Vic Company, 1957–61

Date	Play	Role	Theatre
1957	*Hamlet*	Ophelia	Old Vic
	Measure for Measure	Juliet	Old Vic
	A Midsummer Night's Dream	First Fairy	Old Vic
1958	*Twelfth Night*	Maria	Old Vic
	Henry V	Katharine	Old Vic

(Both plays also on tour to North America)

Date	Play	Role	Theatre
1959	*The Double Dealer*	Cynthia	Old Vic
	As You Like It	Phebe	Old Vic
	The Importance of Being Earnest	Cecily	Old Vic
	The Merry Wives of Windsor	Anne Page	Old Vic
1960	*Richard II*	Queen	Old Vic
	Romeo and Juliet	Juliet	Old Vic

(Also Venice Festival)

Date	Play	Role	Theatre
	She Stoops to Conquer	Kate Hardcastle	Old Vic
	A Midsummer Night's Dream	Hermia	Old Vic

(And walk-ons in *King Lear* and
Henry VI)

The Royal Shakespeare Company, 1961–2

Date	Play	Role	Theatre
1961	*The Cherry Orchard*	Anya	Aldwych

Date	Play	Role	Theatre
1962	Measure for Measure	Isabella	Stratford
	A Midsummer Night's Dream	Titania	Stratford
	A Penny for a Song	Dorcas Bellboys	Aldwych

The Nottingham Playhouse Company, 1963

1963	Macbeth	Lady Macbeth	Nottingham
	Twelfth Night	Viola	Nottingham

(Both plays also on tour to West Africa)

1963	A Shot in the Dark	Josefa Lautenay	Lyric

The Oxford Playhouse Company, 1964–5

1964	Three Sisters	Irina	Oxford
	The Twelfth Hour	Anna	Oxford
1965	The Alchemist	Dol Common	Oxford
	Romeo and Jeannette	Jeannette	Oxford
	The Firescreen	Jacqueline	Oxford

The Nottingham Playhouse Company, 1965–6

1965	Measure for Measure	Isabella	Nottingham
	Private Lives	Amanda	Nottingham
1966	The Country Wife	Margery Pinchwife	Nottingham
	The Astrakhan Coat	Barbara	Nottingham
	St Joan	Joan	Nottingham

The Oxford Playhouse Company, 1966–7

1966	The Promise	Lika	Oxford
	The Rules of the Game	Silia	Oxford
1967	The Promise	Lika	Fortune

1968	Cabaret	Sally Bowles	Palace

The Royal Shakespeare Company, 1969–71

1969	The Winter's Tale	Hermione/Perdita	Stratford
	Women Beware Women	Bianca	Stratford
	Twelfth Night	Viola	Stratford

Date	Play	Role	Theatre
1970	*London Assurance*	Grace Harkaway	Aldwych
	Major Barbara	Barbara Undershaft	Aldwych
1971	*The Merchant of Venice*	Portia	Stratford
	The Duchess of Malfi	Duchess	Stratford
	Toad of Toad Hall	Fieldmouse, Stoat, and Mother Rabbit	Stratford
1973	*Content to Whisper*	Aurelia	Royal, York
1973	*The Wolf*	Vilma	Playhouse, Oxford

(Also at Apollo, Queen's & New London)

1974	*The Good Companions*	Miss Trant	Her Majesty's
1975	*The Gay Lord Quex*	Sophy Fullgarney	Albery

The Royal Shakespeare Company, 1975–80

1975	*Too True to be Good*	Sweetie Simpkins	Aldwych
1976	*Much Ado About Nothing*	Beatrice	Stratford
	Macbeth	Lady Macbeth	Stratford

(Also Donmar and Young Vic)

	The Comedy of Errors	Adriana	Stratford
	King Lear	Regan	Stratford
1977	*Pillars of the Community*	Lona Hessel	Aldwych
1978	*The Way of the World*	Millamant	Aldwych
1979	*Cymbeline*	Imogen	Stratford
1980	*Juno and the Paycock*	Juno Boyle	Aldwych
1981	*A Village Wooing*	Young woman	New End

The National Theatre Company, 1982

1982	*The Importance of Being Earnest*	Lady Bracknell	Lyttelton
	A Kind of Alaska	Deborah	Cottesloe
1983	*Pack of Lies*	Barbara Jackson	Lyric

The Royal Shakespeare Company, 1984–5

1984	*Mother Courage*	Mother Courage	Barbican
1985	*Waste*	Amy O'Connell	Barbican and Lyric

Date	Play	Role	Theatre
1986	Mr and Mrs Nobody	Carrie Pooter	Garrick

The National Theatre Company, 1987–9

1987	Antony and Cleopatra	Cleopatra	Olivier
	Entertaining Strangers	Sarah Eldridge	Cottesloe
1989	Hamlet	Gertrude	Olivier
1989	The Cherry Orchard	Ranevskaya	Aldwych
1991	The Plough and the Stars	Bessie Burgess	Young Vic

The National Theatre Company, 1991

1991	The Sea	Mrs Rafi	Lyttelton
1992	Coriolanus	Volumnia	Chichester

The Royal Shakespeare Company, 1992

1992	The Gift of the Gorgon	Helen Damson	Barbican and Wyndham's

The National Theatre Company, 1994–8

1994	The Seagull	Arkadina	Olivier
1995	Absolute Hell	Christine Foskett	Lyttelton
	A Little Night Music	Desirée Armfeldt	Olivier
1997	Amy's View	Esmé	Lyttelton
1998	Amy's View	Esmé	Aldwych

Director

Date	Title	Companies / Venues
1988	Much Ado About Nothing	Renaissance Theatre Company
1989	Look Back in Anger	Renaissance Theatre Company
	Macbeth	Central School of Speech and Drama
1991	The Boys from Syracuse	Regent's Park Open Air Theatre
1993	Romeo and Juliet	Regent's Park Open Air Theatre

Television

Date	Title	Company
1960	*Z-Cars*	BBC
1960	*Henry V – Age of Kings*	BBC
1962	*Major Barbara*	BBC
1963	*The Funambulists*	ATV
1966	*Talking to a Stranger*	BBC
1968	*On Approval*	Yorkshire
1970	*Confession – Neighbours*	Granada
1972	*Luther*	BBC
1973	*Keep an Eye on Amelie*	BBC
1977	*The Comedy of Errors* (RSC)	Thames
1978	*Macbeth* (RSC)	Thames
1978	*Langrishe Go Down*	BBC
1978	*A Village Wooing*	Yorkshire
1979	*On Giant's Shoulders*	BBC
1979	*Love in a Cold Climate*	Thames
1980–3	*A Fine Romance*	London Weekend
1980	*The Cherry Orchard*	BBC
1980	*Going Gently*	BBC
1982	*Saigon – Year of the Cat*	Thames
1985	*The Browning Version*	BBC
1985	*Mr & Mrs Edgehill*	BBC
1985	*Ghosts*	BBC
1986	*Make and Break*	BBC
1988	*Behaving Badly*	Channel 4
1990	*Can You Hear Me Thinking?*	BBC
1990	*The Torch*	BBC
1991	*Absolute Hell*	BBC
1991–8	*As Time Goes By*	BBC

Films

Date	Title	Director
1964	*The Third Secret*	Charles Crichton
1965	*He Who Rides a Tiger*	Charles Crichton
1965	*A Study in Terror*	James Hill
1965	*Four in the Morning*	Anthony Simmons
1965	*A Midsummer Night's Dream*	Peter Hall
1973	*Dead Cert*	Tony Richardson
1984	*Wetherby*	David Hare
1985	*A Room with a View*	James Ivory
1986	*84 Charing Cross Road*	David Jones
1987	*A Handful of Dust*	Charles Sturridge
1988	*Henry V*	Kenneth Branagh
1994	*Jack and Sarah*	Tim Sullivan
1995	*Goldeneye*	Martin Campbell
1995	*Hamlet*	Kenneth Branagh
1996	*Mrs Brown*	John Madden
1997	*Tomorrow Never Dies*	Roger Spottiswoode

Index

307

Index

Index